Cargoes for Crusoes

❧ ❧ ❧

GRANT OVERTON

By GRANT OVERTON

About Books and Authors

CARGOES FOR CRUSOES
AUTHORS OF THE DAY
AMERICAN NIGHTS ENTERTAINMENT
WHEN WINTER COMES TO MAIN STREET
THE WOMEN WHO MAKE OUR NOVELS
WHY AUTHORS GO WRONG AND OTHER
    EXPLANATIONS

Novels

THE THOUSAND AND FIRST NIGHT
ISLAND OF THE INNOCENT
THE ANSWERER
WORLD WITHOUT END
MERMAID

Cargoes
for Crusoes

By GRANT _Martin_ OVERTON

New York: D. Appleton & Company
New York: George H. Doran Company
Boston: Little, Brown, and Company

8.50
net

Press of
J. J. Little & Ives Company
New York, U. S. A.
———
Bound in Interlaken-Cloth

"Let's Give Him a Book."
"He's Got a Book."

THIS BOOK IS DEDICATED TO
ALL THOSE WHO, THOUGH HAVING
ONE BOOK, SOMETIMES ENJOY ANOTHER

Preface

*Being a True Account of How a Priceless Cargo Was
Delivered to a Desert Islander*

How that I, Robinson Crusoe, came to be wrecked
with others of the ship's company on a Desert
Island, all being lost save my unworthy self, hath
in a precise manner been narrated by one D. Defoe
in the book he saw fit to entitle with my name; but
his ending is indifferent.   For novels like Defoe's
must have the Happy Ending, so styled.   Yet is the
truth often happier far than fiction.   Being no hand
to invent a tale, I am content to set down in this
place events as I humbly took part in them.

Let me declare, then, that here on my Desert
Island I for long suffered great loneliness and con-
sequent distress of soul.   This went on many days.
Howbeit, while sunk very low in my spiritual state
and with expectation nearly gone, a huge ship passing near labored painfully with a storm by the mercy
of God being compelled to throw overboard—or, as
they say at sea, to jettison—the greater part of her
cargo.   And being thus lightened she stood away
from the Island and went on her course safely.   The
same storm cast upon the shore the rich treasure
wherewith she had been laden, so many wooden
boxes or cases, packed tightly and well-lined, which
for the most part were washed up undamaged and,

within, scarcely dampened except it may be for an inch or two. Coming down to the shore the morning after I stood transfixed with astonishment at the sight of something lying on the sand. It was a book.

When I had a little recovered from my amaze, my joy and ecstasy knew no way to communicate itself, and almost immediately, my eye falling on the cases strewn along the beach, I capered with delight. I brake open the boxes, one after the other fast as I could work. All, *all*, were brimmed with the newest books!

Since that day I have not lacked instruction and entertainment, and deem that Providence, at trifling expense to the maritime insurers, hath rescued me from boredom forevermore. And this I deem the only rescue worth a fingersnap in this life of ours, and one that a great majority of people do never accomplish. My days and nights have been and yet are filled with most various delights, my walks are taken with a great company of authors and my conversations are held with them.

With such profit and satisfaction do I read that more than once, being sighted by a vessel which then stood by to take me off my Island, I have waved the sailors to proceed without me, which they have done with doubt and difficulty; yet finally I have convinced them of my meaning, they proceeding with their voyage, I with mine. . . .

Contents

[ix]

CONTENTS

Portraits

Cargoes for Crusoes

CARGOES FOR CRUSOES

1. The Knightliness of Philip Gibbs

i

THEN one said: "Rise, Sir Philip——" but the terms in which the still young man received ennoblement were heard by none; for all were drawn by his face in which austerity and gentleness seemed mingled. A pale young man with a nicotine-stained third finger whom Arnold Bennett had once warned authors against (he asks you to lunch and drives a hard bargain over the coffee). A good reporter for Alfred Harmsworth, Lord Northcliffe. A war correspondent with seven-league boots. A man standing on a platform in Carnegie Hall which rings with riot "looking like a frightfully tired Savonarola who is speaking in a trance." His thin, uncompromising nose; the jut of the chin; the high cheekbones and the hollow cheeks, long upper lip and mouth with drawn-in, straight corners (yet a compassionate mouth); the deep-set eyes; the ears placed so far back, and the raking line of the jaw—if these were all he might be nothing better than a fine breed of news hound with "points." They are nothing; but the clear shine of idealism from eye and countenance is the whole man. Great Britain had knighted a reporter, but Philip Gibbs had been born to knighthood.

For when chivalry would have died, he first succored and then revived it; when men wished to forget, he compelled them to remember. He actually proves what men have forgotten how to prove, and so have turned into a copybook maxim. Perhaps the reason his pen is mightier than any sword is because he wields it as if it were one.

In the eyes of the world he is the D'Artagnan of Three Musketeers who are also three brothers. They are Philip (Hamilton) Gibbs, Cosmo Hamilton (Gibbs), and A(rthur) Hamilton Gibbs, the mutations of name arising from choice and even from a certain literary necessity; for an author's name should be distinctive and is usually better not to be too long. The father, Henry Gibbs, was an English civil servant, a departmental chief in the Board of Education. The mother had been Helen Hamilton. The family at one time consisted of six boys and two girls. Henry Gibbs had "a delicate wife, an unresilient salary, and his spirit of taking chances had been killed by heavy responsibility, the caution and timidity growing out of a painful knowledge of the risks and difficulties of life, and the undermining security of having sat all his working years in the safe cul-de-sac of a government office."[1] It was the office in which Matthew Arnold worked and in which an obscure temporary clerk, W. S. Gilbert, stole moments to compose some verse called *Bab Ballads*. Henry Gibbs was a famous afterdinner speaker and it was certainly he who preserved the Carlyle House for London, but the nature of the case forbade him to encourage the marked adventurous strain in his boys.

Philip Gibbs was educated privately and was an editor before he was 21. He was, in fact, only 19 when

---

[1] *Unwritten History*, by Cosmo Hamilton. Page 3.

PHILIP GIBBS

he became "educational editor" for the large English publishing firm of Cassell at a salary of a hundred and twenty pounds a year. "With five pounds capital and that income, I married"—Agnes Rowland, daughter of the Rev. W. J. Rowland—"with an audacity which I now find superb. I was so young, and looked so much younger, that I did not dare to confess my married state to my official chief, who was the Right Honorable H. O. Arnold-Forster, in whose room I sat, and one day when my wife popped her head through the door and said 'Hullo!' I made signs to her to depart.

" 'Who's that pretty girl?' asked Arnold-Forster, and with shame I must confess that I hid the secret of our relationship." [2]

He was both timid and bashful; yet like many men of his stamp, he was to show on many occasions a lion-like courage. A hundred and a thousand times he was to pass as close to death as a man may pass and yet live; in general, he was to be quite as badly scared as a chap can be in such circumstances; and without exception he was to persist in what he was doing, for there was and is in him something stronger than fear.

ii

Philip Gibbs's earlier career differed little from that of Arnold Bennett or the first years of dozens of Englishmen who have made their start in Fleet Street. After several years with Cassell, he applied for and got a job as managing editor of a large literary syndicate. In this post he bought Bennett's early novel, *The Grand Babylon Hotel*, and other fiction and articles to be sold to newspapers in Great Britain and the colonies. While with Cassell he had written his first book,

[2] *Adventures in Journalism,* by Philip Gibbs. Page 84. Harper.

Founders of the Empire, a historical text still used in English schools. As a syndicate editor he wrote articles on every conceivable subject, particularly a weekly essay called "Knowledge is Power." But his job was outside of London, for which he hankered; and finally he wrote to Alfred Harmsworth, who was later to become Lord Northcliffe and who had founded the Daily Mail. The result was a job under a brilliant journalist, Filson Young, whom Gibbs succeeded a few months later as editor of Page Four in the Mail (devoted to special articles). Here he learned all about the new journalism and had a chance to observe Northcliffe closely. In the seventh chapter of his *Adventures in Journalism*, Philip Gibbs gives a brief but well-etched portrait of the man who transformed the character of the English newspaper. Northcliffe's genius, his generosity, his ruthlessness—which was often the result of indifference and sometimes sprang from fatigue and bad temper—are very well conveyed in a half dozen pages. Gibbs suffered the fate of nearly all this man's temporary favorites. When he was dismissed from the Daily Mail he went for a few months to the Daily Express before beginning what was to be a long association with the Daily Chronicle.

His connection with the Chronicle was broken by the sad experiment of the Tribune, a newspaper founded by a melancholy young man named Franklin Thomasson as a pious carrying out of his father's wishes. As literary editor of this daily, Philip Gibbs bought work by Rudyard Kipling, Joseph Conrad and Gilbert K. Chesterton, but the paper as a whole was dull and doomed. When it went down, Philip Gibbs thought he saw a chance to throw off the bondage of offices. He took his wife and little son and retreated to a coast-guard's cottage at Littlehampton. "There,

[18]

in a tiny room, filled with the murmur of the sea, and the vulgar songs of seaside Pierrots, I wrote my novel, *The Street of Adventure*, in which I told, in the guise of fiction, the history of the Tribune newspaper, and gave a picture of the squalor, disappointment, adventure, insecurity, futility, and good comradeship of Fleet Street." There was need of money, but the novel cost Gibbs more than it earned. His narrative had not disguised sufficiently either the newspaper or members of its late staff. The point is a little difficult for American readers to take in, and rests on English libel law, which is quite different from the American. In England, "the greater the truth, the greater the libel." A libel action was instituted, and although it was finally withdrawn, the bills of costs were heavy and the sale had been killed. But when published in the United States after the war, *The Street of Adventure* had a very good success.

"I knew after that the wear and tear, the mental distress, the financial uncertainty that befell a free lance in search of fame and fortune, when those mocking will-o'-the-wisps lead him through the ditches of disappointment and the thickets of ill luck. How many hundreds of times did I pace the streets of London in those days, vainly seeking the plot of a short story, and haunted by elusive characters who would not fit into my combination of circumstances, ending at 4,000 words with a dramatic climax! How many hours have I spent glued to a seat in Kensington Gardens, working out literary triangles with a husband and wife and the third party, two men and a woman, two women and a man, and finding only a vicious circle of hopeless imbecility! At such times one's nerves get 'edgy' and one's imagination becomes feverish with effort, so that the more desperately one chases an idea, the more resolutely it eludes one." [3]

Yet he counts himself, on the whole, to have been lucky. He was able to earn a living and to give time and labor to "the most unprofitable branch of literature, which is history, and my first love." Years later he was to have a thrill of pleasure at seeing in the windows of Paris bookshops his *Men and Women of the French Revolution*, magnificently illustrated with reproductions of old prints. He wrote the romantic life of *George Villiers, First Duke of Buckingham*, and discovered in the murder of Sir Thomas Overbury "a plot with kings and princes, great lords and ladies, bishops and judges, poisoners, witch doctors, cutthroats and poets," the incomparable material for his *King's Favorite*. These books brought him only a few hundred dollars apiece, though perhaps more in reputation and friendships.

iii

He returned to journalism, eventually, as special correspondent and descriptive writer for the Daily Chronicle. He was rather frequently in charge of the Paris office and had all sorts of adventures in that city, both those derived from saturating himself in French history and others incident to his daily work. After the Portuguese revolution he was sent to Portugal to explore the condition of those political prisoners that the republicans had in some cases interred alive. His greatest feat was the revelation of Dr. Cook's fraud in claiming the discovery of the North Pole. This was a triumph of sheer intuition, in the first instance, and both dogged persistency and remarkable courage were necessary before Philip Gibbs could be proved right.

[3] *Adventures in Journalism.* Page 113.

It began with a late start, twenty-four hours behind the other correspondents. When Gibbs got to Copenhagen, the vessel bringing Dr. Cook had not arrived, owing to fogs. Through a chance meeting in a restaurant with Mrs. Rasmussen, wife of the explorer, Gibbs got to Elsinore and aboard a launch which was putting out to meet the delayed ship. Thus he was the only English-speaking person present at the first interview, on shipboard. As it happened, Dr. Cook had not yet acquired that magnificent poise and aplomb which he was to display from the moment he set foot ashore. His eyes evaded Gibbs, he explained that he had no papers to prove his claim and not even a diary, and when pressed for some sort of written record or notes he exclaimed: "You believed Nansen and Amundsen and Sverdrup. They had only their story to tell. Why don't you believe me?" Later Cook had a moment of utter funk, hiding in his cabin. It passed quickly and after that he was outwardly all that a hero should be.

But Gibbs had had his chance. His seven-column story to the Daily Chronicle caused him to be denounced everywhere and even put him in jeopardy of his life in Copenhagen; yet a few weeks were to show it to be one of the greatest exclusive newspaper stories, "beats" or "scoops," ever written.

IV

In September, 1912, war started in the Balkans. Gibbs went as a correspondent and this experience, lamentable and laughable, comical and extremely repellent, was his first direct preparation for work soon to follow. The year following he had occasion to go to Germany and study the state of mind, popular and official, toward England. He was, therefore, exceptionally well fitted to be a correspondent at the front when the World War began. It would be impossible as well as improper to try to abbreviate here the story of his experience told so brilliantly and with so much movement (and with far too much modesty) in his *Adventures in Journalism*. At the outset of the war no newspaperman had any official standing. The correspondent was unrecognized—or it would be more accurate to say that he was recognized only as a dangerous nuisance, subject to arrest at sight. Gibbs and two other very distinguished newspapermen, H. M. Tomlinson and W. M. Massey, worked together for weeks and months and were three of a small group of correspondents who risked their lives constantly in the war zone and their liberty on every occasion when they stepped out of it. There came a time when the game seemed to be up. "I had violated every regulation. I had personally angered Lord Kitchener. I was on the black books of the detectives at every port, and General Williams solemnly warned me that if I returned to France I would be put up against a white wall, with unpleasant consequences." [4] The solution came with the appointment of five official war correspondents, of whom Gibbs was one from first to last. These men covered the war, not for one newspaper but for the newspapers of Great Britain and America. They were attached to General Headquarters and among the men of distinction who were assigned to them as friends, advisers and censors was C. E. Montague, editor of the Manchester Guardian and author of *Disenchantment*, *Fiery Particles*, *A Hind Let Loose*, etc., a meditative writer of exquisite prose who, at the outbreak of the war, had dyed his white hair black, enlisted as a

[4] *Adventures in Journalism.* Pages 245-246.

private, served in the trenches, reached the rank of sergeant, finally surviving when the dugout which sheltered him was blown up. . . .

After the war the five correspondents received knighthood, and Philip Gibbs is properly Sir Philip Gibbs, K. B. E. (Knight of the British Empire). On journalistic commissions he visited Ireland and Asia Minor and revisited most of the countries of Europe, including Russia. He came to America twice to lecture on the war and conditions resulting from it, and his book, *People of Destiny*, is a critical but admiring account of America as he found it. Pope Benedict XV., against all precedent, accorded Gibbs an interview on the reconstruction of Europe and this interview was naturally printed in all the principal newspapers of the world. He had become, more truly than any other man has ever been, more fully than any other man is, the world's reporter. His title was splendidly established by his summarizing book on the war, *Now It Can Be Told*, and was strikingly reëmphasized with his novel, *The Middle of the Road*, concerning which a few words are in order.

v

Although Philip Gibbs had published, in 1919, a novel, *Wounded Souls*, which contains much of the message of *The Middle of the Road*, the world was not ready for what he had to tell. He therefore set to work on a canvas which he determined should include all Europe. His visits to Ireland, France, Germany and even Russia had placed at his disposal an unparalleled mass of authentic firsthand material. He knew, better than most, what existed, and what lay immediately ahead. Using fiction frankly as a guise to present facts, both physical facts and the facts of emotion and attitude, he wrote his story.

When the novel was published in England and the United States at the beginning of 1923 it leaped into instant and enormous popularity. This was partly the result of prophetic details, such as this speech of one of of the characters (from page 317 of *The Middle of the Road*):

" 'France wants to push Germany into the mud,' said Dorothy. 'Nothing will satisfy her but a march into the Ruhr to seize the industrial cities and strangle Germany's chance of life.' "

When the novel was published the French invasion of the Ruhr had just begun.

There was a sense of larger prophecy that hovered over the story. But even more of the instant success of the book was due to the terrible picture it painted, minute yet panoramic, ghastly but honest. People sat up, literally, all night to finish the book. People read it with tears running from their eyes, with sobs; they went about for days afterward feeling as if a heavy blow had stunned them, a blow from which they were only slowly recovering. Although every effort was made in advance of publication to insure attention for the book, it is doubtful whether such effort counted at all in the book's success. For none who read it failed to talk about it in a way that fairly coerced others to become Philip Gibbs's readers. Month after month the sale of this book rolls on. It is not, as a piece of literary construction or considered as literary art, a good novel; it is something much bigger than that—a piece of marvelous reporting and a work of propaganda charged to the full with humane indignation and pity and compassion.

[24]

vi

As if he had found his field at last in the roomy spaces and manifold disguises of the novel, Philip Gibbs followed *The Middle of the Road* with a very keenly-observed study of young people. *Heirs Apparent* deals with the generation which was too young to take any active part in the World War but which has come to a somewhat unformed maturity since. The gayety of the novel does not prevent the author, with his usual thoroughness, from presenting the more serious aspects of his young people's misbehavior. There is incidentally an exactly drawn study of that newer, sensational journalism which Philip Gibbs tasted under Northcliffe and which is familiar enough, though on the outside only, to most Americans. But the delightful thing about *Heirs Apparent* is the author's unfailing sympathy with his youngsters; and the optimism of the ending—the book closes with a character's cry: "Youth's all right!"—is the sincere expression of Philip Gibbs's own perfect faith.

The tales in his new volume, *Little Novels of Nowadays*, are brothers to *The Middle of the Road*. What proportion of these stories is fact and what fiction is irrelevant, since in atmosphere and emotion all are true. Each of these poignant pieces is a document of the calamitous war more significant to humanity than the treaty sealed at Versailles. Whether in Russia or stricken Budapest or flaming Smyrna or some far-off corner of lonely starvation, Philip Gibbs has seen all, felt all . . . and can convey all.

vii

In fine, a bigger man than any of his books. One of the greatest reporters the press has ever had, one of the half-dozen—if so many—best masters of descriptive writing now alive. A chap who suffered nervous breakdowns prior to 1914 and who turned to iron in the moment of crisis. A militant pacifist because he has really seen war waged. A lover and fighter for justice, and a preacher of mercy. There is about him, despite the abolition of miracle and the rapid transformation of the world into a factory and a machine, some of that lost radiance of a day when men set forth to conquer in the name of their faith, or to spread a gospel which might redeem the world.

BOOKS BY PHILIP GIBBS

FICTION:

1908	*The Individualist*
1908	*The Spirit of Revolt*
1909	*The Street of Adventure*
1910	*Intellectual Mansions, S. W.*
1911	*Oliver's Kind Women*
1912	*Helen of Lancaster Gate*
1913	*A Master of Life*
1914	*Beauty and Nick*
	In England: *The Custody of the Child*
1920	*Wounded Souls*
	In England: *Back to Life*
1922	*Venetian Lovers*
1923	*The Middle of the Road*
1924	*Heirs Apparent*
1924	*Little Novels of Nowadays*

HISTORICAL:

1899	*Founders of the Empire*
1906	*The Romance of Empire*
1906	*Men and Women of the French Revolution*
1908	*The Romance of George Villiers, First Duke of Buckingham*
1909	*King's Favorite*
1912	*Adventures of War with Cross and Crescent*

[26]

THE KNIGHTLINESS OF PHILIP GIBBS

1915 *The Soul of the War*
1917 *The Battles of the Somme*
1918 *The Struggle in Flanders*
        First title: *From Bapaume to Passchendaele*
1919 *The Way to Victory*
        In England: *Open Warfare*
1920 *Now It Can Be Told*
        In England: *Realities of War*
1920 *People of Destiny*
1921 *More That Must Be Told*
        In England: *The Hope of Europe*
1924 *Adventures in Journalism*

Essays:

1903 *Knowledge Is Power*
1905 *Facts and Ideas*
1913 *The Eighth Year: A Vital Problem of Married Life*
1913 *The New Man: A Portrait of the Latest Type*

SOURCES ON PHILIP GIBBS

His *Adventures in Journalism* is autobiographical in the best sense of the word, and only needs to be supplemented by the formal particulars in *Who's Who* (England). There are interesting references in Cosmo Hamilton's *Unwritten History*. For a not wholly friendly reference, see Clement K. Shorter's page in *The Sphere*, London, for 6 October 1923. Mr. Shorter was one of a few who believed themselves libelled in *The Street of Adventure*, and he has had various literary feuds.

Address: Sir Philip Gibbs, Ladygate, Punch Bowl Lane, Dorking, England.

2. The Trail Blazers

i

THESE paths are strange and exciting. One leads into the midst of wild beasts, another into the depths of the sea. A third goes laboriously some few feet underground and erases three thousand years in three months. One or two, keeping to the present, are sources of innocent merriment; several employ the mode of fiction to vivify fact; and at least one is a continuous pageant in colors of the American West.

There is no order in which these paths are to be taken; you may go half across the world to follow one, or you may begin by merely stepping outside your door. America or Arabia, ferns or fishes, dogs or diggings, history, hunting . . . outdoor books are the best of indoor sports.

The alphabet is an immense convenience and I start with Adventurousness and America. For some time Joseph Lewis French has been busy selecting from various American authors the best accounts of the discovery of gold in California, the days of the pony express and the stage coach, the cowboy, the trapper, the guide, the bad man, and other phases of our history. He has drawn upon the works of Francis Parkman, Mark Twain, Bret Harte, Hamlin Garland, Bayard Taylor, General George A. Custer, Owen Wister, Theodore Roosevelt, Emerson Hough and a good many others in the task. Mr. French calls his book *The Pioneer West: Narratives of the Westward March of*

[28]

Empire, and Hamlin Garland has written a foreword for it. Also Remington Schuyler has done illustrations in color. As an anthology, the volume has no exact parallel in my knowledge. The nuggets it contains are otherwise for the most part found with considerable difficulty in half a hundred somewhat inaccessible places. It is, for example, not easy to find what you want in either Parkman or Roosevelt without risking a long hunt; and books by other earlier writers, even one so perfectly well-known as Bayard Taylor, are often hard to come by. It is no wonder that Mr. Garland calls *The Pioneer West* a real service in recovery. Mr. French spreads a satisfactory panorama before the reader, for his selected narratives run from the time of Lewis's and Clark's discovery of Oregon down to the last of the Indian uprisings.

A projected alliance between the Hudson's Bay Company and the Russian American Fur Company led, in 1867, to a great piece of foolishness on the part of an American Secretary of State. Congress was induced to pay some millions of dollars to purchase a fancy refrigerator and everyone was scornful of "Seward's folly." Edison Marshall has taken the phrase for the title of his new novel dealing with that period in Alaskan history. *Seward's Folly* relates how Major Jefferson Sharp, late of the army of the Confederate States of America, was sent to Sitka by Seward. Major Sharp liked an aristocratic society, and he found it in Sitka where Russians, Englishmen, Americans and Indians were colorfully combined. He also encountered, in Molly Forest and her uncle, two Americans undisturbed by any doubts as to the superiority of American character and the value of American ideas of liberty and opportunity.

The fact that Major Sharp was still loyal to the

spirit of the Confederacy and had no intention of serving the Union did not tend to simplify matters. He was, however, no scoundrel; and he came to recognize, beneath the glitter of Alaskan surfaces, much that his nature could not countenance. Mr. Marshall has managed an extremely good story. But he has brightened a portion of history in doing so.

William Patterson White's *The Twisted Foot* and B. M. Bower's *The Bellehelen Mine* are novels of the cattle rancher and the miner, respectively. Mr. White's story has almost every ingredient of an exciting yarn—a love interest, an independent young woman who doesn't believe in explanations, a mystery, an open enemy, a set of foes whose methods are mean and underhanded, and a couple of young men who think quick and shoot quick. The impetuous Buff Warren, cowboy, is sent to drive off the range a family of "nesters." He finds that the father is blind and that the family is making a very brave fight against severe odds. He also meets Gillian Fair. Instead of putting the Fairs off the range, Buff takes them under his protection. This means the loss of his job, and when, by a trick, he gets himself made deputy sheriff, his state of mind is not helped by the fact that all clues to a bandit who is terrorizing the region seem to lead to Gillian Fair.

B. M. Bower tells of a silver mine named by a prospector after his two baby daughters, one of whom, grown to womanhood, is the heroine of *The Bellehelen Mine*. Helen Strong, left alone to carry out plans that she and her father had made together, returns to Goldfield and assembles a crew from among her father's old miners. It is the beginning of an unanticipated battle, for the Western Consolidated is determined to make Helen Strong sell out.

[30]

THE TRAIL BLAZERS

The Bellehelen Mine is to an extent a departure from the author's previous books, a story of mine-working and not of ranch life. But it should be realized that B. M. Bower, or Mrs. Cowan, has been for some years a mine owner and manager. It would be surprising if she did not use this phase of her experiences in her fiction. She lives at El Picacho Mine, Las Vegas, Nevada; and after twenty years of writing Western fiction it is high time she gave us a mining story.

B. M. Bower is a woman but by no means a tender-foot. Mary Roberts Rinehart's account of her tender-footage, in *The Out Trail*, is the most amusing record of a woman in the West on my shelf of recent books. But the most amusing record of America in general is, I think, *Cobb's America Guyed Books*, that series of small volumes with drawings by John T. McCutcheon, a book to each State. These attach themselves with a burr-like tenacity to the memory in a series of epigrams. You remember that Irvin S. Cobb said of New York City: "So far as I know, General U. S. Grant is the only permanent resident," and of Indiana: "Intellectually, she rolls her own," and of Kansas: "A trifle shy on natural beauties, but plenty of moral Alps and mental Himalayas." Such priceless remarks are more to be cherished—and are more cherished—than State mottoes; but the *Guyed Books* have a claim to respect as well as affection. Each presents, along with various State demerits, partly humorous and partly real, the honest claim of the people of one section to be considered as individual, characterizable, with a personality not lost in the American mass. And Mr. Cobb has not failed to give the people of each State credit for State achievement.

Yet, because they contain humor, the *Guyed Books*

will always be classed as works of humor. A little leaven is a dangerous thing. On the other hand, a little knowledge leaveneth the whole lump. Donald Ogden Stewart has that little knowledge, and the result is the perfection of his new work, *Mr. and Mrs. Haddock Abroad*. It is the fault of authors of books of family life that they almost always know too much. Mr. Stewart (as reviewers say) has avoided this shortcoming. And in fiction, as in any other game, the element of surprise is invaluable. Surprise, conjecture, suspicion—especially suspicion! It was because she was above suspicion that Caesar's wife was not well received in the best Roman circles. *Mr. and Mrs. Haddock Abroad* would have helped her. . . . But, all seriousness for once aside, Mr. Stewart's treatise on the American family unit is masterly. It will give Americans a new status in Paris. There are many irrelevances and illustrations throughout the book.

ii

Five—usually five and a fraction—per cent. of the people in any community are confirmed fishermen. The greatest living authority on fishes is David Starr Jordan, for so many years president of Leland Stanford Junior University. He is the author of the most important book on its subject, a piscatorial Bible, in fact, which now appears in a new revised edition. It has forty-six chapters, and 673 illustrations, of which eighteen are full-page plates in color. It is by Dr. Jordan, now a man past seventy. Its title is *Fishes*. It has no other title, and no subtitle. It needs none.

This marvellous book makes the heart leap as the trout leaps. Nothing so delightful or complete is found elsewhere. One may know nothing about fishes—I don't—and yet turn these pages in a perfect enchantment. I suppose, in a way, it is the emotion of a first youthful visit to the Aquarium, but an emotion incredibly magnified. Dr. Jordan speaks of his volume with what must seem to the reader a ridiculous modesty. He says it is a non-technical book that may still be valuable to those who are interested in the study of fishes as science. He says his chief aim has been "to make it interesting to nature-lovers and anglers, and instructive to all who open its pages. The fishes used as food and those caught by anglers in America are treated fully, and proportionate attention is paid to all the existing as well as all extinct families of fishes." This may be true, but it no more explains the book than a conjuror's account explains his magic.

Beginning with the fish as a form of life, Dr. Jordan goes through every attribute of fishes and then, in an incomparable sequence, tells what we know of each species. There are chapters like that on the distribution of fishes which seem to transform the world in somewhat the fashion in which Jules Verne's Captain Nemo transformed it; other chapters, like that on the fish as food, are of vital importance; and such a chapter as that on the mythology of fishes (including the sea serpent) have a charm irresistible and without equal. At length one plunges into the sea, swimming through a myriad of sea creatures whose very names— elasmobranchii or shark-like fishes, the salmonidae, the mailed-cheek fishes, the dactyloscopidae—are as curious and as evocative as those strange shapes that float in green water behind aquarium glass.

Dr. James A. Henshall's *Book of the Black Bass*, an acknowledged masterpiece, is practically a new book as the result of rewriting and enlargement. Nearly all the illustrations, including those in color, are new. In addition to a complete scientific and life history of the fish, Dr. Henshall gives the last word regarding tools and tackle for catching what is "inch for inch and pound for pound the gamest fish that swims."

Let us continue for a little with the authorities on these very special subjects of sport. Dr. William A. Bruette is one on dogs. He is well-known as the editor of Forest and Stream, and various particular books on the dog—or perhaps I should say, on particular dogs—preceded *The Complete Dog Book*. There is not an opportunity for anything of its sort to follow it unless some one may be moved to write a canine encyclopædia in some number of volumes. For *The Complete Dog Book*—illustrated with photographs, of course—describes the dogs of the world and very fully describes all the breeds recognized by the American Kennel Club. It is, throughout, a carefully comparative description, giving the standards for judging each breed and the good and bad points of each. The care of dogs in health and their treatment in disease, as well as their training and general management are gone over in detail; but Dr. Bruette's prime service is his wisdom on the subject of buying puppies. Here are the pages which will save the reader most, both in dollars and disappointment.

Birds are hard to learn, not easy to observe, and must be taken largely on trust for an acquaintance. On the other hand, if you will take George Henry Tilton's *The Fern Lover's Companion* with its 188 illustrations, go over it carefully, use its glossary of terms and keep an eye about you in your walks, you may learn the names and the chief characteristics of our most common ferns in a single season. There is about ferns something of the fascination there is in fishes—a great variety of form, and forms of exquisite coloration and beauty of pattern. Mr. Tilton's handbook is progressive; if consulted attentively, it can be followed from beginning to end without confusion or the need of going again over the same ground. Ground in the book, I mean!

When it comes to covering ground, Charles C. Stoddard's *Shanks' Mare* is a superior article. This book about walking—really, about the joys of walking— moves without haste and with an easy rhythm of prose and sentiment. It is one of the few books that have the impelling quality of fine spring weather. As Stewart Edward White said: "That is the main thing—to get 'em out." The remark occurred in a letter to Dr. Claude P. Fordyce, a letter which forms the introduction to Dr. Fordyce's capital book on *Trail Craft*. "I am glad you are publishing the book," wrote Mr. White. "All your articles on the out-of-doors life have seemed to me practical, sensible, and the product of much experience, plus some discriminative thought." He followed his words about getting people out of doors with: "If, in addition, you can give them hints that will, through their interest or comfort, keep 'em out, the job is complete." *Trail Craft* will do a finished job for a good many who read it. Dr. Fordyce has the considerable advantage of knowing American wildernesses; he writes with equal knowledge of practical mountaineering and desert journeys; tenting, motor camping, the use of balloon silk in camp, camera hunting, medical improvization, even the possibilities of leather working for the outdoor man are included in *Trail Craft*.

What percentage of American vacations are now accomplished with the aid of the automobile must be left for the census of 1930 to determine; but it is large, and will be larger then. In fact, motor camping is a distinct department of a magazine like Outers' Recreation, attended to along with other editorial duties by F. E. Brimmer, whose *Autocamping* is rather more necessary than the Blue Book. For a missed road is remediable, but a non-existent hotel isn't. Besides, a hotel isn't camping.

Having lived outdoors with his family, including small children, for as long as five consecutive months, Mr. Brimmer has met most of the contingencies you will have to meet. *Autocamping* is the difference between a vacation and a disaster.

Here are two short works of fiction by one of the best living storytellers whose subjects are drawn from sport. *A Wedding Gift*, by John Taintor Foote, is annotated by its subtitle, "A Fishing Story." Mr. Foote's *Pocono Shot* needs no recommendation to those who know his fine dog story, *Dumb-Bell of Brookfield*. *A Wedding Gift* is the tale of a confirmed fisherman, aged forty, who marries a young and beautiful girl. The story is told by a friend whose wedding gift to the pair consisted of hand-painted fish plates each with a picture of a trout rising to take a fly. The bride had packed three trunks with frilly clothes in expectation of a honeymoon at Narragansett. She was wrong. She was taken to the Maine woods.

The narrative of what followed is of such a character that the fisherman's friend, having heard him out and remembering the dozen plates, each with a trout painted on it, does not wait to meet the bride.

A Wedding Gift is pure amusement, if you like, but *Pocono Shot* is written with an emotion that the reader feels whether he cares for dogs or not. It has also—owing, perhaps, to its being told in the first person—an accent of reality. The dog of the story is a black and white setter, the best bird dog in the Pocono Hills,

[36]

and better on a scent than any hound in the country round about. It was this aptitude which got Pocono Shot into trouble; tracking a man who had caused the death of a girl, the setter received a terrible axe wound from the fugitive's father. The dog is marked by a great shoulder scar. We make acquaintance with his history at this point, step back for a little to learn his career, go with him in the field and find out for ourselves his extraordinary qualities, and then follow him to his reunion with the master who had shot to kill when the setter's life was imperilled.

iii

Surely the most exciting trail blazed in our day was the short and obscure one leading a few feet underground which took Howard Carter and Lord Carnarvon into Tut.Ankh.Amen's royal chamber. The second volume of Howard Carter's and A. C. Mace's *The Tomb of Tut.Ankh.Amen*, now impending, will round out the record of a discovery which exists, and is likely to remain, without parallel. The odds against a similar find are too great for anyone but a mathematician to calculate, and would be meaningless in any calculation. The first volume of *The Tomb of Tut.Ankh.-Amen* surpassed most other official and authentic records of its sort simply because the authors forgot they were archæologists and—told the story. In the presence of that priceless gift of fortune, standing where they had stood and breaching a blank wall to find it the threshold of the inner chamber with its nested gold shrines, who could have thought of anything but the supreme human and dramatic values of that scene and fateful moment? Not Howard Carter, certainly. He remembered then the six long and barren years of unrewarded searching, the first faint hint that he might be on the right track, the mounting excitement chilled at regular intervals by the worry of doubt and the littleness of disappointed hopes. Yet here lay a king of Egypt, his body cased in gold and his tomb and its seals protected by his gods. It was a story that could not be told except in all its simplicity. One could no more dress it up in lore and learning than permit the excesses of emotional description. *The Tomb of Tut.Ankh.Amen* is the modern romance of the conquistador.

While we are on the path of adventure in strange lands I want to draw attention to a book which transcends the interests of sportsmen. A fourteen-year-old boy, a circus trainer of animals, Dr. W. T. Hornaday, of the New York Zoo, Courtney Ryley Cooper, the novelist, and in fact persons of all ages and occupations will find themselves utterly absorbed in the pages of A. Blayney Percival's *A Game Ranger's Note Book.* This handsome book, illustrated with photographs, has been arranged and edited by E. D. Cuming from the great mass of observations, both written and verbal, made by Mr. Percival during nearly thirty years spent in Africa, of which about twenty-two were passed in the Game Department of what is now the Kenya Colony. It opens with seven chapters on the lion, followed by one or more chapters apiece on the leopard; cheetah, serval and caracal (one chapter); hunting dogs; hyænas; elephant; rhinoceros; hippopotamus; buffalo; giraffe; swine; zebra, and antelope. Most of Mr. Percival's material about the antelope has had to be reserved for a separate volume, so copious is it. The book closes with chapters on hunting and photographing big game. It is utterly untechnical, extremely modest, occasionally humorous, and as meaty with thrills as with information about animal characteristics and habits. *A Game Ranger's Note Book* deserves as a pendant in reading Fred L. M. Moir's *After Livingstone*, a story of adventure and hunting when big game were more numerous than now. The story is told by one of two brothers, business men who were pioneer traders in Africa. It has plenty of bush fighting and Mr. Moir witnessed scenes of savage life that will probably never come within the experience of white men again.

GOING OUT?

Birds of America, edited by T. Gilbert Pearson, John Burroughs, Herbert K. Job and others. Three volumes. Describes and pictures 1,000 species. Over 300 species shown in color from New York State Museum drawings. Eggs of 100 species in actual size and colors.

The Outdoorsman's Handbook, by H. S. Watson and Capt. Paul A. Curtis, Jr. Tested wisdom on hunting, camping, fishing and woodcraft. Indexed.

Lake and Stream Game Fishing, by Dixie Carroll. The author was at the time of his death recently probably the best known fisherman in the United States.

Goin' Fishin', by Dixie Carroll. Pungently written and especially good on the subject of baits. Equally interesting to the expert and the occasional angler.

Streamcraft: An Angling Manual, by Dr. George Parker Holden. Endorsed by Stewart Edward White and pronounced by Henry van Dyke "the best of all modern books on the science of trout-fishing."

Casting Tackle and Methods, by O. W. Smith. Forty years' experience condensed by the fishing editor of Outdoor Life and author of *Trout Lore*.

The Salt Water Angler, by Leonard Hulit, is an invaluable and complete compendium of information for salt water fishermen.

CARGOES FOR CRUSOES

In the Alaska-Yukon Gamelands, by J. A. McGuire. The story of an expedition to gather museum specimens far off the beaten routes. Probably the best authority on the game resources of the territory.

Fishing with a Boy, by Leonard Hulit. The tale of a city man in search of health with, incidentally, much about the ways of the humbler fishes.

Jist Huntin', by Ozark Ripley. Stories told by an expert guide who has fished and hunted from Alaska to the Gulf of Mexico.

Breaking a Bird Dog, by Horace Lytle. Altogether unique is this fascinating account of the process of training, from the author's actual experiences.

What Bird is That? by Frank M. Chapman. The most recent Chapman bird book. Handily divided according to season; every bird pictured in colors.

Handbook of Birds of Eastern North America, by Frank M. Chapman. A standard work, invaluable to the bird lover.

3. The Art of Melville Davisson Post

WHO that read in the Saturday Evening Post of 18 July 1914 a short story called "The Doomdorf Mystery" forgets it now? No one, I think; and it was a very short story, and it appeared over ten years ago. The magazine which published it—if one had read no others—has published 2,500 short stories since. "The Doomdorf Mystery" is one in a thousand, literally.

The creature, Doomdorf, in his stone house on the rock brewed a hell-brew. "The idle and the vicious came with their stone jugs, and violence and riot flowed out." On a certain day two men of the country rode "through the broken spine of the mountains" to have the thing out with Doomdorf. "Randolph was vain and pompous and given over to extravagance of words, but he was a gentleman beneath it, and fear was an alien and a stranger to him. And Abner was the right hand of the land."

About the place were two persons, a circuit rider who had been rousing the countryside against Doomdorf and who had called down fire from heaven for the creature's destruction. A little faded woman was the other.

In his chamber, the door bolted from the inside according to custom, Doomdorf lay shot to death.

The circuit rider asseverated that heaven had answered his prayer. The little, frightened, foreign woman showed a crude wax image with a needle thrust through its heart. She had killed Doomdorf by sorcery.

Randolph exclaimed with incredulity. Murder had been done; he was an officer of justice. But Abner pointed out that when the shot was fired, by evidence of Doomdorf's watch, the circuit rider was on his way to the place, the woman on the mountain among the peach trees. The door was bolted from the inside, the dust on the casings of the two windows was undisturbed and the windows gave on an hundred-foot precipice as smooth as a sheet of glass. Had Doomdorf killed himself? And then got up and put the gun back carefully into the two dogwood forks that held it to the wall? Says Abner: "The murderer of Doomdorf not only climbed the face of that precipice and got in through the closed window, but he shot Doomdorf to death and got out again through the closed window without leaving a single track or trace behind, and without disturbing a grain of dust or a thread of cobweb. . . . Randolph, let us go and lay an ambush for this assassin. He is on the way here."

This masterly tale, so far as the explanation is concerned, could doubtless have been chanced upon by Melville Davisson Post in those old records which he, a lawyer, would need to consult. Its kernel or nubbin could spring from the simplest scientific knowledge, the acquisition of any boy in high school. Its marvellous art is another affair. One might have the explanatory fact and make no more of it than a curious coroner's case. One could narrate it without any use of imagination and the result would be a coincidence without meaning.

The manner of Doomdorf's assassination depends very greatly upon coincidence. But given the series of coincidences, it was due to the operation of a natural law. Mr. Post had, initially, two difficulties to overcome. The first was fiction's rule of plausibility. The second was art's demand for emotional significance, a more-than-meets-the-eye, a meaning.

ii

Truth is stranger than fiction dares to be. Truth compels belief, fiction must court it. To overcome the handicap imposed by the manner of Doomdorf's killing with its conspiracy of chances, Mr. Post plunges his reader [1] at once into coincidences far more improbable—the presence on the scene of the circuit rider, the double confession of circuit rider and the woman to having killed Doomdorf. He storms the reader's stronghold of unbelief, the wall is breached, and no Trojan Horse is necessary later to bring his secret into the city. In fiction, there is no plausibility of cause and effect outside human behavior. The implausible (because unmeaning) manner of Doomdorf's death is superbly supported by two flanks, the behavior of the evangelist and the behavior of a terrified, superstitious and altogether childlike woman.

Art's demand for meaning requires much more than a certain plausibility of occurrence. The manner of Doomdorf's death need not have been dependent on his evildoing; it must be made to seem so. The glass water bottle standing on the great oak table in the chamber where he slumbered and died could as easily have held water as his own raw and fiery liquor. There are two kinds of chance or coincidence in the world. One kind is meaningless; our minds perceive no cause and effect.

---

[1] "The Doomdorf Mystery" is the opening story in Mr. Post's book, *Uncle Abner, Master of Mysteries* (1918).

The other kind is that in which we see a desired cause and effect. The writer of fiction must avoid or overcome the first kind if he is to write plausibly and acceptably; but upon his ability or inability to discern and employ the second kind depends his fortune as an artist.

In other particulars "The Doomdorf Mystery" exemplifies the artistry of the author. If I have not emphasized them, it is because they are cunning of hand and brain, craftsmanship, things to be learned, technical excellences which embellish but do not disclose the secret of inspiring art. The story is compactly told; tension is established at once and is drawn more tightly with every sentence; and the element of drama is much enhanced by the forward movement. Doomdorf is dead, but "Randolph," says Abner, "let us go and lay an ambush for this assassin. *He is on the way here.*" Not what has happened but what is to happen constitutes the true suspense. The prose style, by its brevity and by a somewhat Biblical diction, does its part to induce in the reader a sense of impending justice, of a divine retribution upon the evildoer. But it is also a prose that lends itself to little pictures, as of the circuit rider, sitting his big red-roan horse, bareheaded, in the court before the stone house; or of the woman, half a child, who thought that with Doomdorf's death evil must have passed out of the world; or of Doomdorf in his coffin with the red firelight from the fireplace "shining on the dead man's narrow, everlasting house." The comparative loneliness, the wildness, and the smiling beauty of these mountains of western Virginia are used subtly in the creation of that thing in a story which we call "atmosphere" and the effect of which is to fix our mood. The tale is most economically told; the simplest and fewest means are

[44]

made to produce an overwhelming effect. I have dwelt on it at length because it so perfectly illustrates the art of Melville Davisson Post, so arrestingly different from that of any of his contemporaries—different, perhaps, from anyone's who has ever written.

iii

Mr. Post is one of the few who believe the plot's the thing. He has said: "The primary object of all fiction is to entertain the reader. If, while it entertains, it also ennobles him this fiction becomes a work of art; but its primary business must be to entertain and not to educate or instruct him. The writer who presents a problem to be solved or a mystery to be untangled will be offering those qualities in his fiction which are of the most nearly universal appeal. A story should be clean-cut and with a single dominating germinal incident upon which it turns as a door upon a hinge, and not built up on a scaffolding of criss-cross stuff. Under the scheme of the universe it is the tragic things that seem the most real. 'Tragedy is an imitation, not of men, but of an action of life . . . the incidents and the plot are the end of a tragedy.' [2] The short story, like any work of art, is produced only by painstaking labor and according to certain structural rules. The laws that apply to mechanics and architecture are no more certain or established than those that apply to the construction of the short story. 'All art does but consist in the removal of surplusage.' [3] And the short story is to our age what the drama was to the Greeks. The Greeks would have been astounded at the idea common to our age that the highest form

[2] Aristotle in his *Poetics*.
[3] Walter Pater.

of literary structure may omit the framework of the plot. Plot is first, character is second." [4]

Mr. Post takes his stand thus definitely against what is probably the prevailing literary opinion. For there is a creed, cardinal with many if not most of the best living writers, which says that the best art springs from characterization and not from a series of organized incidents, the plot;—which says, further, that if the characters of a story be chosen with care and presented with conviction, they will make all the plot that is necessary or desirable by their interaction on each other. An excellent example of this is such a novel as Frank Swinnerton's *Nocturne* or Willa Cather's *A Lost Lady*. Yet it is not possible to refute Mr. Post by citing such books for he could easily point to other novels and stories if modesty forbade him to name his own work. Though there cannot and should not be any decision in this matter, for both the novel of character and the novel of incident are proper vehicles, it is interesting to consider plot as a means to an end.

The Greeks used plot in a manner very different from our use today. At a certain stage toward the close of a Greek tragedy the heavens theoretically opened and a god or goddess intervened, to rescue some, to doom others of the human actors. The purpose was to show man's impotence before heaven, but also to show his courage, rashness, dignity and other qualities in the face and under the spell of overwhelming odds. The effect aimed at by the spectacle of Greek tragedy was one of emotional purification, a purging away in the minds of the beholders of all petty and little things, the celebrated *katharsis* as it was

[4] The quotations from Mr. Post are collated from the chapter on him in Blanche Colton Williams's *Our Short Story Writers* (Dodd Mead).

called.[5] To the extent that modern fiction aims to show man's impotence in the hands of destiny or fate, his valiance or his weak cowering or his pitiful but ineffectual struggle, the use of plot in our day is identical with that of the Greeks. One may easily think of examples in the work of Thomas Hardy, Joseph Conrad, and others. The trend has been toward pessimism as an inscrutable destiny has replaced a set of scrutable, jealous, all-too-human deities in the Olympian pantheon.

With Edgar Allan Poe the attempt was begun—indeed, was successfully made, for the time being, at least—to replace the divine with a human agency. Although the Greek drama had perished, all through the Middle Ages and afterward the effort had kept up to preserve the essence of miracle as an invaluable element in human drama. There were both miracles and miracle plays. In place of the Greek *deus ex machina*, "the god from the machine" with his interventions in human affairs, the world had its Francis of Assisi and its Joan of France. But for whatever reason the divine agency was gradually discredited, the force called Providence or destiny came increasingly to be ignored, and even so great a dramatist-poet as Shakespeare, unable or unwilling to open the heavens to defeat Shylock, could only open a lawbook instead.

What men do not feel as a force in their lives cannot safely be invoked in an appeal to their feelings, and Poe, a genius, knew it. In some of his stories he used in place of the Greek *deus ex machina* the vaguely supernatural, impressive because vague. In other stories he took the human intelligence, sharpened it, and in the person of Monsieur Dupin made it serve his

[5] See Gilbert Murray's *Euripides and His Age* in the Home University Library (Holt).

purpose. M. Dupin, not being a god, could not be omniscient; as the next best thing, Poe made his detective omniscient after the event. If the emotional effect of a Dupin remorselessly exposing the criminal is not as ennobling as retributive justice administered by a god from Olympus, or wrought by Christian miracle, the fault is not Poe's. It is we who limit the terms of an appeal.

Mr. Post has himself commented on the flood of detective stories that followed Poe's "until the stomach of the reader failed." Disregarding merely imitative work, let us have a look at such substitutes as have been managed for divinity and fate. We commonly call one type of story a detective story simply because the solution of the mystery is assigned to some one person. He may be amateur or professional; from the standpoint of fictional plausibility he had, in most cases, better be a professional. Poe had his M. Dupin, Gaboriau, his M. Lecoq; Conan Doyle, his Sherlock Holmes. Mr. Post has Abner, his M. Jonquelle, prefect of police of Paris; his Sir Henry Marquis of Scotland Yard; his Captain Walker, chief of the United States Secret Service. If we are looking for Mr. Post's difference from Poe and others we shall not find it here. The use of a detective is not inevitable; when there is none we call the tale a mystery story. The method of telling is not fixed; and it is doubtful if anyone will surpass the extreme ingenuity and plausibility of Wilkie Collins in a book like *The Moonstone*, where successive contributed accounts by the actors unfold the mystery at last. One of the few American writers whose economy of words suggests a comparison with Mr. Post was O. Henry. And O. Henry was also a believer in plots, even if the plot consisted, as some-

MELVILLE DAVISSON POST

times it did, in little more than a few minutes of mystification.

Poe had replaced the god from the machine with the man from the detective bureau, but further progress seemed for some time to be blocked. All that anyone was able to do was to produce a crime and then solve it, to build up a mystery and then explain it. This inevitably caused repetition. The weakness was so marked that many writers tried to withhold the solution or explanation until the very end, even at the cost of making it confused, hurried, improbable. Even so, no real quality of drama characterized the period between the crime at the commencement and the disclosure at the finish of the tale. I do not know who was the first to discover that the way to achieve drama was to have the crime going on, to make the tale a race between the detective and the criminal. The method can, however, be very well observed in Mary Roberts Rinehart's first novel, *The Circular Staircase* (1908); and of course it is somewhat implied in the operations of Count Fosco in Wilkie Collins's *The Woman in White*, many years earlier. But this discovery constituted the only technical advance of any importance since Poe. As a noticeable refinement upon this discovery Melville Davisson Post has invented the type of mystery or detective-mystery tale in which the mysteriousness and the solution are developed together. Not suitable for the novel, which must have action, this formula of Mr. Post's is admirable for the short story, in which there is no room for a race with crime but only for a few moments of breathlessness before a denouement.

This refinement of Mr. Post's whereby repetition is avoided, the development of the mystery and its solution side by side, is usually hailed as his greatest achievement. I happen to think that he has in certain of his tales achieved something very much greater. It seems to me that in some of his work Mr. Post has put the *deus ex machina* back in place, has by a little lifted the mere detective story to the dignity of something like the old Greek tragedy, and in so doing has at least partially restored to the people the purge of pity and the cleansing of a reverent terror.

iv

For whatever tribute one may pay him on the technical side, and every book of his increases the tribute that is his due, the thing that has remained unsaid is his use of plot for ennobling the heart and mind of the reader. He is right, of course, when he says that the primary business of the writer must be to entertain; but more rightly right when he adds that it is possible to do the something more in a work which may aspire to be called a work of art. Anna Katharine Green once wrote: "Crime must touch our imagination by showing people like ourselves but incredibly transformed by some overwhelming motive." The author of *The Leavenworth Case* and all those other novels which have entertained their hundreds of thousands, despite appalling technical shortcomings which she never ceased to struggle with but was never able to overcome, was one of the terribly few to command our respect and our admiration in this crucial affair. She was one of the few with whom plot was never anything but a means to an end, and that end, the highest. Of others, it is easy to think at once of O. Henry; it is in this that I would compare him with Mr. Post, and not in any lesser detail such as the power to tell a story with the fewest possible words. All the emphasis that has been put on short story construction in America, all the trumpeting that has proclaimed American writers as the masters of the short story on the technical side will ultimately go for nothing if the fact is lost sight of that a short story is a cup to be brimmed with feeling. And as to the feelings poured into these slender chalices, by their effects shall ye know them.

There is a curious parallel between Mr. Post and another contemporary American writer, Arthur Train. Both began as lawyers, and both showed unusual ability in the practice of the law. Both are the authors of books in which the underlying attitude toward the law is one of that peculiar disdain which, perhaps, only an experienced lawyer can feel. Mr. Train's stories of Ephraim Tutt display an indignation that is hot enough under their surface of weathered philosophy and levity and spirit of farce. But as long ago as 1896 Mr. Post had published *The Strange Schemes of Randolph Mason*, his first book of all and one that must detain us a moment.

His career up to that time may be dealt with briefly. Born in Harrison County, West Virginia, 19 April 1871, the son of Ira Carper Post and Florence May Davisson Post, he was graduated (A.B.) from West Virginia University in 1891 and received his LL.B. from the same institution the year following. He was very shortly admitted to the bar of the Supreme Court of West Virginia, of the United States Circuit Court of Appeals, and of the Supreme Court of the United States. He served as a Presidential elector and secretary of the Electoral College in 1892. A young man not yet twenty-five, he conceived that "the high ground of the field of crime has not been explored; it has not even been entered. The book stalls have been filled to weariness with tales based upon plans whereby the detective or ferreting power of the State might be baffled. But, prodigious marvel! No writer has attempted to construct tales based upon plans whereby the punishing power of the State might be baffled." And he reflected that the true drama would lie in a duel with the law. He thereupon created the figure of Randolph Mason, a skilled, unscrupulous lawyer who uses the law to defeat the ends of justice. Of these stories the masterpiece is probably "The Corpus Delicti." Well-constructed, powerful, immensely entertaining, surely these dramas are of the essence of tragedy, surely they replace Poe's detective with somebody far more nearly approaching the Greek god from the machine. In considering the effects of these remarkable tales we can hardly lose sight of their moral purge of pity and terror, their sense of the law man makes as a web which man may slip through or break or brush aside. Why, a true god from the machine, Mr. Post implies, is not necessary to us; we can destroy ourselves; heaven has only to leave us alone. This, in its turn, produces the much stronger secondary effect: the cry for a true god to order and reward and punish us.

Uncle Abner (1918) has been well contrasted with *The Strange Schemes of Randolph Mason.* "He has demonstrated that wrong may triumph over man-made laws, which are imperfect after all the centuries; but that right must win under the timeless Providence of God." [6] In *Uncle Abner* the *deus ex machina* is fully restored. When it was known how Doomdorf had died, "Randolph made a great gesture, with his arm extended. 'It is a world,' he said, 'filled with the mys-

---

[6] Blanche Colton Williams in the chapter on Mr. Post in *Our Short Story Writers.*

terious joinder of accident!' 'It is a world,' replied Abner, 'filled with the mysterious justice of God!' "

V

Mr. Post married, in 1903, Ann Bloomfield Gamble, of Roanoke, Virginia. Mrs. Post died in 1919. The political career which seemed possibly to be opening before him in his twenties has been neglected for one more fascinating as an author; although he has served as a member of the board of regents of State Normal schools, as chairman of the Democratic Congressional Committee for West Virginia in 1898, and as a member of the advisory committee of the National Economic League on the question of efficiency in the administration of justice (1914-15). He lives at The Chalet, Lost Creek, R. F. D. 2, West Virginia, rides horseback and enjoys the company of his dog, and reads the classics. He is the author of other books besides *Uncle Abner* which reveal his love for the West Virginia countryside and his power to make his stories take root and grow in that setting. Of his *Dwellers in the Hills* (1901) Blanche Colton Williams says, in *Our Short Story Writers*: "To read it is to ride in memory along a country road bordered by sedge and ragweed; to note the hickories trembling in their yellow leaves; to hear the partridges' call, the woodpecker's tap, and the 'golden belted bee booming past'; to cross the stream fringed with bulrushes; to hear men's voices 'reaching half a mile to the grazing steers on the sodded knobs'; to meet a neighbor's boy astride a bag of corn, on his way to the grist mill; to stop at the blacksmith's, there to watch the forging of a horseshoe; or at the wagoner's to assist in the making of a wheel; to taste sweet corn pone

[53]

and the striped bacon, and to roast potatoes in the ashes. . . ."

With the exchange of West Virginia for Kentucky, this is also the background and the mood of *The Mountain School-Teacher* (1922), but this short novel is an allegory of the life of Christ. A young schoolteacher appears in a mountain village. We first see him striding up a trail on the mountain, helping a little boy who is having trouble with an ox laden with a bag of corn. In the village the schoolteacher finds men and women of varied character. Some welcome him, and they are for the most part the poor and lowly; some regard him with suspicion and hate. The action parallels the life of Christ and is lived among people who are, despite nineteen centuries, singularly like the people of Christ's time. In the end comes the trial of the schoolteacher on trumped-up charges. "If He came again," the author seems to say, "it would happen as before."

Such fiction does not come from a man who is primarily interested in railroads and coal, education and politics, nor from one whose final interest is to provide entertaining fiction.

vi

In recent books Mr. Post has allowed his fiction to follow him on his travels about the earth. *The Mystery at the Blue Villa* (1919) has settings in Paris, Nice, Cairo, Ostend, London, New York and Washington; the war of 1914-18 is used with discretion as an occasional background. Mr. Poe's mysticism can be quickly perceived in certain stories; the tragic quality is ascendant in such tales as "The Stolen Life" and "The Baron Starkheim"; and humor is not absent from "Lord Winton's Adventure" and "The Witch of Lecca." A story of retributive justice will be found in "The New Administration." The scenes of most of the episodes in *The Sleuth of St. James's Square* (1920) are in America; the central figure about whom all the cases turn is Sir Henry Marquis, chief of the investigation department of Scotland Yard. The material is extremely colorful—from all over the world, in fact. *Monsieur Jonquelle, Prefect of Police of Paris* (1923) has the same characteristics with the difference of the central figure and with various settings. The reader will observe in these books that the narrative standpoint is altered from story to story; to take *Monsieur Jonquelle*, some of the tales are related by the chief character, some by a third person, some by the author. The reason for the selection inheres in each affair and is worth some contemplation as you go on. *Walker of the Secret Service* (1924) is pivoted upon a character who appears in "The Reward" in *The Sleuth of St. James's Square.*

This new book of Mr. Post's is a brilliant example of his technical skill throughout; it has also a special interest in the fact that the first six chapters are really a compressed novel. Walker, of the U. S. Secret Service, is introduced as a mere boy of vigorous physique who falls under the influence of two expert train robbers. The several exploits he had a share in are related with a steady crescendo of interest. At the end of the sixth chapter we have a clear picture of the fate of the two chiefs he served. The peculiar circumstances in which young Walker was taken into the Secret Service are shown; and the rest of the book records some of the famous cases he figured in. The motivation is that of *Uncle Abner*. " 'Crime always fails. There never was any man able to get away with it. . . . Sooner or later something turns up against which he is wholly unable to protect himself . . . as though there were a power in the universe determined on the maintenance of justice.' "

Two of the most striking stories, "The Expert Detective" and "The 'Mysterious Stranger' Defense," are developed from courtroom scenes—indeed, "The Expert Detective" is a single cross-examination of a witness. Probably this tale and one called "The Inspiration" must be added to the shorter roll of Mr. Post's finest work, along with "The Corpus Delicti" and "The Doomdorf Mystery."

The general method has been said, correctly, to combine the ratiocination of Poe's stories with the dramatic method of the best French tellers of tales. The details of technique will bear and repay the closest scrutiny. But in certain stories Melville Davisson Post has put his high skill to a larger use than skill can accomplish; for those of his accomplishments an endowment and not an acquisition was requisite. When one says that of the relatively few American writers with that endowment in mind and heart he was able to bring to the enterprise in hand a skill greater than any of the others, one has indeed said all.

BOOKS BY MELVILLE DAVISSON POST

1896 *The Strange Schemes of Randolph Mason*
1897 *The Man of Last Resort*
1901 *Dwellers in the Hills*
1909 *The Corrector of Destinies*
1910 *The Gilded Chair*
1912 *The Nameless Thing*
1918 *Uncle Abner, Master of Mysteries*
1919 *The Mystery at the Blue Villa*
1920 *The Sleuth of St. James's Square*

THE ART OF MELVILLE DAVISSON POST

SOURCES ON MELVILLE DAVISSON POST

Mr. Post's own two articles on the short story are of the highest value, not only to an understanding of his method, but as a contribution to the theory of literary structure—a contribution, unlike most, allied to and realized in practice.

His first article appeared under the title, "The Blight," in the Saturday Evening Post for 26 December 1914. A shorter article on "The Mystery Story" appeared in the same magazine, 27 February 1915.

In April, 1924, while in New York for a short time Mr. Post dictated the following notes which amplify a little his written articles:

"The modern plan for the mystery or detective story can no longer follow the old formula invented by Poe and adopted by Gaboriau, Conan Doyle, etc. All life has grown quicker, the mind of the reader acts more quickly, our civilization is impatient at delays. In literature, and especially literature of this type, the reader will not wait for explanations. All explanations must be given to him in advance of the solution of the mystery.

"It became apparent upon a very careful study of the mystery story that something must be done to eliminate the obvious and to get rid of the delay in action and the detailed and tiresome explanation in the closing part. It occurred to me that these defects could be eliminated by folding together the arms of the Poe formula. Instead of giving the reader the mystery and then going over the same ground with the solution, the mystery and its solution might be given together. The developing of the mystery and the development toward the solution would go forward side by side; and when all the details of the mystery were uncovered the solution also would be uncovered and the end of the story arrived at. This is the plan which I followed in my later mystery-detective stories

—the *Uncle Abner* series, *Monsieur Jonquelle*, and *Walker of the Secret Service*. This new formula, as will at once be seen, very markedly increases the rapidity of action in a story, holds the reader's interest throughout, and eliminates any impression of moving at any time over ground previously covered.

"It requires a greater care and more careful technique, for *every explanation which the reader must receive in order to understand either the mystery or the solution must be slipped into the story as it proceeds without any delay in its action.* There can be no pause for explanation. Each explanation must be a natural sequence and a part of the action and movement. The reader must never be conscious that he is being delayed for an explanation, and the elements of explanation must be so subtly suggested that one receives them as he receives the details of a landscape in an adventure scene, without being conscious of it.

"In undertaking to build up a story on this modern formula, one must first have a germinal or inciting incident upon which the whole story may turn as upon a hinge. Out of this controlling incident, the writer must develop both the mystery and its solution and must present them side by side to the reader in the direct movement of the story to the end. When the mystery is finally explained, the story is ended. There can be no further word or paragraph; there can be no added explanation. If a sufficient explanation has not preceded this point, the story has failed. If the reader has been compelled to pause at any point in the story long enough to realize that he is receiving an explanation, the story has failed.

"But it will not be enough if the writer of the mystery-detective story is able cleverly to work out his story according to this formula. He must be able to give this type of story the same literary distinction that can be given to any type of story. To do this he has only to realize a few of the primary rules of all literary structure. He must remember that everything, every form of character, has a certain dignity. This dignity the writer must realize and respect. Flaubert told Maupassant that in order to be original he had only to look at the thing which he wished to describe long enough and with such care that he saw in it something which no one had seen in it before. That rule ought to be amended to require the writer to look at every character and every situation long enough and with sufficient care to realize the dignity in it—that element of distinction which it invariably possesses in some direction—and when he has grasped that, to respect and convey it in his story.

"It may as well be said that no one form of literary structure is superior to another. The story dealing with the life and action of our highest types does not in itself result in any better literature than the story dealing with the lowest or most abandoned types; nor are physical adventures to be graded below metaphysical adventures. The mystery-detective story may be structurally so excellent and its workmanship so good that it is the equal of any form of literature.

"The obvious is at the base of all boredom. The thing that provides our perpetual interest in life is that the events lying just ahead of us cannot be determined. It is the mystery in the next moment, the next hour, the next day that we live to solve. If by any mental process we could ascertain the arrival of events ahead, no human being could endure the boredom of life. Something of this mystery, this uncertainty, must be caught up for the reader in the short story if his interest is to abide to the end. The skill of the author in preserving this uncertainty and mystery in events—in this imitation of life—will indicate the place to be assigned to him in the art he has undertaken."

To an interviewer (by letter) who asked for the principal events of his life, Mr. Post once made a suitably whimsical answer:

"I was born like the sons of Atreus in the pasture land of horses. I was reared by a black woman who remembered her grandmother boiling a warrior's head in a pot. I was given a degree by a college of unbeautiful nonsense. I have eaten dinner with a god. And I have kissed a princess in a land where men grind their wheat in the sky."

4. Jeffery Farnol's Gestes

i

A GESTE is a great exploit or an heroic achievement; the thing that has today pretty generally dwindled to a gesture. But although the fiction of Jeffery Farnol is full of gestures—of ladies who cry, "La!" and of ladies who swoon; of gentlemen who draw swords as naturally as they draw breath, or even more so—the succession of his work is a series of gestes. For one point, he followed his bent in the teeth of literary fashion and scored, at the outset, an enormous popular success. For another point, he kept his head when success was upon him. Although a favorite scene in his stories is one full of lightning fence, swifter guard and dexterous riposte, the true portrait of the author is decidedly different: It shows him in the patient and laborious attitudes of his own Black George, in the toil the young Farnol was himself committed to for a period in his youth, the heavy work of the forge and the foundry, the slow heating to malleability and the shape hammered out before cooling. After *The Broad Highway* had captured the fancy of England and America, in an incautious moment Farnol the smith, Farnol the patient artificer, contracted to furnish his next tale as a serial in an American magazine. The editor blithely began publication with only part of the manuscript in hand. Dissatisfied with his work, the author at one stage tore up ten completed chapters. For several months he worked under pressure. In the end he kept the editor supplied. The experience did not lead him into the misconception that his smithy was a Ford factory. Nor has the fact that he can write one kind of tale ever led him to suppose that he ought to succeed with another variety; he followed *The Definite Object* with *Our Admirable Betty*. It is surprising to reflect that he made his first hit by reviving a species of romance when romance of that species, and of pretty nearly every species, was justly considered to have breathed its last; but it is vastly more surprising to realize that he has continued to succeed by the same tactics. Almost ten years later another young man, similarly self-willed, was to score an equal success in America (though not in England) by the same sort of reckless behavior, only the title of the book was to be *Main Street* and not *The Broad Highway*. But Sinclair Lewis, although unaware of his advantage, was setting a fashion, not defying one. Both Mr. Lewis's novel and Mr. Farnol's were the products of that kind of saturation which, while it cannot be relied upon to produce enduring literature, can nearly always be counted upon to produce literary phenomena. Such a phenomenon, certainly, was the Kentish tale of Peter Vibart, Charmian, the Tinker, Black George, and the Ancient, appearing as a book early in 1911 and rolling rapidly up to a sale of 500,000 copies in England and America. And though perhaps not a portent, as *Main Street* has been a portent, it was a sign of far more significance than the appearance on the scene of a new individual writer. But let us tell the story of that story in orderly fashion.

ii

It begins with two little boys in their nightshirts listening furtively but eagerly outside the door of a

[61]

room in which their father was reading aloud to their mother, whose eyes were on her needle. The book was *The Count of Monte Cristo*. The name of the older boy—he was eight—was John Jeffery Farnol; of the younger, who was to fall in the Boer War, Ewart Farnol. The family had removed from Birmingham, where Jeffery was born, to Lee, in Kent. The reading proceeded until a sneeze betrayed the boys. But after that they were admitted for an extra hour to the evening readings. The senior Farnol read excellently, varying his voice to suit the characters. He made the stories live, for Jeffery at least. From Cooper, Scott, Dickens, Dumas, Thackeray and Stevenson heard at home, Jeffery became a schoolboy who invented tales to entertain his fellows; in particular he started a story which he carried on for three months, winding it up with the close of term. When he had finished school he wanted to become a writer, but as there was not money to send him to one of the universities, his father thought the ambition foolish, and at 17 the boy was set to work in Birmingham with a firm of engineers and brassfounders. Manual labor at the forge was varied by a great deal of fighting with fists. He was short and thickset; he spent the lunch hour either telling stories to the other men, "stories from the classics," as he says, "vividly touched up, no doubt, or making a rough drawing of some scowling diffident sitter." As he sat drawing one noon, a man of the crowd looking over his shoulder remarked: "Ah, that's all very well, but drawing ain't manliness." A test of manliness, inquiry developed, was the feat of a chap who had climbed up the inside of the big chimney. Farnol laid five shillings to half a crown that he could duplicate the deed. Says one account: "The chimney towered up, one hundred and twenty feet of blackness, choked with the soot of four years and with insecure stanchions, several of them broken." He fastened his handkerchief at the top for all to see; it is easy to believe that the worst of the thing was the climb down with soot tumbling in his eyes. The men refused to pay their bets, he had to fight one of them, though sick and giddy, and was beaten. But a climax was near at hand. Farnol kept a notebook in which he was forever jotting down ideas and impressions. The foreman most reasonably objected to these interruptions of work. There were blows. Leaving the foreman "reclining in a daze against an anvil"—the words aren't Farnol's—the last Farnol saw of the place was his handkerchief fluttering from the chimney top.

"No good for work, always writing." How singularly right the foreman's verdict had been, some years were required to prove. For a time Farnol stayed at home and wrote stories, poems, whatnot. A few stories got printed. His father was unimpressed, except by the unanimity of family relatives in declaring that he was encouraging Jeffery to grow into an idle fellow. It seemed as if something might be constructed from his son's natural aptitude for drawing. Jeffery began the study of line and figure drawing under Loudon at the Westminster Art School. He found everybody else at the school so much more clever that he became discouraged.

"I think I'll write."

"You can't write," said his father. "You've not had a University education."

He went into his father's business, but as he continued to write stories, and as some of them continued to get accepted, this arrangement was a failure. At this time his favorite recreation was cycling. "All the highroads and byroads of Kent, Surrey and Sussex became familiar to me. I wheeled between the flowery hedgerows and quenched my thirst at the wayside taverns. It was then, while watching villagers wending their way to church, that I first saw the Ancient. There he was, tall hat, smock-frock, shrewd, wrinkled face, and gnarled hands grasping his knobbly staff just as I have described him in *The Broad Highway*. And that was the first inception of the book, though it was not until several years afterward that it came to be written." Black George was fashioned out of his own time spent at the Birmingham forge.

Farnol wasn't yet twenty-one when he married Blanche Hawley, daughter of F. Hughson Hawley, a New York artist. The pair set out for America. The bride of seventeen had been sent to England on a visit. It was hoped that Mr. Hawley would take the news well. It was also hoped that Jeffery might sell stories more successfully in the United States. He had a negligible amount of money. The seven, and more than seven, lean years were beginning.

iii

Mr. Hawley received them well. In an interview a year ago[1] Mr. Farnol, recalling the New York period, is quoted as saying:

"I hadn't a cent in the world. My wife had paid for the wedding ring and the honeymoon, and it seemed to me that after that it was up to me to do something. It has been said that her father remained adamant when we arrived, but that isn't true. I'm expecting a knock on the bean from him when he reads that. On the contrary, I found him a delightful old cove, and we were forgiven.

[1] The Evening Telegram, New York, 21 October 1923, page 20.

Photograph by E. Hoppé, London.

JEFFERY FARNOL,

"After that I went to work, living alone in a room at Thirty-eighth Street and Tenth Avenue. One night, about 3 o'clock in the morning, I came across a man down by the river whose face was all covered with blood.

" 'What's the matter?' I asked him.

" 'I'm dying, kid, I'm dying!' he told me.

"I took him home and fixed him up. It turned out that he was the leader of a notorious gang. I've never known a finer chap than he. I've found out in this life that if you scratch deep enough you'll always find true worth.

"About a week after that night he came around and took me to a notorious saloon. He took me into the back room and introduced me to the bunch. Several of them have gone to the chair since, but they were good fellows.[2] I've gone into that saloon without a nickel in my pocket, and looking it. I've had one of the gang say to me: 'Stony up against it, kid? Will a fiver help?' and before I could know what happened the gang would have taken up a collection of $25 and given it to me.[3]

"My wife was living with her family at that time, but often she would come to bring me baskets with

[2] Identified by a correspondent of the Boston Herald (18 October 1923) as Dago Frank, Lefty Louie, Whitey Lewis, Gyp the Blood—figures in the Becker case.

[3] "Tammany ruled through the corner saloon," Farnol is quoted as saying, in an interview appearing in the New York Tribune, 19 October 1923. "Dear me, yes, we used to vote ever so many times. I always went out with my Hell's Kitchen gang, and we voted for Tammany as often as we were told, changing our coats and going in time and time again. That was when we were voting against Jerome.

"I've surprised my American friends by saying I thought prohibition was a good thing. I've seen too much tragedy and sordidness, too many babies born of drunken parents. I used to love my cups as well as anybody, and I used to say that regeneration could not be forced on a drunkard by law, but now I think the law will help give him his start anyway."

chicken and all sorts of delightful little delicacies.
The neighborhood was a terrible one in those days,
and I was afraid at first to have her come there. I
told some of the boys about it. They told me never to
worry again. They arranged that an unseen body-
guard should follow her from the street car and escort
her to my room and back again when she was ready
to leave. . . . She believed in me even then when
it meant more to me than anything in the world. People don't know it, but I am naturally a timid man.
She gave me confidence in myself, and with it came the
ability to succeed."

The room at Thirty-eighth Street and Tenth Avenue was a studio, "dismal, rat-haunted," where a job
as a painter of theatrical scenery compelled him to
spend a great many of his nights and days. In intervals of scene-painting he began *The Broad Highway*.
"I met O. Henry several times in the offices of Ains-
lee's Magazine. I think it was Will Irwin who introduced us. O. Henry was unusually taciturn for an
American, and I—well, I am an Englishman. So
though we saw each other frequently, never more than
'How d' ye do' passed between us.

"The pleasantest recollections I have of those old
days was the time I spent in dabbling in painting and
theatricals at the old Astor Theatre. One day a down-
and-out young man got past the doorkeeper and
strolled on the stage. 'I've got a fortune here in my
pocket,' he said. 'We all have that,' I replied.

"The young fellow said he had been a cub reporter
in Chicago, but now he was hungry and looking for a
job. Finally he got the attention of the producer at
the theatre. He pulled out a manuscript and began
reading. The producer at first paid no attention, but
gradually became more and more interested. When

the first act had been read the producer said, 'All right, I'll take it.' The starving dramatist was Eugene Walter and the manuscript was that of 'Paid in Full.' " [4]

Farnol wrote in the studio and also at Mr. Hawley's home, in Englewood, New Jersey. When *The Broad Highway* was the best seller, Mr. Hawley rounded out the picture of the New York period.[5] "Farnol," he said, "is a dreamer and a bookworm, and has just about as much practical idea of time and money as that type is popularly supposed to have. He kept right on writing, and night was the time he had to do it. Many a time when I've been detained late with a press of work I'd get home at midnight or thereabouts to find a light supper waiting for me and Jeffery up working, only waiting to be called to entertain me while I ate. For he is the most entertaining talker I've ever known and loves to talk. His natural speech is the phraseology in *The Broad Highway*.[6] It has become natural to him through many years of living with the characters in the books of that period he loves so well. And he is a born storyteller. He always kept us sitting overtime at meals, just as he used to keep me sitting up till 2 or 3 o'clock in the morning on the occasion of the midnight suppers. When he gets to spinning a yarn, whether telling it or writing it, he loses all knowledge of the flight of time. Often when I've come down to breakfast before catch-

[4] Interview in Boston Herald, 18 October 1923.

[5] Interview in The Sun, New York, 21 October 1911, page 16.

[6] " 'B'gad, no!' Yes, Mr. Farnol talks that way. He has had his characters do it for so long that it comes to him naturally and is in nowise an affectation."—The Evening Telegram, New York, 21 October 1923, page 20.

"Glasses are a part of his expressive equipment, as much as 'dammit man' is, and probably more so than a vest which seems to have acquired a habit of coming unbuttoned."—Interview by John Anderson in The Evening Post, New York, 23 October 1923, page 12.

ing my early train to New York I've found him just
finishing his night's work, fresh and enthusiastic. Even
when his days are full of leisure he likes best to work
at night. Then, he says, his brain is clearer, and there
are no interruptions. His power of concentration and
absorption is the most marvellous thing I've ever encountered. I remember once taking him to the Players
Club with me for luncheon. After luncheon he wan-
dered into the library and was delighted to see the
work of Aphra Behn, an early writer I'd never heard
of, but belonging to his favorite period and well known
to him. I left him there renewing her acquaintance
with delight. I forgot all about him, but chancing to
go back for dinner, on entering the library to my
amazement I saw him sitting there in exactly the same
posture in which I'd left him hours before. He didn't
know whether ten minutes or as many hours had
elapsed."

Farnol succeeded in selling a number of short
stories and had some work as an illustrator. He wrote
two light romances, *My Lady Caprice* and *The Money
Moon*, which magazines bought. For two years he
put all his spare time on *The Broad Highway*, the
history of which is among the curiosities of book publishing.

iv

Like *Main Street* a decade later, *The Broad Highway* was possibly conceived and certainly executed in
a spirit of revolt. Such rebellions are common, and the
only wisdom that can be uttered in respect of them is
embodied in that proverb which says that one man's
meat is another man's poison. Editors and publishers
endeavor to give the public what the public wants.
The public, very naturally, never knows what it wants

until it tastes it. The public is like a husband sitting down to his wife's dinner. He may like everything or nothing; he may enormously relish the unexpected, placed before him with inward perturbation and in a spirit of desperate doubt. He may pounce with appetite upon, and sing loudly the praise of, some dish denounced by him and refused by his palate the week before. If a writer attempt to please editors or publishers, who, in turn, are attempting to please their publics, he will be successful with the entrepreneurs and possibly with the audiences. And his temperament may make such a course the very best thing. If his temperament is otherwise, sooner or later he will please himself; and if he can then get published a large public may just possibly discover that he greatly pleases them.

The completed manuscript of *The Broad Highway* was submitted to the Century Company and Charles Scribner's Sons in New York, both of whom failed to come to terms and returned it shortly. It was then submitted to Dodd, Mead & Company, who indicated a conditional acceptance and asked the author to come in and discuss possible changes. The firm's readers offered their suggestions and Farnol took notes. The principal result was that he cut 20,000 words out of the book, which still remained of 200,000-word length, or twice the length of the usual "full-length" novel. The alterations were not enough to give the publisher the necessary confidence; the year was 1907, the year of the money panic; and the manuscript was finally returned to Farnol with a definite declination. The reasons were sound: There had been a bad slump in Wall Street, the book was formidably long, the author was unknown, the interest of the tale might be almost wholly for English readers. But there was another reason in the nature of the novel to which a few words should be devoted.

Robert Louis Stevenson had died in 1894. His work spawned a school of historical fiction, much of it pseudo-historical, which had dominated the American book market for years. The public taste did not discriminate during that decade between the good and the bad; *To Have and To Hold* and *When Knighthood Was in Flower* were equally hailed as masterpieces and alike elevated to the top of the heap. From that day, indeed, dates the name and the peculiarity of the "best seller." The term remains, but it has only in very recent years begun to undergo a transformation of meaning, the idea of relativity having crept in. With a truer perception and a better sense of proportion, we now tend to speak of a book as a best seller *in its class*, or in relation to the literary merit of the work or the record of the author or generally with an eye to what sale could be expected in the circumstances. The fact of a sale in so many figures remains; but the estimation in which the fact is held is quite different. A sale of 20,000 copies that would have passed unregarded twenty years ago is now likely to be accounted as of the greatest significance.

What was fundamentally the trouble in 1907 was not to be stated with vigor until 1914, when Frank Swinnerton's critique of Stevenson [7] was to appear with such concluding sentences as these: "Stevenson . . . created a school which has brought romance to be the sweepings of an old costume-chest. . . . If romance rests upon no better base than this, if romance is to be conventional in a double sense, if it spring not from a personal vision of life, but is only

[7] *R. L. Stevenson: A Critical Study,* by Frank Swinnerton. Pages 189, 190.

a tedious virtuosity, a pretence, a conscious toy, romance as an art is dead. And if it is dead, Stevenson killed it." Such, even in 1907, was in various quarters uneasily felt to be the fact. In 1907, it is true, George Meredith was spending his declining years in poetry, and Thomas Hardy was at work on *The Dynast;* but *The Way of All Flesh* had been published four years earlier, Shaw's plays were being staged, the dead George Gissing was at last coming into attention, Mr. Galsworthy had just given us *The Man of Property*, Mr. Wells was brewing *Tono-Bungay*, and Mr. Bennett was at work on *The Old Wives' Tale*. If the lid of the costume-chest was still raised, it had every appearance of being propped most insecurely. All cogent and immediate reasons aside, the publisher of books had every psychological and intuitive reason for doubting the appeal of a volume of 500 closely printed pages, much of it in dialect and all of it concerned with Kentish scenes of a hundred years earlier.

To return to *The Broad Highway*: An actor with whom the author had become acquainted at the Astor Theatre was about to play an engagement in Boston, and offered to show the manuscript to friends in the office of Little, Brown and Company. Farnol waited for some word in vain; after several months he learned that the actor had returned to New York, and sought him out. The actor had visited the publishing house but had completely forgotten the manuscript. . . . It was taken from the bottom of his trunk, where it had lain all the while, and Farnol was minded, first to sell it, with all rights, for $500. Mr. Hawley said Farnol would do no such thing, "if I have to buy it myself." Farnol's next impulse was to burn the cumbersome bundle. He finally gave it to his wife, and Mrs. Farnol sent it to her husband's mother in England. Shir-

ley Byron Jevons, at that time editor of The Sportsman, was the next to see it. He took it to the publishing house of Sampson Low, Marston & Company,
introducing it with: "Here is another *Lorna Doone*"—
Blackmore's novel having been the firm's greatest fiction success. The publishing house accepted the book
and had drawn an agreement with Mr. Jevons as Mr.
Farnol's agent when the author appeared unexpectedly.
In fact, Farnol, discouraged by his fortunes in America, had simply got on the boat with his wife and
little daughter. A new agreement was drawn with him
direct, and signed. Then, but some time before the
book was set up in type, the publisher showed it to
Clement K. Shorter, editor of The Sphere, whose
devotion to the work of George Borrow was well
known. Mr. Shorter's account of the incident em-
bodies an interesting estimate of the book:[8]

"I read *The Broad Highway* with avidity, and recognized at once—as who would not have done?—that
here was a striking addition to picaresque romances,
that the author had not read *Don Quixote*, *Gil Blas*
and the best stories by Defoe and Fielding for nothing,
nor had he walked along the broad highways of England without observation and profit any more than
had the creator of *Lavengro* and *Romany Rye*. For the
vast multitude of readers of each epoch the dictum of
Emerson stands: 'Every age must write its own books.'
It is of no use for the pedantic critic to affirm, with
pontifical fervor, that Cervantes and Le Sage and
Defoe are masters of literature and that our contemporaries are but pigmies in comparison. The great
reading public of any age will not be bullied into reading the authors who have reached the dignity of
classics. The writer who can catch some element of

[8] The Book News Monthly, Philadelphia, November, 1915.

the spirit of the 'masters' and modernize it is destined
to win the favor of the crowd. And thus Mr. Jeffery
Farnol has entered into his kingdom. . . . *The Broad
Highway* sold in hundreds of thousands. It is a breezy,
healthy book, as unpretentious as it is sincere. Neither
its author nor his friends need to worry themselves
as to whether it is a masterpiece of literature. For
our day, at least, it has added to the stock of harmless
pleasures. To the critic who complains that 'it is but
an exercise in archæology,' and that the author 'has
never felt what he has written but has gathered it up
from books, one can reply in the language of Goldsmith's Mr. Burchell, 'Fudge.' It is still possible in
England, in spite of its railway trains and its mechan-
ical development, to feel the impulse which inspired
Charles Dickens, George Borrow and all the masters
of the picaresque romance, who have in days gone by
traveled with delight through the countryside, seeking adventures and finding them. 'I felt some desire,' says Lavengro, 'to meet with one of those adventures which, upon the roads of England, are as plenti-
ful as blackberries in autumn.' Mr. Farnol has a talent for recreating such adventures, and he is perfectly
frank with his readers, anticipating a certain type of
criticism. 'Whereas the writing of books was once a
painful art,' he makes Peter Vibart say in *The Broad
Highway*, 'it has of late become a trick very easy of
accomplishment, requiring no regard for probability
and little thought, so long as it is packed sufficiently
full of impossible incidents through which a ridiculous heroine and a more absurd hero duly sigh their
appointed way to the last chapters. Whereas books
were once a power, they are of late degenerated into
things of amusement, with which to kill an idle hour,
and be promptly forgotten the next.' "

The letter killeth, but the spirit giveth life. On a famous occasion the late Maurice Hewlett tore to shreds the historicity of the work of James Branch Cabell, and Mr. Cabell completely lost his temper. Mr. Farnol's hero in *Beltane the Smith* "finds himself in an England which from the internal evidence of friars, bowmen, arms and armor we might vaguely describe as Edwardian (Edward I., II., III.)—the pikes he appears to have borrowed from a later period. And yet it is not Edwardian either; for there is no hint of a king in it all, and never, never was there such an anarchical England, save in the reign of Stephen of Blois." [9] Mr. Farnol's Latin, says J. P. Collins, "gives one the shivers. He mixes his *thee's* and his *ye's*, and precisians may murmur at his forms of archaic diction. But . . . if Farnol makes a slip in the way of detail, or lapses into excess, he preserves the most important thing, and that is atmosphere.[10] Everyone will recall Scott's inaccuracies in *Ivanhoe*, of which the most serious was the depiction of a state of feeling between the Saxons and Normans existing a century earlier than the time of the novel.

Mr. Shorter has made us longer; it remains to say that *The Broad Highway*, accepted in England, was offered by the English publisher in America, in one instance to Dodd, Mead & Company, who again declined it. Little, Brown and Company were the acceptors, learning for the first time of the actor's delinquency a few years earlier. The book was published on both sides of the ocean and sprang into instant success. In the midst of the smother of applause, appeals, money and golden prospects Mr. Farnol had

[9] A writer in the London Times, quoted in the Boston Evening Transcript, 24 November 1915.
[10] "The Romance of Jeffery Farnol," by J. P. Collins. The Bookman, New York, July, 1920.

a moment. He ejaculated: "Just think! I've lost four years of my life!"[11]

v

He was 33—ten years older than it has been done, and thirty years younger than it has been done, also.[12] Mr. Henry Sydnor Harrison achieved *Queed* at 31, Sinclair Lewis was 35 when *Main Street* appeared. On the whole, the four years seem not an excessive price to have paid for a coup, nor thirty-three years long to have found oneself. The point was neither in the success nor the time taken to reach it; it was in Mr. Farnol's ability to keep his head on his shoulders. This he proceeded to do; although he sold, while yet unwritten, the serial rights to his next work, pressure upon him did not prevent his destroying ten unsatisfactory chapters, as has been related, and although as he said at the time, "I really cannot blame the magazine people," he was emphatic in saying, "I never wish to undergo such an experience again." [13] Two years elapsed after the publication of *The Broad Highway* before the appearance of *The Amateur Gentleman;* and except for the publication of a piece of work written before *The Broad Highway* [14] and his effort to help in the war (*Great Britain at War*), he has had only nine books brought out in the dozen years since he raised the curtain. And of these one, *The Geste of Duke Jocelyn*, a romance in prose, blank verse and

[11] Quoted by Henry C. Shelley in his article, "Jeffery Farnol and 'The Broad Highway,'" in The Independent, New York, 7 September 1911.

[12] Rudyard Kipling was 23 when *Plain Tales from the Hills* was brought out in Calcutta; recognition came a few years later. Mr. F. Scott Fitzgerald wrote *This Side of Paradise* at 23. William De Morgan was well past sixty when *Joseph Vance* made its success.

[13] Interview in the Boston Sunday Globe, 28 May 1912 (London correspondence printed without a date line).

[14] *The Honourable Mr. Tawnish* (1913).

rhyme, is a novelty written for his daughter, Gillian, published because what had entertained one girl might very conceivably entertain others. Mr. Farnol's method of keeping his head on his shoulders has been to practise industry without becoming industrial. Although homesick at first on his return to England, he settled in Kent, at Lee, with a den at the top of the house where he could work from midnight to breakfast. Old English books lined two walls of this refuge; another wall was given up to a collection of old pistols and sabres; and on the desk there usually lay a dictionary of slang dated 1812. More recently the Farnols have lived at the seashore at Brighton, but the winters are generally spent at Ospedaletti, which is on the Italian Riviera.

Except for a short visit to report for the London Daily Mail the fight between Jack Dempsey and Georges Carpentier in 1921,[15] Mr. Farnol had not revisited America until autumn, 1923. At that time visitors met a shortish man, anything but a figure of romance, whose outstanding trait was his genuine friendliness, "a friendliness which is not an affectation with which he tries to put strangers at their ease, but an actual part of him." [16] To see him rehearse and enact, rather than merely outline, his next novel was an exceptional experience, for at such times he suits his voice to his characters and displays a considerable range of dramatic skill. Interviewers developed evidences of a struggle in the romancer's mind between

[15] "A better selection than Mr. Farnol the Daily Mail could not have made," said W. B. ("Bat") Masterson, in The Morning Telegraph, New York, 24 July 1921. "Mr. Farnol's narrative was not only interesting, but for the most part extremely thrilling. I would like to give the whole story as Mr. Farnol wrote it." He does, however, quote the salient passages of Farnol's story.
[16] Interview by John Anderson in The Evening Post, New York, 23 October 1923, page 12.

the type of woman he writes about and the types more usual today; however, chivalry, or perhaps the romantic vision, enabled him to come through the ordeal by newsprint without dishonor. He denied the possibility of platonic love and friendships. "After a certain point, such friendships are bound to be no longer platonic. Mark me! I know they wouldn't be in my case, anyway." [17] A subject he did not tire of discussing was the wonder of America.[18] To several who talked with him he expressed the intention of writing another novel about New York City.[19] "New York should be called 'The City of Great Adventures,' " he said, with characteristic enthusiasm, "because anything *might* happen in New York." [20]

More expressive of the man is the story of how his slightest novel came to be published. He was discussing with his mother the advisability of bringing out work written before *The Broad Highway*. "Look here," he said to her, "why not rout out *Mr. Tawnish?* You have been very good to me, and I can never properly repay you, but if you can do anything with *Mr. Tawnish* you shall have it." The tale—one that reminds most readers of Tarkington's *Monsieur Beaucaire*—was taken out of a drawer, touched up and added to, and accepted for book publication. The advance royalties, constituting a generous gift, were handed over to Mrs. Henry Farnol. This was in the autumn of 1913.

[17] Interview in The Evening Telegram, New York, 21 October 1923, page 20.

[18] "An Attic Salt-Shaker," by W. Orton Tewson in The Public Ledger, Philadelphia, 3 November 1923.

[19] Interviews in The Evening Telegram, New York, 21 October 1923, page 20; in The New York Tribune, 19 October 1923; in The Boston Herald, 18 October 1923. *The Definite Object* (1917) is laid in New York.

[20] Interview by Fay Stevenson in The Evening World, New York, 24 October 1923.

vi

In an article appearing at the height of Mr. Farnol's first success, Henry Keats wrote: *"The Broad Highway* has seemed to the critics to invite comparison with so many different masters of the English novel—George Borrow, Blackmore, Le Sage, Dickens, Stevenson, Thackeray, to mention a few—that I asked him about his 'foster-father.' Mr. Farnol smiled. 'I would not know my own literary parent if I met him out here in the broad highway of Kent,' he exclaimed. Judging from his subsequent confessions, the creator of Peter Vibart and Charmian is under greater indebtedness to Laurence Sterne than to any of the immortals named above. And that was owing to the friend of his 'boyish ambitions,' to whom *The Broad Highway* is dedicated. Mr. Shirley Byron Jevons was the first, some years since, to call Mr. Farnol's attention to the supreme difficulty of writing a book dealing with the abstract, citing, as a rare example of success in that line, Sterne's *Tristram Shandy*. A copy of that unusual book was speedily procured by Mr. Farnol, and he recalls as though an impression of yesterday the manner in which he was 'enthralled' by its pages. 'Then,' he adds, 'I went on to The Spectator and The Tatler, the reading of which showed me how great is the loss of those who are unacquainted with the Queen Anne essayists.' " [21] This settles the matter of style.

Certain books by Mr. Farnol—*The Honourable Mr. Tawnish*, *Great Britain at War*, and *The Geste of Duke Jocelyn*, each outside the true succession of his work—have been incidentally characterized. A de-

[21] "Jeffery Farnol at Home," by Henry Keats, The Book News Monthly, September, 1911.

scriptive note on his principal novels may perhaps fittingly conclude this account.

The Broad Highway (1911) has probably already been sufficiently described, as it must be familiar to many who may read these lines. *The Amateur Gentleman* (1913) has for hero Barnabas, son of a retired and famous boxing champion of England. Having come into a legacy, the young man resolves to journey to London to become a gentleman. The period is that of the Prince Regent. There is a rapid series of adventures on the journey; Barnabas meets Cleone, the heroine; he acquires a valet and establishes himself with the quality, and the fashionable world loses him, for he returns home again. *Beltane the Smith* (1915) concerns a golden-haired giant and matchless swordsman whose odyssey of adventure is lived in a much earlier England. *The Definite Object* (1917) is the story of a young New Yorker whose wealth has taken from him all incentive to action. For want of a definite object in life he is toying with the thought of suicide when he surprises a youthful burglar in the act of entering his rooms. Then, as "Mr. Geoffrey," he takes up lodgings with the housebreaker in the old Hell's Kitchen district of New York—which was the region between Thirty-fourth and Forty-second Streets and west of Sixth Avenue. *Our Admirable Betty* (1918) is a return to the dimension of *The Broad Highway* and *The Amateur Gentleman*. *Black Bartlemy's Treasure* (1920) and *Martin Conisby's Vengeance* (1921) are tales of piracy and the Spanish Main, the second novel completing the first. *Peregrine's Progress* (1922) more closely than any other book approximates the scenes and action of *The Broad Highway;* it is laid in Kent, it relates a boy's adventurings on the road and by the roadside, and it re-

introduces the Tinker. *Sir John Dering* (1923) keeps
to the same period. A skilled swordsman who has in-
curred the enmity of the Lady Herminia Barrasdaile
is forced to fight duel after duel which she has insti-
gated in the hope that he will meet his death.

The dictum of Mr. Shorter best fits the case of this
friendly writer and honest workman. We have already
quoted the words: "The great reading public of any age
will not be bullied into reading the authors who have
reached the dignity of classics. The writer who can
catch some element of the spirit of the 'masters' and
modernize it is destined to win the favor of the
crowd." The love of a fairy tale, delight in action,
pleasure in such characterizations as Black George, the
Tinker, and the Ancient—picturesque; in outline
broadly simple—have been potent. Stevenson was
dead; the good as well as the bad of his legacy had
been swallowed up in a flood wherein the sound could
no longer be distinguished from the meretricious; what
we loosely call realism was in the ascendant. Years
were to go by before "realism" could be seen to be
the necessary clearing of paths to an exploration of
the romantic impulse more intelligent as well as more
subtle. In the meantime an age-old thirst found these
draughts to quench itself. On the porch of the "Bull"
at Sissinghurst the readers of Mr. Farnol have sat for
many an afternoon, washing the dust from their throats
with a pleasant ale and enjoying the surprising procession of knights, scholars, gipsies, gallants, pirates
and simple maids and ladies of fashion which has
passed before them, coming from and returning to a
world without end, truly.

JEFFERY FARNOL'S GESTES

BOOKS BY JEFFERY FARNOL

1907 *My Lady Caprice*
       In England: *The Chronicles of the Imp*
1911 *The Broad Highway*
       The Money Moon. Earlier, in point of composition,
       than *The Broad Highway.*
1913 *The Amateur Gentleman*
1913 *The Honourable Mr. Tawnish.* Earlier, in point of
       composition, than *The Broad Highway.*
1915 *Beltane the Smith*
1917 *The Definite Object*
1918 *Great Britain at War*
       In England: *Some War Impressions*
1918 *Our Admirable Betty*
1920 *The Geste of Duke Joçelyn*
1920 *Black Bartlemy's Treasure*
1921 *Martin Conisby's Vengeance*
1922 *Peregrine's Progress*
1923 *Sir John Dering*

SOURCES ON JEFFERY FARNOL

The Novels of Jeffery Farnol. Booklet published by LITTLE,
BROWN & COMPANY, Boston, 1923.
   The Country of "The Broad Highway," by Henry C. Shel-
ley. THE BOOK NEWS MONTHLY, October, 1912.
   Jeffery Farnol's Life and Career, by Herbert F. Jenkins.
THE BOOK NEWS MONTHLY, September, 1911.
   How I Began, by Jeffery Farnol. Booklet published by
SAMPSON LOW, MARSTON & COMPANY, LTD., London. The
text is reprinted from T. P.'s Weekly of 14 February 1913.
   *Love Still Ruling Motive in Life of the Modern Youth and
Maiden.* Interview by Marguerite Dean in The Evening
World, New York, 28 June 1921. Note especially: "As a
matter of fact I knew a charming fellow who did, in real life,
just what my hero did in *The Definite Object*—took a little

girl from the New York slums, educated her, loved and married her."

Other references will be found in the footnotes to the text of this chapter. They do not include, by any means, all the interviews in newspapers.

5. Adults Please Skip [1]

i

NOT that age has anything to do with it. A man is as young as he feels and a woman is as young as her imagination keeps her. The idea of never growing up is a mistake. Everyone wants to grow up, but that's no reason for not keeping youthful.

There's something in fellows like Irvin S. Cobb and Owen Johnson and Ralph Henry Barbour which is just as good at forty as at fourteen—maybe better. And there's something in books like *Little Women* that you keep coming back to. . . .

S'pose we'd better begin with the Bedtime Story Man. Half the children in the United States of America are willing to call it a day when Thornton W. Burgess says the word. Mr. Burgess owes his success to the fact that he was born in a place called Sandwich in the State of Massachusetts. It made him realize that something was needed "between the dark and the daylight," as Longfellow said. Having splendid eyesight and some excellent connections, he was able to enter the best animal circles, and early met Peter Rabbit, Lightfoot the Deer, and loads of others. The way to meet them is by all means under Mr. Burgess's auspices, in *The Burgess Animal Book for Children.* Sammy Jay, Bob White and the feathered companions

[1] Several of the prime favorites among authors of books for boys and girls are discussed in Chapter 14.

who have more or less dealings with Striped Chipmunk
and Johnny Chuck are introduced in *The Burgess Bird
Book for Children*. It is a point of honor with Mr.
Burgess always to let his animal friends tell their own
stories. Louis Agassiz Fuertes illustrates these books
with pictures in full colors. For example, he shows
fifty-eight birds in all their glory. *The Burgess Bird
Book for Children* brought cries of joy from Dr. W. T.
Hornaday, who is America's leading naturalist and who
presides over more animals at the New York Zoo than
went into the ark with Noah. But wait! Here's a
third volume to put with these two, *The Burgess
Flower Book for Children*, also illustrated in color and
black and white and showing 103 flowers. You should
see the color pictures, for instance, of the yellow
adder's-tongue and the wild columbine! Let it be
stressed: the books by Burgess are the most popular and
most successful published for *little* children. Their
interest and joy is communicable to the child of four
years—and they are read and re-read by boys and girls
up to twelve, and sometimes by their elders.

Rose Fyleman, with *Fairies and Chimneys*, *The
Fairy Flute*, and *The Fairy Green*, won some time ago
chief honors as the children's poet; and now she seems
to be on the path to distinguished honors for her prose
stories. *The Rainbow Cat*, whose color scheme included orange hind legs and a red, red tail, gave the
greatest satisfaction, and so will *Forty Good Night
Tales*, in which errant fairies explain themselves. But
probably the most ambitious book is the new *Rose
Fyleman's Fairy Book*. Rose Fyleman for fairies, as
the advertisers would say.

Did you see *Number One Joy Street*, ever? At any
rate, you will see *Number Two Joy Street*, won't you?
Like the first book, it has a jolly cover and endpapers,

[84]

and plenty of illustrations in color and otherwise. The collection of prose and verse for boys and girls in *Number Two Joy Street* is from writers whose names will make even older people prick up their ears— Gilbert K. Chesterton, Walter de la Mare, A. A. Milne, Hilaire Belloc, Hugh Walpole, Laurence Housman and Rose Fyleman are some of them. With such an array of contributors, you will have very hard work to keep your copy of this book for your very own. It will be necessary to speak nicely but firmly to older people.

You will also need to explain that you must be left alone with Edna Geister's new book, *What Shall We Play*. Grownups are almost certain to think that they ought to stick around and tell you how to go about the fifty best games in this book. They are wrong. Miss Geister herself says so. She says she took the very best out of her hundreds of inspirations for play and took pains to explain them so that children can play them without help or direction, and at sight. *Let's Play* is another one of her game books written especially for boys and girls. *It Is To Laugh* is a little more grown-up (not a great deal).

The Velveteen Rabbit, by Margery Williams, has remarkable pictures. As you look at William Nicholson's drawings (they were made on stone, which gives them their peculiar texture) you can really see the sawdust hero come to life and leap for joy! We will come in a moment to other books with glorious pictures, but first let us see if we have one or two more books for four and five and six years. Yes. Here is *Mother Hubbard's Wonderful Cupboard*, by Maude Radford Warren and Eve Davenport, who also wrote *Tales Told by the Gander* and *Adventures in the Old Woman's Shoe*. The scheme in each of these books is the delightful one of continuing the Mother Goose stories. Mother Goose, with her unfinished tales, is extremely tantalizing. Probably the good woman told all she knew, but it is by no means enough. For instance, she appeared to know nothing of the circumstances in which Mother Hubbard acquired her dog. They were highly interesting. You see, she needed some one to work for and be interested in, and as no child was available she took Diccon, who was a trained, performing dog attached to a circus, but so ill that his owner thought he wouldn't live long anyway. C. A. Federer has made the many illustrations, some of them in color.

The Wiggly Weasel and Other Stories, by Mabel Marlowe, is another book with many pictures that is full of the fun of clever animals, brownies, and their kin.

Perhaps you take part in plays? Then, if you are young enough, I think you will be enthusiastic over the seven gay masques in *The Magic Sea Shell and Other Plays*, by John Farrar. There is probably a place in the garden that looks as though a play were about to begin there, or a spot down the meadow or a roomy chimney-corner in the house. Home-made music and costumes, please!

For seriousness, and in moments when you want to know more about the world you live in, and how men came to live in it, anyway, the two most helpful books are likely to be Frederic Arnold Kummer's *The First Days of Man* and *The First Days of Knowledge*. These relate the *true* fairy story of Creation and man's coming-to-know. Moreover, it is told in such a way that any boy and most girls can make for themselves the simple tools that man first began by making.

ii

I spoke of books with pictures. If you are so lucky as to have the *Fairy Tales by Hans Andersen*, illustrated by Kay Nielsen, or those other books for which he made the illustrations, *The Twelve Dancing Princesses* and *East of the Sun and West of the Moon*, I hope you will say a word to your older friends about this artist. They are likely to be as ecstatically happy as yourself, in the contemplation of the pictures, but not to know what it is they admire. Then you must tell them that Kay Nielsen is a Dane, the son of an actor and a famous actress, who was brought up in a home where the rich furnishings and beautiful colors came from Constantinople and the East. He went to London and saw drawings by Aubrey Beardsley in which all the lines combined elegance, suavity (or great smoothness), power (or sureness and ease), and a certain austerity (bareness, simplicity). And so, by what he had seen and by the nature received from his parents, he became a great artist who could do fiery work with an occasional effect of grim strength; but in these pictures you know he is riotously playful with his lines and his colors alike.

Edmund Dulac and Arthur Rackham are other great artists who have done much of their finest work in illustrating children's books. You may have Hawthorne's *A Wonder Book*, illustrated by Rackham, or *Edmund Dulac's Fairy Book*, or *Stories From the Arabian Nights*, *The Sleeping Beauty and Other Fairy Tales*, or *Stories from Hans Andersen*, each with Dulac's pictures. Perhaps the most wonderful of all Dulac's books is the edition of Shakespeare's comedy of *The Tempest*.

[87]

iii

You are old enough to be thinking about going away to school. You can't get too many school stories. In particular, you are keen for a new book by Ralph Henry Barbour. Nobody writes better school sport books! *The Fighting Scrub*, Mr. Barbour's latest, is a picture of life at a famous New England school; and the fellows and the incidents of the tale are just as actual as the setting. Clif Bingham and Tom Kemble are boys everyone can recognize among his friends, and while Loring Dean, a cripple confined to a wheel-chair, is a new character in a story of boys, his splendid head-work in planning a forward pass play that makes the winning touchdown for the school is proof that a boy need not be an athlete to count.

There are some very pretty points about *The Fighting Scrub*. It has been usual to write only about a fellow who "made the team." The scrub team has been an unsung, unhonored aggregation on which the first team sharpened its teeth. Mr. Barbour's hero is only a scrub; but even a scrub has been known to play in the big game and with crucial results. Here's another thing: people have begun to recognize the fact that we are in danger of losing sight of football and other games as sport, and of thinking only of winning. Nothing could show better than the history of Clif Bingham and Tom Kemble in *The Fighting Scrub* that the real joy of football lies in the spirit in which you play. Every fellow can see himself in Clif or Tom or Loring Dean.

Again, there are thousands of boys who will be able to see themselves in Joe Kenton, the hero of Mr. Barbour's *Follow the Ball*. Joe is a fellow who is far from having things all his own way, but he is a sticker.

[88]

He has to earn the money to get through school, and that never made it easier to make a record in athletics. But he shows up well, and *Follow the Ball* has baseball, skating, hockey and camping in its pages as well as football.

The proved classics in the way of school stories are assuredly Owen Johnson's. It is sixteen years since the first publication of his first book of Lawrenceville stories, but Hickey Hicks, Dink Stover, Doc Macnooder, Hungry Smeed, the Gutter Pup, the Tennessee Shad and Lovely Mead are as "generally and specifically bully" as when Booth Tarkington hailed them. Mr. Johnson's success in *The Prodigious Hickey*, *The Varmint* and *The Tennessee Shad* is as great as Mr. Tarkington's own in *Penrod;* immeasurably greater than Kipling's effort in *Stalky & Co.* It is true to say that the Lawrenceville stories blend speed, surprise, mischief and humor with a smoothness and a perfection untouched by anything else of their sort. They avoid the utter priggishness and complacency of *Tom Brown's School Days*, while having the same positive value of a real school, under its own name and with its own tradition, as their background. "The only real prep school story ever written," said George Ade, crisply, after reading *The Varmint*. Why? No doubt the fact that the Lawrenceville stories are semi-autobiographical has much to do with it. For Johnson was a Lawrenceville boy in the 1890s; there is extant a picture showing him with the original (but somewhat older) Brian de Boru Finnegan, Turkey Reiter, the Old Roman, and the Prodigious Hickey. Johnson himself it was who held the skeleton while Hickey attached it to a rope hung from a ventilator. Johnson sat on the roof when Old Ironsides—afterward a New York real estate broker—slid off and got

[89]

filled with gravel. It was Johnson who experienced the agony of muffing a ball and being attacked by the whole baseball team, which he has described as the Varmint's first discouraging experience with Lawrenceville athletics.

And after a dozen years, Mr. Johnson recently returned to the Lawrenceville scene in *Skippy Bedelle*, which tells how Skippy planned to invent a foot regulator for bathtubs and of certain deplorable experiments which were to produce mosquito-proof socks. *Skippy Bedelle* is largely the story of a sentimental progression and includes the first dress suit and Skippy's first girl.

In the days when professional ballplayers still had mustaches and you could give people a thrill by riding down the post-office steps on a high-wheel bicycle, Irvin S. Cobb was goin' on fourteen. And in *Goin' on Fourteen*, his new book with pictures by Worth Brehm, the artist for Tarkington's Penrod stories, Cobb has cut a few cross-sections out of a year in the life of an average boy. Now without in any respect being literal reminiscences, these chapters accurately and joyously reflect a scene and a period and a boy most unmistakably American. For Johnny Custer, otherwise John C. Calhoun Custer, Jr., is neither Tom Sawyer nor Penrod Schofield—though perhaps more like Tom and Huck Finn than Penrod—but he is as instantly recognizable and as entirely "boy" as either. And Johnny Custer was his own trained investigator; he did not depend upon others to tell him what would happen in untried circumstances, no, sir! The account of how he and Mr. Simons short-circuited the fowls of a chicken fancier should be read with caution; it is likely to leave you in the same condition of happy helplessness in which it left Johnny.

[90]

Albert Payson Terhune, like John Taintor Foote,[2] writes a capital dog story, and Mr. Terhune's stories of collies, Buff and Lad and the others, are known wherever the dog has his due. In *The Heart of a Dog*, Terhune's new book, there are one or two tales in which a collie is not the hero, but Lad and Buff and Treve and Lochinvar Bobby are familiar friends of the breed which Mr. Terhune himself raises and takes prizes with. Marguerite Kirmse has made the eight pictures in color and others in black and white. This is another book that grown-ups will borrow and neglect to return, if you don't watch out.

Every boy and girl knows how hard it is to find a good, readable history. The difficulty was pointed out to Sidney Dark, who set to work at once to do something about it. And so far he has done magnificently, producing, in *The Book of Scotland for Young People*, *The Book of England for Young People*, and *The Book of France for Young People*, three histories more clear and interesting to boys and girls of ten to sixteen than any similar accounts. (I do not even except Charles Dickens's *A Child's History of England*, which is one-sided in spots.) Each of Mr. Dark's books has sixteen illustrations from famous paintings of historic scenes.

iv

There is an Everyman's Library—why not an Everychild's Library? Well, one has been begun. It is called The Beacon Hill Bookshelf and already eight volumes are to be had. One of them, *The Boy Whaleman*, has never been published before; the others are all established favorites stamped with the approval of librarians and parents as well as of children themselves.

[2] See Chapter 2.

But even the old ones are printed from new type and all the books are illustrated in color by well-known artists—five to eight color plates apiece.

The first book on The Beacon Hill Bookshelf is the book that still is first on children's bookshelves everywhere throughout America. It is the book which, in a recent wide competition conducted by The Bookman, led all other "juveniles." Its author was Louisa M. Alcott, and its title is *Little Women: or Meg, Jo, Beth and Amy*. Nowadays when you ask people like Hugh Walpole and Frank Swinnerton what American books they have read they have a way of recalling at once that Louisa M. Alcott was one of the first, and—without prejudice to other writers—has remained one of the most memorable. The Beacon Hill *Little Women* has pictures by Jessie Willcox Smith, and is properly companioned in the series by its sequel, *Little Men: Life at Plumfield with Jo's Boys*. Reginald Birch has done the pictures for *Little Men*.

Of the other six books, I must draw your attention especially to two: the one which is published for the first time and one by John Masefield. George F. Tucker's *The Boy Whaleman* has a place in the series because it deals with the experiences of an American lad more than sixty years ago—almost as far back as Richard Henry Dana's *Two Years Before the Mast*. Based on fact, Mr. Tucker's book is a thrilling account of a New Bedford boy's three years' voyage on a whaling ship.

Mr. Masefield's book, *Martin Hyde, the Duke's Messenger*, is illustrated by T. C. Dugdale, and is a spirited story of a boy who served the Duke of Monmouth in his attempt to gain the throne of James II. The tale is therefore one of the Monmouth Rebellion, as the rebellion of 1685 in England is most often called. Owing to the distinction with which Mr. Masefield writes, this book is one of the very best of adventure stories for boys' or girls' reading.

Besides the four books of which I have tried to tell something, the Beacon Hill Bookshelf also holds these four to date:

What Katy Did, by Susan Coolidge. This is the most popular of Susan Coolidge's books, the story of a girl who would not let illness and invalidism keep her from doing things.

The Story of Rolf and the Viking's Bow, by Allen French. Rolf avenges his father's murder and earns the viking's bow in a story with incidents drawn from the Icelandic sagas.

Nelly's Silver Mine, by Helen Hunt Jackson. This book by the author of *Ramona* is as popular to-day as forty years ago. It is the story of Rob and Nelly, twins in New England, who take a long journey to a new home in Colorado, where Nelly finds the mine of the title.

A Daughter of the Rich, by Mary E. Waller. The story is a great favorite with girls, who never fail to be interested in the account of a year spent on a farm in Vermont by a rich young city girl. Elizabeth Shippen Green Elliott has made the pictures in color.

AND HERE ARE A FEW OTHERS

Billy Mink, by Thornton W. Burgess, illustrated in color by Harrison Cady. The first volume in a new series of Burgess books which deals with the animals living in and around the Smiling Pool. For boys and girls of four to twelve.

Ruffs and Pompoms, by Beulah King, illustrated by Maurice Day. Finney Foo, the clown doll in the toy shop, goes out into the world to find a smile for the little Chinese Lady and has the strangest adventures that ever happened to a toy. For boys and girls of six to ten.

The Valley of Color-Days, by Helen B. Sandwell, illustrated in color by Alice Bolam Preston. The strange adventures of Jane and David, who were taken in charge by Burr, the fairy, while their parents were away for a few days. For boys and girls of six to ten.

Round the Year in Pudding Lane, by Sarah Addington, illustrated by Gertrude Kay. Twelve original and whimsical tales of the adventures that happened to the Mother Goose children who lived in Pudding Lane. For boys and girls of six to twelve.

The Goblin's Glen: A Story of Childhood's Wonderland, by Harold Gaze, illustrated in color by the author. Ruth and Norman and their Uncle Hal are taken by the fairies to unusual regions—the heart of Japan, Cloudland, the Arctic Circle and the Happy Isles. For boys and girls of seven to twelve.

The Friends of Diggeldy Dan, by Edwin P. Norwood, illustrated in color by A. Conway Peyton. The wonderful circus clown and his animal friends go to visit the king of Jungleland. For boys and girls of seven to twelve.

Fifty New Poems for Children. Here are verses about the things every child knows, such as dandelions, swallows, the wind, and the scissors-grinder, mixed with poems about the things of every child's wish and fancy—cloud houses, magic wall-paper, goblins and ring-a-ring fairies. The poets include Robert Graves, Katharine Tynan, Eleanor Farjeon, Edith Sitwell, Wilfrid Blair and Madeleine Nightingale.

Egyptian Tales of Magic, by Eleanor Myers Jewett, illustrated in color by Maurice Day. The oldest stories in the world, full of magic and mystery, which make the kings and sailors and priests and peasants of ancient Egypt come alive again before our eyes. For boys and girls of ten to fifteen.

Medicine Gold, by Warren H. Miller. A story of adventure, of big game hunting and fishing and life in the open in the great north woods. Indians figure in the story and there is an exciting mystery ingeniously solved. Mr. Miller is known as a writer of boys' fiction and of outdoor books for boys.

Scott Burton in the Blue Ridge, by Edward G. Cheyney. You can read this book alone or as the fourth of a series about a young forester. Assigned to government service in North Carolina, Scott plays an exciting part in the settlement of a mountaineers' feud. The author has worked with the United States Forestry Service and is a professor in and director of the University of Minnesota College of Forestry.

Rat's Castle, by Roy Bridges. The fascination of pirate gold hangs in the background of a slashing, well-told story.

Fourteen Years a Sailor, by John Kenlon. The Chief of the New York Fire Department tells the picturesque story of his boyhood and young manhood on deep water, including shipwreck on the desolate Crozet Islands.

The Listening Man, by John A. Moroso. A companion volume to the author's *Cap Fallon: Fire Fighter*. This book shows how a retired detective of the New York City force still takes an interest in and aids in solving mysteries and in bringing criminals to justice. Cap Fallon is one of the characters. Mr. Moroso is a novelist who, as a New York newspaper reporter, covered many big police stories.

The Boy Scout's Own Book, edited by Franklin K. Mathiews. This gathers into one volume those articles and stories from Volumes I-IV of *The Boy Scouts Year Book* having to do particularly with Scouting. A book of especial interest to boys who expect to become Scouts. Joseph A. Altsheler, Henry van Dyke, Robert E. Peary, Dr. Grenfell and Warren H. Miller are a few of the authors represented in the book.

The Boy Scouts Year Book (1924), edited by Franklin K. Mathiews. This year's book features fiction, though the special article and handicraft features are well maintained. Dan Beard's how-to-make-it articles, and stories by P. G. Wodehouse, Homer Croy, Dr. W. T. Hornaday, Joseph B. Ames, Richard Connell, Raymond L. Spears and William James are included.

CARGOES FOR CRUSOES

David Blaize of King's, by E. F. Benson. The story of David Blaize, hero of Mr. Benson's *David Blaize* and *David Blaize and the Blue Door*, at Cambridge.

The Story Key to Geographic Names, by O. D. von Engeln and Jane McKelway Urquhart. Takes geography out of the boredom of lists and figures and tells the stories back of place names.

And for Parents—

New Roads to Childhood and *Roads to Childhood: Views and Reviews of Children's Books*, both by Anne Carroll Moore, supervisor of work with children in the New York Public Library; and *A Century of Children's Books*, by Florence V. Barry.

6. The Twentieth Century Gothic of Aldous Huxley

i

IN that closing chapter, classical in its quality, which rounds off his *Antic Hay*, Aldous Huxley writes:

"Shearwater sat on his stationary bicycle, pedalling unceasingly like a man in a nightmare. . . . From time to time his dog-faced young friend, Lancing, came and looked through the window of the experimenting chamber to see how he was getting on. . . . The sweat poured off him and was caught as it rained down in a water proof sheet, to trickle down its sloping folds into a large glass receptacle. . . .

"Lancing expounded to the visitors all the secrets. The vast, unbelievable, fantastic world opened out as he spoke. There were tropics, there were cold seas busy with living beings, there were forests full of horrible trees, silence and darkness. There were ferments and infinitesimal poisons floating in the air. There were leviathans suckling their young, there were flies and worms, there were men, living in cities, thinking, knowing good and evil. And all were changing continuously, moment by moment, and each remained all the time itself by virtue of some unimaginable enchantment. . . .

"In his hot box Shearwater sweated and pedalled. He was across the channel now; he felt himself safe. Still he trod on; he would be at Amiens by midnight if he went on at this rate. He was escaping, he had escaped. He was building up his strong light dome of life. Proportion, cried the old man, proportion! And it hung there proportioned and beautiful in the dark confused horror of his desires, solid and strong and durable among his broken thoughts. Time floated darkly past."

This is not the Aldous Huxley, you will say, of *Limbo*, or of *Crome Yellow*, nor even of the collection of tales called *Mortal Coils*. No, it isn't. The intelligent child, the studious Oxford youth, the young man in maiden meditation fancy free, have gone somewhere. (We need not mind where.) The person that emerges in their place has a mind vaulted and full of pointed arches. His thoughts are lighted through stained glass, glass that singularly resembles the colored microscopic slides with which Grandfather Huxley was intently preoccupied. It is a Gothic mind with a special twentieth century illumination through the windows of applied science; the lighting is not very satisfactory nor is the source entirely congruous; but this mind-place is one of many and singular pleasures. A sense of airy spaciousness exists, and there is a comfortable feeling that one is not too closely observed, except by God. The delight of sanctuary would be perfect if one were not forced to go outside, now and then. However, there is the sense of escaping, of having escaped—from Grandfather, with his courage and his science and his controversies; from Aunt Humphry Ward with her formula for writing novels; from Laforgue and the French school; from Oxford and the English school; from Applied Religion; and this goes some way to compensate for the necessity of living in London and struggling to build up a strong light dome of life with stories, critiques, poems, books, essays, *feuilletons*.

[98]

ALDOUS HUXLEY

To understand Aldous Huxley's work it is only necessary to have been born too late. This includes practically everybody. But to appreciate his writing requires more of a background than is possessed by those who would make a cult of him. He has nothing to do with cults, though perhaps something with literary cultures. His roots are very far back, the smallest at least as far back as the Elizabethans. Not many can identify the passage in Marlowe from which are taken the two lines on the titlepage of *Antic Hay*. There is more than a suspicion that the grandson of T. H. Huxley is acquainted with Greek and Latin literature and with the spectacles of the Renaissance. But the alcoves of the Bodleian Library are well-lined and not too much frequented. The truth is that Huxley is the child of the nineteenth century far more than of the twentieth, or the seventeenth, or even the first. And the nineteenth century is so much in the foreground as to be most unfamiliar ground for many readers of today. Their backgrounds are too far back, and their foreground is too far forward; the scene is lost in the middle. One of the most significant facts about Aldous Huxley is his almost indiscriminate fondness for the works of Charles Dickens, just as another in his nephewship to Mrs. Humphry Ward. Consider his two grandfathers. The renowned scientist, T. H., whose name is still anathema to the simple fundamentalist, was yet a human, an all too human creature, who, as he told Henry Holt, tried vegetarianism but had to abandon it because he found he could no longer think. The father of Julia Arnold (who became Mrs. Leonard Huxley, Aldous's mother) was the subject of considerable conversion and re-conversion by the

Church of England and the Church of Rome. Julia Arnold was a niece of Matthew Arnold, whose doctrine of sweetness and light wasn't wasted on a desert air—was, indeed, caught up and echoed with diminishing but sympathetic outcries. As for Mary Arnold, who became Mrs. Humphry Ward, the author of *Robert Elsmere* was by taste and temperament a scholar whose true monument is possibly her encyclopædia articles on theologians in Spain.

What, then, is the character of a man barely thirty whose horoscope belongs to 1894? His sisters and his cousins and his aunts are not to be left out of the reckoning any more than those of W. S. Gilbert's admiral. Brought up to admire Wordsworth, Mr. Huxley has lived to enjoy him; [1] a child of eminent Victorians, he has a perspicacious eye for the limitations of Lytton Strachey as a biographer. [2] The inner truth, of course, is something more important than these details of taste, which might be accidental. The inner truth is itself an accident—quite possibly an accident in design. And it is due to the shape of Huxley's head, not the outer shape but the shape inside—as we have said, all curious vaultings, pointed arches, mediæval, constructed for all the rites of a ceremonious mysticism but constrained by the circumstances of his era and the exigencies of daily living to be used rather as a laboratory than a cathedral. One must eat. When Grandfather Huxley gave over eating meat, he was unable to think, and his grandson, obliged to use a beautiful brain in journalism and letters, can hardly dedicate it to worship.

"Worship." The word may seem strange to be used in speaking of the author of *Antic Hay*, in which there

[1] See *On the Margin*, page 32, bottom, *et seq.* and page 150 *et seq.*
[2] *On the Margin*, page 16 *et seq.*

[100]

is much genial blasphemy; but what the careless
reader may not see is the bitter cry beneath the surface
of a stony contempt. The cry is there, nor is it always
embittered. "God as a sense of warmth about the
heart, God as exultation, God as tears in the eyes, God
as a rush of power or thought—that was all right,"
reflected Theodore Gumbril Junior. "But God as
truth, God as 2 plus 2 = 4—that wasn't so clearly all
right." [3]   And a few moments later the young man is
recalling, with passion and pain, the death of his
mother. Those familiar with the story of the two
dwarfs, Sir Hercules and Filomena, in *Crome
Yellow* [4] know what pathos and tenderness Huxley can
command in a narrative of entire simplicity undisturbed by the self-conscious tendency of much of his
work. For it is true, as Michael Sadleir said some
time ago, that there are (have been?) several Huxleys. [5]   But although the artificer in words who is
"almost omnipresent" will never vanish, the "amateur
in garbage, pierrot lunaire, the cynic in ragtime, the
fastidious sensualist" are numbered of days. The
young man in his twenties who provoked "consternation and respect" knows as well as Mr. Sadleir that he
has no time to waste. His position is clear, being that
of a man whose time is being wasted, not by himself
but by others; and a man whose impatience is becoming
very great. The portrait of Coleman in *Antic Hay*
is perhaps the most concentrated expression of that
. . . impatience. Of the several attitudes assumed in
the world to-day by gifted writers whose core of feeling is mystical, Huxley's, I think, has the most courage
to commend it. Mr. Sinclair Lewis clicks the shutter

[3] See *Antic Hay*, page 8.
[4] See *Crome Yellow*, page 121 *et seq.*
[5] See *When Winter Comes to Main Street* (Grant Overton), page 34
et seq.

of a mental camera; Mr. James Branch Cabell tries to glue our eyes to a series of romantically-colored stereoscopic slides; Mr. Joseph Hergesheimer paints in oils; Mr. James Joyce uses chalk on the sidewalks or even on the walls of less advertised, but not less public, places. Huxley, however, has learned from Dickens the art of caricature. As he draws, his really vast erudition comes crowding through the aisles of his strange and beautiful mind. Like little imps, like twisted gargoyles come to life, figures of the past fling themselves on the haft of his pen, to move it this way and that. A heavier stroke here, to show the semblance of a satyr; this curve a little thinned by pity; a blot here for the spirit made flesh. . . . So you have gradually assembled his company, grotesque, exaggerated, wretched, bizarre, inhuman-human, like drawings by Cruikshank or Phiz, like illustrations to a new *Nicholas Nickleby*, or *Pickwick*, repulsively true, their meaninglessness carrying their deepest meaning. That meaning is so significant that only a mystic can be expected to grasp it. It goes back to the struggle between paganism and Christianity which led into what we call the Dark Ages. Mr. Huxley has looked at his world and seen with disgust—but also with anguish and pity—how the wheel has come full circle, how for the mystical mind a Dark Age is again come upon us. Must, then, the old and crucial warfare be waged all over again? If we are to worship at Greek shrines, he will remind us that Priapus was the god of gardens. And he quotes the Latin of Odo of Cluny [6] to show how excess breeds counter-excess. The whole point with Huxley is his perfect grasp of the historical analogy to the present mood and tense—or tension. He is savage in his picture of London, the modern city, in

[6] *Antic Hay*, page 305.

Antic Hay; unsparing in his representation of the manifestations of the spirit we affect—jazz, prevailing dances, rages in new art, stupidities in experimental science. Possibly his comprehension of the last is his most relentlessly hostile view; he is the grandson of a scientist, a very great thinker, pathetically dependent upon a flesh diet for intellectual accomplishment. Grandfather's thinking, though possibly not futile, seems to have got no farther than the God of 2 plus $2 = 4$. For such a God, the grandson has little use; for such an age as impends over us, he has even less.

This young man has been everywhere and seen everything. He writes, not that he who runs may read, but that he who reads may run. He subtly, but more and more urgently, invites us to flee—the wrath to come? No, the madness already here. Does his generation fancy itself as pagans and revel in its paganism? He will show them their precedents and quote for them their texts—which they may ponder before passing out to the vomitorium. One might divide Aldous Huxley's work to date into two classes: and if one class is juvenilia, most certainly the other division, led by *Antic Hay*, is Juvenalia. The Goth laid waste, even as this young Goth from Oxford is laying waste; and then the Goth built churches. They are the incomparable, those edifices. The son of the Arnolds and the Huxleys, the Oxford scholar, the pupil of London, is preparing for us his twentieth century Gothic.

iii

"Huxley, Aldous Leonard, writer," recites *Who's Who*, "born 26 July 1894; third son of Leonard Huxley, whom see, and Julia Arnold; married, 1919, Maria Nys; one son. Educated at Eton and

Balliol College, Oxford. Worked on the editorial staff of the Athenæum, 1919-1920; dramatic critic of the Westminster Gazette, 1920-1921. Publications: *The Burning Wheel*, 1916; *The Defeat of Youth*, 1918; *Limbo*, 1920; *Leda*, 1920; *Crome Yellow*, 1921; *Mortal Coils*, 1922. Recreation: reading. Club: Athenæum."

A short private letter dated 13. vii. 22 adds one or two details. "I was educated very conventionally at Eton & at Oxford (the only break in the process being two or three years of partial blindness, from 17 to 19½, when I learned to read Braille embossed writing). I took English Literature at Oxford, under the professorship of the late Sir Walter Raleigh. I have worked on a good many papers—doing literary journalism, art criticism, music criticism & dramatic criticism. I am a close student of French literature & have many acquaintances in Paris. I travel as much as I can—which is not nearly so much as I should like. My ideal at the moment is to be completely idle for three years—but, alas, I see no prospect of its being fulfilled!" The letter also says, in answer to a specific inquiry about *Mortal Coils: "Mortal Coils*, like *Crome Yellow*, was chiefly written in Italy last summer (tho' there are two stories in it of considerably earlier date)—in extreme heat by the Mediterranean."

Here is a reminiscence of Huxley written in June, 1922:

"Aldous Huxley had tea with me at the Savoy in February, 1922, when London was being raided by a series of particularly nasty fogs. All the salt exhaled by the neighboring sea is sucked in by these fogs, which apply it patiently to the eyes of London, causing the people sore eyes and a weary outlook. Out of one of these fogs Huxley stepped into the writing room of the hotel, where I instantly recognized him. He is very tall and thin, walks with a visible stoop, and looks about him with the uncertainty of those who are new to the extreme of near-sightedness. One of his eyes is almost all white.

"He is very much interested in America and professes to envy us our exuberance and Henry L. Mencken, which seems to me sheer affectation. He also entertains the view that the invasion of Europe by American soldiery during the late war has caused a revolution in European social intercourse, which is a little more reasonable. I have made a complete record of this conversation in a manuscript book of mine entitled 'In Georgian England,' which is unlikely ever to find a publisher.

"About him personally I know only what one can gather from a purely impersonal discussion. He has a slight income, and that was why he was leaving for Italy with his wife, and that was why he was very anxious about an American market, and that was why he was writing some plays which, judging by some play work of his I saw, must be pretty bad. But it should interest you to know that at a luncheon of young Oxford poets to which I was invited he was referred to several times as the most learned man in England." [7]

Huxley's personal appearance and agreeable manner have been frequently described [8] and his conversational gift is not aptly epitomized by that very famous English novelist who recently said of him: "He looks clever. He says nothing—he has no need to say anything. It suffices for him to sit silent, looking clever." The same novelist, a very penetrating analyst of literary powers, added: "But this young man is almost the

[7] Letter of Samuel Roth, 500 Fifth Avenue, New York, 28 June 1922.
[8] *American Nights Entertainment* (Grant Overton), pages 34 and 35.

only 'white hope' in English literature at present."
Huxley is at his best, conversationally, in a small company. One of his close friends is Frank Swinnerton
whose judgment of Huxley's gifts as a writer strongly
confirms the novelist's estimate just quoted.

iv

The Burning Wheel (1916) and *The Defeat of
Youth* (1918) were volumes of poems, as was *Leda*
(1920). Only *Leda* has been published in America.
Although it is not ten years since the appearance of
Mr. Huxley's first book, the first (London) editions of
all of them are held at a premium by dealers and
collectors. One may pay, for a particular item, anywhere from ten to fifteen pounds in some instances—
or certainly not less than $60 or $75 in New York.
A first edition of a new Huxley is something to put
aside carefully. The distinction is unusual among
living writers and, in the case of a man under thirty,
possibly unique.

The title poem of *Leda* is an affair of nearly 600
lines, iambic pentameter with an occasional variant,
written in rhymed couplets as a continuous narrative
with the occasional "paragraphing" usual in narrative
blank verse. The subject is the classical myth of
Jupiter's disguise as a swan:

> Couched on the flowery ground
> Young Leda lay, and to her side did press
> The swan's proud-arching opulent loveliness . . .
> And over her the swan shook slowly free
> The folded glory of his wings, and made
> A white-walled tent of soft and luminous shade
> To be her veil and keep her from the shame
> Of naked light and the sun's noonday flame.

ALDOUS HUXLEY

The poems which follow, including the "First Philosopher's Song," are among the earliest and most perfect expressions of Huxley's perception of the futility of science:

> But oh, the sound of simian mirth!
> Mind, issued from the monkey's womb,
> Is still umbilical to earth.

The deliberate attempt, with a delicate savagery, to hold the mirror up to his generation was begun in "Frascati's":

> Bubble-breasted swells the dome
> Of this my spiritual home,
> From whose nave the chandelier,
> Schaffhausen frozen, tumbles sheer.
> We in the round balcony sit,
> Lean o'er and look into the pit
> Where feed the human bears beneath,
> Champing with their gilded teeth.
> What negroid holiday makes free
> With such priapic revelry?
> What songs? What gongs? What nameless rites?
> What gods like wooden stalagmites?
> What steam of blood or kidney pie?
> What blasts of Bantu melody?
> Ragtime. . . . But when the wearied Band
> Swoons to a waltz, I take her hand.
> And there we sit in blissful calm,
> Quietly sweating palm to palm.

A number of poems written in prose form—though without the special effects of Amy Lowell's "polyphonic prose" in *Can Grande's Castle*—follow. Of these "Soles Occidere et Redire Possunt" is the only one arranged as verse. Preceded by a short foreword it offers us the record of a day in the life of John Ridley. "Ridley was an adolescent, and suffered from that instability of mind 'produced by the mental conflict forced upon man by his sensitiveness to herd suggestion on the one hand and to experience on the other' (I quote from Mr. Trotter's memorable work on Herd Instinct)." It is a study in "the anguish of thinking ill of oneself":

> "Misery," he said, "to have no chin,
> Nothing but brains and sex and taste:
> Only omissively to sin,
> Weakly kind and cowardly chaste."

But of these prose poems the most significant is "Gothic," fashioned around the nursery couplet:

> Upon Paul's steeple stands a tree
> As full of apples as can be.

From the opening sentence: "Sharp spires pierce upwards, and the clouds are full of tumbling bells" to the evocative closing image—"he had it in turn as an alms from the grave knight who lies with crossed legs down there, through the clouds and the dizzy mist of bell-ringing, where the great church is a hollow ship, full of bright candles, and stable in the midst of dark tempestuous seas"—the piece is a true glimpse into that mind which no more resembles the other minds of its day than St. Paul's resembles a shop on Bond Street.

v

Much unwisdom has been uttered concerning Huxley's prose. The applausive enthusiasm of the ordinary Huxley devotee may be dismissed without comment; superficiality (not to say shallowness) may call for pity but certainly not for censure. A misapprehension of what the author was doing in *Antic Hay*, though common enough and a more serious matter, will rectify with time. A comparison of such poetry as "Leda" to Keats is better ignored than made the subject of delicate differentiation; but what shall we say of these? "The wittiest man, after Beerbohm, now writing in English." [9] "His humor is hot as well as shining." [10] "He is finished and fastidious, sophisticated and diverting." [11] "There's no doubt about it. Huxley is brilliant." [12] Mr. Clement K. Shorter, in the London Sphere, pronouncing *Mortal Coils* the best book Huxley had yet written, said: "There's a great deal of brilliancy in it, although one or two of the stories are too chaotic for my taste, and one, 'Nuns at Luncheon,' is too morbid. The best are 'The Gioconda Smile' and 'The Tillotson Banquet.' . . . One thing is clear, that Mr. Aldous Huxley has a career in front of him and some of his gifts are hereditary. . . . Mrs. T. H. Huxley had distinct gifts as a poet, and I have a volume of her verse I highly value. The son, Mr. Leonard Huxley, is a man of varied talent and the editor of the Cornhill Magazine. Mr. Aldous Huxley's talents have taken a widely different turn, but they should carry him far." If they are to carry him much farther, one grieves for Mr. Shorter, already lagging a little. It was commonly remarked that *Crome Yellow* derived from Peacock—a modernized *Headlong Hall* with the slapstick eliminated and the addition of overtones on the (then) current sex motif.

[9] Mr. F. Scott Fitzgerald.
[10] Mr. Henry L. Mencken.
[11] The New Republic.
[12] Mr. John V. A. Weaver.

CARGOES FOR CRUSOES

Let us glance at the prose and test some of these characterizations.

Limbo opens with a novelette, "Farcical History of Richard Greenow," the account of a young man whose mental hermaphroditism explained the fact that in certain states he was Pearl Bellairs, a highly sentimental novelist. The lady takes increasing possession of his faculties; he dies, a conscientious objector to war service, engaged in writing perfervid patriotic appeals to the girls and women of England. "Happily Ever After" deals with an inveterate feminine propensity toward the disguise of love by allurements. "Eupompus Gave Splendour to Art by Numbers" is a historical precedent offered to Cubists and other innovators in art. "Happy Families," "Cynthia," and "The Death of Lully" are all studies in the immature, adolescent attitude toward sex and love; and "The Bookshop" is a study in pity.

In *Mortal Coils*, "The Gioconda Smile" deals with Miss Spence, who poisons her rival quite vainly. "Permutations Among the Nightingales," in form a play, is a study in promiscuity. "The Tillotson Banquet," though longer, is of the same genre as "The Bookshop" in *Limbo*. "Green Tunnels" is the episode of a young girl's heartbreaking disappointment. "Nuns at Luncheon" is the effective portrait of a writer of fiction whose god of realism identifies himself to the worshipper only in his aspect of brute. The original, like most Huxley originals, is a composite. For Mr. Huxley is not so much engaged in hitting heads as in hitting what is in the heads.

The novels, *Crome Yellow* and *Antic Hay* exhibit the same characteristics and underlying intention as the shorter pieces; they have the added value of unity of form (in *Crome Yellow*, of time and place as well).

[110]

Crome Yellow is more varied in its emotional presentation as well as lenient; *Antic Hay* is sterner, more peremptory—the rapier driven home. But where is the likeness in all this or in any of this, to Max Beerbohm? Mr. Huxley is witty—incidentally. His humor, described as "hot as well as shining," is no more humor than the work of Mark Twain in *The Mysterious Stranger*. No doubt his prose is a "finished" prose; but "fastidious, sophisticated and diverting"! The picture conjured up by such adjectives is one of an elegant trifler. Yet hardly a man writing can use such uncompromising, Old-Testamentary speech; and if the bulk of Huxleyana is diversion, then Savonarola should be considered with reference to his possibilities as a vaudeville entertainer. And "brilliant." It is a word from the outermost darkness, spreading darkness around.

vi

Perhaps as a result of these singular misapprehensions, the remark was general, when Huxley's book of essays, *On the Margin*, appeared, that here was a volume which might be the work of any gifted young man. Not quite. The display of learning was rather too great for gifted young men to manage, as it were, without parade. Yet the very ones who made the comment —and this writer must number himself among them— could have learned more concerning what a conventional biographer would love calling "the real Aldous Huxley" from a re-perusal of *On the Margin* than from any other of his books. Said one reviewer: "Mr. Huxley can be fantastic enough, though his is never the fantasy of the cloudy dreamer, but the fantasy of a thinker whose mind is enchanted by the logical devel-

[111]

ʋpment of a happy thought; but his clarity was never better shown than in this collection. . . . Even in his lesser marginalia, he has a winning and graceful conversational manner, whether he be commenting on a quaint book, on pantomime songs, on the contrast between amorous poetry (of the second class) in French and in English, or upon boredom as a literary inspiration through the ages. . . . The one thing which Mr. Huxley cannot stand is mistiness and insincerity; and what he means by clarity and sincerity he amply shows in his essays on Edward Thomas, Sir Christopher Wren, Ben Jonson, Chaucer, and the centenary of Shelley's death." [13] Here is a greater degree of percipience than has been shown since Mr. Sadleir offered his criticism (now perhaps obsolescent, but penetrating at the time). In fact, the essay on "Sir Christopher Wren" in *On the Margin* is the single most self-illuminatory bit of writing Mr. Huxley has offered us. Like the great architect of London, Aldous Huxley is a designer who prizes in his work a quality peculiar and individualizing; and as with Wren, the quality is not æsthetic but moral.

It is explicit, for all its unobtrusiveness, in the title story of his new collection, *Young Archimedes and Other Sketches*. Comedy and irony in various proportions are the material of five of the six tales, but the principal story, in length a novelette, is a charming narrative of a child in Italy, a child with a beautiful forehead and eyes that could flash ripples like the sunshine on clear pale lakes. The young Guido showed an extraordinary penchant for music; but when he was a little older, like Archimedes, his mind turned to the theorems of mathematics; it was evident that his genius was larger. The tragedy of his life in the hands of a

[13] The London Times, 3 May 1923.

grasping woman is told with an affectionate sadness. Undoubtedly this piece of his fiction, austere and tender, will give to thousands of readers a new conception of Aldous Huxley. They will perhaps see that the mind of the child, Guido, is a miniature of the mind of the one who writes about him; and that there is even a profound likenesss between both those minds and the one of which Emerson wrote:

> The hand that rounded Peter's dome,
> And groined the walls of Christian Rome,
> Wrought in a sad sincerity . . .

BOOKS BY ALDOUS HUXLEY

1916 *The Burning Wheel.* Published in England only.
1918 *The Defeat of Youth.* Published in England only
1920 *Limbo*
1920 *Leda*
1921 *Crome Yellow*
1922 *Mortal Coils*
1923 *On the Margin*
1923 *Antic Hay*
1924 *Young Archimedes and Other Sketches*
        In England, *Little Mexican and Other Stories.*

SOURCES ON ALDOUS HUXLEY

In addition to the sources referred to in the text of the chapter or in footnotes, the reader should consult the READER'S GUIDE TO PERIODICAL LITERATURE for the years since 1920.

7. In Every Home:
A Chapter for Women

i

IN addressing this chapter to you, I do what I can to notify other men that they may find it uninteresting. Indeed, as you and I know, if all the truth were told they would find it, many of them, most unpalatable reading. There are things we need not go into, such as the indubitable fact that the success of the home depends solely upon the woman. A man may contribute to it, but he cannot make it; and whatever his behavior, if the woman is steadfast, he cannot absolutely wreck it. The home is a form of government and a form of human society. We are familiar with the larger forms of government men have tried, the best of them only partly successful. But the home has been a complete success, times innumerable. Men may call it a benevolent despotism, but the fact remains. It is perhaps significant that the government of the home is not conducted by the use of the Australian or the Massachusetts ballot. Women have accepted the vote and will use it; but their grasp of certain essentials of society is more clear than men's, and if the ballot cannot safeguard the home, and the health and welfare and opportunity of children, then government will have to be transformed into something that will.

But this is understood; my purpose is simply to tell of a few books which are, in type, indispensable to the homemaker. The types are really only two: the cook book and the handbook of motherhood. It so happens that there is one volume of each type so complete, so thoroughly tested, so practically perfect that it stands alone on an eminence above all others of its sort— and the best of the others make no pretensions to do more than add wings, columns, buttresses, and chapels to the main edifice. If I could talk about *The Boston Cooking-School Cook Book* and *The Care and Feeding of Children* in the same breath, I should do so. I can, anyway, talk about them in the same chapter!

The Boston Cooking-School Cook Book, by Fannie Merritt Farmer, first appeared in 1896 and was most recently revised last year. It has over 800 pages and still is a volume of little more than ordinary size, no thicker than a rather long novel. The 122 illustrations are so treated as to be intelligible—and if you have ever tried photographing food, you will appreciate what this means. The pictures have been used to show what the words of the text could not make so clear; one sees at a glance the differences between kidney lamb chops, rib chops and French chops, or the precise effect of capon in aspic, rather elaborately garnished with cooked yolks and whites of eggs cut in fancy shapes, pistachio nuts, and truffles.

The book opens with a simple scientific account of the kinds of food (food being "anything which nourishes the body") and follows with a chapter on cookery including invaluable timetables. After a chapter on beverages with its recipes there are chapters on everything from bread to ice cream, from soup to jam and jelly-making and drying fruits. Then comes a long selection of menus, a chapter on food values with the necessary tables, and a forty-eight page index which has all the utility of an absolute, all-inclusive bill-of-fare.

The chief thing, of course, is that every teaspoonful and every direction in the book is exact, and standard. Nor, without going into the more recondite French cookery, or into special Italian, Spanish, German and other foreign dishes, is it possible to think of any dish which *The Boston Cooking-School Cook Book* omits. The variety of each kind of dish is often extraordinary. For example, I have just counted seventy hot puddings. In every case there is first the table of ingredients, then the simple directions. If a personal word will add anything to the force of what has been said, I will say that the superb cook who honored me by becoming my wife tells me that in no case when following *The Boston Cooking-School Cook Book* formula has she failed to cook with success.

Specialized, or partly specialized, cook books are many, and one of the best and most recent is *Fannie Fox's Cook Book*, by Fannie Ferber Fox, with the assistance of Lavinia S. Schwartz. Mrs. Fox is a sister of Edna Ferber, and the novelist has written an introduction for *Fannie Fox's Cook Book* which has all the richly human interest of her own fiction. In a paragraph which need hurt no feelings, Miss Ferber points out the tendency to over-emphasis in one or another direction which characterizes the cookery of most lands; and she gives with humorous eloquence her personal tribute to the toothsome torte, that cake of rich and crumbling particles which is included in Mrs. Fox's recipes. This is a cook book that covers all kinds of foods but is distinctive by its preservation of the finest recipes from Jewish cookery.

Another valuable addition to the kitchen bookshelf is Bertha E. L. Stockbridge's *Practical Cook Book*, in which a notable feature is the great number of practical suggestions for menus.

The Care and Feeding of Children appeared in 1894 and was also revised last year. More than a million mothers have used it, and beyond question it has saved thousands of lives in infancy. Within the last half-dozen years, a generation which was raised on the book has, in turn, begun to raise its own children with its aid. It constituted its author, Dr. L. Emmett Holt, the foremost authority on babies in America; and as the years passed he returned to the book, in its various revisions, the fruit of a wonderful experience which its prestige had brought to him. Physicians have for years bought *The Care and Feeding of Children* in quantity to present to their patients. The hundreds of questions that every mother must have answered are all answered in this marvelous work. Bathing, nursing, artificial feeding, changes in food, substitutes for milk, under-nourishment, health habits, weaning, diet after weaning, the training of older children, children's diseases—nothing is left out. This, to be sure, is largely possible because of the nation-wide and prolonged use of the book, and the constant additions and slight reconstructions it has undergone. The book has always been kept of handy size and at a low price. The thought of what Dr. Holt's book has done and is doing tempts to eloquence; but the only eloquence which is tolerable is the eloquence of the immense fact. We talk about services to humanity; but the writing and publishing of this book was possibly the greatest service to humanity in our time.

The Home Care of Sick Children, by Dr. Emelyn Lincoln Coolidge, is likely to be as helpful to mothers who have the care and feeding of sick children as Dr. Holt's book has been to mothers generally. Dr.

Coolidge lived for many years in the Babies' Hospital, New York, and worked there under the personal direction of Dr. Holt. As editor of the department on babies of the Ladies' Home Journal she has had an enormous correspondence with mothers throughout America and even in foreign countries. And *The Home Care of Sick Children* has one great merit: it does not stop where most other books of its kind stop, with: "Give a dose of castor oil, and call a doctor." It tells in every instance what a mother can and should do, and it invariably tells when to call the doctor in. Not only does it avoid calling the doctor unnecessarily, but it gives many detailed instructions that a physician generally has not time to give. Recipes to tempt the sick child's appetite, amusement, clothing and the hygiene of the sick-room are all dwelt upon.

There is a book with which it would be wise to precede Dr. Holt's. *Healthy Mothers* is by Dr. S. Josephine Baker, consulting director, Children's Bureau, United States Department of Labor, an authority on babies, whose articles regularly appear in the Ladies' Home Journal and who is constantly asked for advice by women throughout the country. *Healthy Mothers* deals almost entirely with the mother's care of herself, and tells explicitly how she may best meet her responsibility to her baby, how she may have better health for herself, and the finer mental attitude that comes with physical well-being. The relation of a mother to her unborn child implies a responsibility greater than that entailed in any other human relationship. It is very largely within the power of the mother to determine not only her own condition and future health, but to decide whether or not her baby is to be healthy and strong. *Healthy Mothers*, without going into technical discussion, sufficiently explains the general course of pregnancy and childbirth so that the mother may have an intelligent understanding of how to care for herself, safeguard her child, and make every requisite preparation.

iii

And the growing child? *Child Training*, by Angelo Patri, is the book for parents who look unhappily at the child and ask themselves despondently: "What in the world makes him do that?" Or, "What is the matter with her now?" Or, "Why does he disobey me?" Or, "Why does she have such bad manners?" Or, "Why doesn't he study?" And, at one or another time, practically all parents are faced with these questions.

Angelo Patri has been training children, and helping fathers and mothers to train them, for twenty-five years. He is principal of Public School 45, New York. This school faces a garden centered about a sun dial and fed by a tiny greenhouse. Across the street is a whole block given over to a playground, its cinder floor padded firm by the play-winged feet of thousands of children who play on it every day. The school is unusual in having a great variety of shops and work-rooms as well as the usual classrooms; a swimming pool; and a library. It is constantly visited by teachers from all over the world, men and women who are anxious to see the principal and talk with him. Some of them have heard him talk to audiences, big and little; some have read his widely published articles on children; others merely know of the remarkable way in which he has brought home and school together, so that parents constantly come to him to work out the problem of their child.

There are about two hundred chapters or sections—chapterettes, rather—in Angelo Patri's *Child Training*. Each of them is so short that it can be read in five minutes or less. Each carries pointed wisdom about the child, and not only for the father or mother but for the uncle, aunt, teacher, or anyone having to do with children. Very often the point is conveyed by an anecdote—there are a good many smiles and chuckles in the book. But Mr. Patri can speak out with definiteness. Perhaps his finest wisdom is shown in a point that he makes more than once: children do certain things that bother us because it is time for them to do these things. When this is true, Mr. Patri is bent on showing just what should be done to help the youngster over a hard place. *Talks to Mothers* is another treasury of Mr. Patri's helpful wisdom.

Another new book on child training which will appeal to all those who believe in the power of suggestion is *Auto-Suggestion for Mothers*, by R. C. Waters, lecturer in English to the Nancy School of Applied Psychology. This is a practical book on the application of Emil Coué's method. The technique to be used is explained clearly and simply. The possibilities of Coué's method of auto-suggestion when applied to the correction of habits, to disease, to education and play are set forth and examples are cited. *Auto-Suggestion for Mothers* has been translated into French by Mme. Coué and has been adopted by the Coué School as a text.

iv

Every home should have one or more books on keeping well. The old family medical book, a chamber of horrors, has been made obsolete by a few general books with, thank heaven, a greatly different emphasis. But among recent books on the art of keeping well, I know of none more satisfactory than Dr. S. M. Rinehart's *The Commonsense of Health*. Dr. Rinehart, who is the husband of Mary Roberts Rinehart, was a general practitioner in Pittsburgh for over twenty years. Later he was in charge of tuberculosis hospitals in western Pennsylvania, and during the war he was put in charge of all army tuberculosis hospitals in the United States. Recently he has been in the United States Public Health Service. His book is wholly popular in character, cheerful, good-natured, and not in the least afraid of an occasional joke. It is precisely the thing for general reading by both sexes at all ages. Common and worrisome ailments, such as colds, are dealt with, as well as certain fairly common and serious diseases, like pneumonia and tuberculosis. But the range of the book is wide, and there are discussions of nerves, how hard one should work, and besetting fears. The information is sound and the style is entertaining. One class of unfortunate will be particularly helped by the book—the unhappy man or woman termed by Dr. Rinehart a "symptom hunter." We each know at least one!

v

I cannot close this chapter without a short word about books and the home. You who make the home, you women who are overwhelmingly the book readers of America, know how necessary books are to make the home complete. Read yourself, and discuss what you read. Never urge or compel a child to read a book. If you read the right books and talk about them afterward (they ought to move you to talk about them) the boy or girl will read them also. Buy books. In general, never buy them in "sets." You ought to know an author, even a classic author, a little better than to have to do that. Keep abreast of the new books—one of the easiest things in the world to do, and one of the most fascinating. It is fair that you should ask that at least as much money go into the purchase of books for the home as goes into the purchase of magazines, or radio apparatus, or as is expended in mere diversions such as the picture shows. Last year thirty cents per person was spent for books in America—far too little. You can change all that, and no simple change that I can think of will pay you better.

BOOKS FOR THE HOMEMAKER

Choice Recipes for Clever Cooks, by Lucy G. Allen. More than 500 original recipes for those who already know how to cook and appreciate the best in food and flavor. By the director of the Boston School of Cookery. Illustrated.

Table Service, by Lucy G. Allen. A concise exposition of the waitress's duties by the director of the Boston School of Cookery. New revised edition, with illustrations and diagrams.

The Candy Cook Book, by Alice Bradley. A new edition, revised, containing over 300 recipes and covering the subject completely. By the principal of Miss Farmer's School of Cookery. Illustrated.

One-Piece Dinners, by Mary D. Chambers. Recipes for dinners where the meat, vegetables and other accessories are cooked all together and make a complete, well-balanced and sufficient meal. Directions are also given for optional salads and fruit desserts. Illustrated.

Cooking for Two: A Handbook for Young Housekeepers, by Janet McKenzie Hill. Instructions for young housekeepers and a collection of practical recipes for two, grouped according to food values. Fully illustrated.

Colette's Best Recipes: A Book of French Cookery, by Marie Jacques. This new cook book, by a Breton whose culinary achievements have won her renown in France, contains recipes for the most delicious and palate-tickling dishes, from French consomme to the French pastries, of crispness or creaminess unsurpassed. Illustrated.

The Science of Eating, by Alfred W. McCann. A comprehensive book by an authority on foods; what to eat and why.

What to Eat and How to Prepare It, by Elizabeth A. Monaghan. This combines very definite information on food values with many recipes and instructions for cooking.

What to Drink, by Bertha E. L. Stockbridge. Recipes for several hundred beverages—ades, punches, fizzes, shrubs, milk drinks, icecreams, sundaes, sherbets, etc.

Food and Cookery for the Sick and Convalescent, by Fannie Merritt Farmer. A book for those whose duty it is to care for the sick, and of equal importance to those who see in correct nutrition the way of preventing much of the illness about us. Important chapters on infant and child feeding and suggestions as to diet in special diseases. By the author of *The Boston Cooking-School Cook Book*. Illustrated.

Canning, Preserving and Jelly Making, by Janet McKenzie Hill. "Aims to present the latest ideas on the subject using the methods found to be simplest and shortest by the experiments of the U. S. Department of Agriculture, State universities, and cooking experts."—Booklist of the American Library Association. Illustrated.

Marketing and Housework Manual, by S. Agnes Donham. Clear and concise information on these everyday subjects.

Spending the Family Income, by S. Agnes Donham. "A guide to wise use of the family or personal income by means of a carefully thought-out and tested budget. Principles are laid down which apply equally well to large and small incomes."—Booklist of the American Library Association. Illustrated with eight pages of charts in color.

The Prospective Mother, by J. Morris Slemons, M.D. Written especially for women who have no knowledge of medicine by a physician who has made this subject his specialty. Food, exercise, clothing, the adaptation of daily work, and recreation are fully covered.

[123]

Healthy Babies, by S. Josephine Baker, M.D., Consulting Director, Children's Bureau, U. S. Department of Labor. The methods and advice given are intended to be used in keeping babies well, from the minute they are born until they are past the babyhood stage. The book shows how mother-love can be directed into the wisest and sanest channels. It contains three sets of baby record forms. Illustrated.

Healthy Children, by S. Josephine Baker, M.D., Consulting Director, Children's Bureau, U. S. Department of Labor. Deals with the period of childhood between babyhood and school age. As its purpose is to accentuate health, it shows the mother how she may give the child of pre-school age the same health care available for the baby. Illustrated.

The Mothercraft Manual, by Mary L. Read. A young mother's guide written by the former director of the School of Mothercraft, Peoria. Some of the chapters are on heredity and eugenics, the care and feeding of children, home nursing, education of the child, games, toys, and story telling for children. Illustrated.

Nutrition and Growth in Children, by William R. P. Emerson, M.D. Dr. Emerson has won nation-wide recognition by his pioneer work in organizing nutrition clinics in American cities. His study of the mal-nourished child is of the highest importance alike to the mother, the social worker and the public official. Illustrated.

How to Know Your Child, by Miriam Finn Scott. "A book that should be in every home where there are children. It is comprehensive and authoritative, and represents years of experience and study by a foremost expert. The very best manual on its subject obtainable at any price."—Ladies' Home Journal.

A Text-Book of Nursing, by Clara S. Weeks-Shaw. A book on home nursing which gives the non-professional nurse full directions for the hygiene of the sick-room, bathing, observance of symptoms, medicines and their administration, disinfection, surgical nursing, the care of sick children, etc. Illustrated.

Sewing and Textiles, by Annabel Turner. All the stitches,

seams and finishes which go to make up the fundamentals of good sewing. Patching, sewing and darning are taught on samplers, but otherwise the methods are applied on useful garments. Materials are also studied and tests for shoddy are given. The author is instructor in home economics in the University of Wisconsin.

Tinkering With Tools, by Henry H. Saylor. Comment on tools and their care, with many suggestions as to their use for those who like to set their hands to such crafts as woodworking, painting, plumbing, masonry, electric wiring, etc. With illustrations and diagrams.

8. A Great Impersonation by
E. Phillips Oppenheim

i

THE other evening I picked up a novel called *The Lighted Way*, which, although it was published in May, 1912, I hadn't chanced ever to read. The page blurred slightly before my eyes, I think, because in going back over it some of the names and particulars seemed entirely changed. But this, as I took it in first, was the way it ran:

"Mr. E. Phillips Oppenheim, sole proprietor of the firm of E. Phillips Oppenheim & Nobody, wholesale entertainers of London and Europe, paused suddenly on his way from his private office to the street. There was something which until that second had entirely slipped his memory. It was not his title, for that, tastefully chosen, was already under his arm. Nor was it the Plot, for that, together with the first chapter, was sticking out of his overcoat pocket, the shape of which it completely ruined. As a matter of fact, it was more important than either of these—it was a commission from his conscience.

"Very slowly he retraced his steps until he stood outside the glass-enclosed cage where twelve of the hardest-worked clerks in London bent over their ledgers and invoicing. With his forefinger—a fat, pudgy forefinger—he tapped upon a pane of glass, and an anxious errand boy bolted through the doorway.

" 'Tell Mr. Reader to step this way,' his employer ordered.

"Mr. Reader heard the message and came hurrying out. He was an undersized man, with somewhat prominent eyes concealed by gold-rimmed spectacles. He was possessed of extraordinary zest for the details of the business, and was withal an expert and careful adviser. Hence his hold upon the confidence of his employer.

"The latter addressed him with a curious and altogether unusual hesitation in his manner.

" 'Mr. Reader,' he began, 'there is a matter—a little matter—upon which I—er—wish to consult you.'

" 'Those American serial rights——'

" 'Nothing to do with business at all,' Mr. Oppenheim interrupted, ruthlessly. 'A little private matter.'

" 'Indeed, sir?' "

Now as I say, at this point I went back and found to my bewilderment at first, but perfect satisfaction afterward, that Mr. Oppenheim seemed to be Mr. Weatherley, a worthy provisioner; the title, an umbrella; the Plot, a copy of the London Times; and the alarming commission from Mr. Oppenheim's conscience, a possibly no less embarrassing commission from Mr. Weatherley's wife. Thereupon everything went smoothly and excitingly through thirty-seven chapters. But afterward it occurred to me that perhaps, after all, my blunder, visual or mental, was not an unnatural one. Who has not had in his mind's eye a picture of Mr. Oppenheim with a Plot, or Plots, bulging from his pockets, and with as many titles in his mental wardrobe as most men have neckties? And what one of his readers has not felt himself, time and again, personally summoned by the author to the consideration of a matter—a little matter—a quite private matter just then upon the author's conscience. . . .

ii

It is the secret of Mr. Oppenheim's success, not detected as such by his readers, very probably not a trifle of which he himself is consciously aware. This engaging gift of confiding something, this easy air, this informality of his beginnings, disarms us and interests us as could no elaborately staged effort to arrest our attention and intrigue our minds. Even when he commences his story dramatically with such a confrontation as that which opens his *The Wrath to Come*, the air of naturalness is upon the scene. And the source of this effect? It comes from the fact that Mr. Oppenheim is imparting to you all that he himself knows at the given moment. Yes, literally. For our notion of him as a man with plots distending his pockets is entirely a mistaken notion. He has no plots; at least, he has no ready-made plots; he does not, so to say, plot his plots. "Just the first chapter, and an inkling of something to follow," was his answer to some one who asked him how much of his leading character he saw when he began a novel.[1] What other method, when you stop to reflect upon it, would be possible for the author of eighty-six published novels? Certainly no one could map out his tales, even in essentials, and then write them to that number, not if he were to do the plots one by one, as occasion arose. He would be a slave, and the book, as written, would soon come to be lifeless. Nor, by such a method, would thirty-eight years afford time. In thirty-eight years the pace would be lost. Only spontaneity is

[1] Literary news note in The Indianapolis Star, 20 March 1922.

[128]

capable of guaranteeing such a record as stands to Mr. Oppenheim's credit. "Two or three people in a crowded restaurant may arouse my interest, and the atmosphere is compelling. I start weaving a story around them—the circumstances and the people gradually develop as I go on dictating to my secretary the casual thoughts about them that arose in me while I was looking at them and their surroundings. First of all I must have a congenial atmosphere—then the rest is easy." [2] And again:

"Writing for the movies is a ghastly business. I speak from experience. I shall never do it again. The picture people came to me and said, 'Next time you have a novel in your head, why not, instead of writing 80,000 words, write a 5,000-word synopsis and let us have it? Then write your novel from the synopsis.'

"Well, they paid well and I did it. I wrote the synopsis first and then set to work on the novel. I have never had a harder job in my life. Some writers, no doubt, do sketch out their plots beforehand, but I never work that way. When I start a story I never know just how it is going to end. All I have to start with is an idea. As I go along the idea grows and develops. So do the characters. I sort of live with them through the story and work out their salvation as it goes along. It is like a game.

"But when you write for the movies you have to reverse the process. In my case, it is fatal. Novels, even the kind that I write—and they are solely for amusement—must have some soul, something that gives them a human quality. This the author puts into the story as he goes along. When, however, he

[2] *Gods of Modern Grub Street,* by A. St. John Adcock. (Stokes.) Page 267.

writes a synopsis and then sits down to enlarge and expand it into a novel, the spell is broken. He has a cold and rigid plan to follow. It nearly killed me to novelize my first scenario." [3]

He dictates his novels, revising the sheets as they come from the typewriter, sometimes re-dictating a passage or chapter. In summer he works outdoors; in winter he may pace up and down his study. "Many a time, earlier in life, when I used to write my stories with my own hand, I have found that my ideas would come so much faster than my fingers could work that I have prayed for some more speedy method of transmission. My present method is not only an immense relief to me, but it enables me to turn out far more work than would have been possible by any other means." [4] Story-writing, he believes, is an original instinct, "just as it is an original instinct with a sporting dog to sniff about in every bush he passes for a rabbit. One writes stories because if one left them in the brain one would be subject to a sort of mental indigestion. As to plots, there are only about a score in the world, and when you have used them all, from A to Z"—which he pronounced "Zed," for this was in an after-dinner speech—"you can turn around and use them from Z to A." [5] A favorite illustration with him is taken from a day's walk in London. "You can take the same walk every day in the year and you will meet a different crowd of people. These people contain the backgrounds of 365 stories a year." One person a day will keep the typewriter in play, for "I create one more or less interesting personality, try to

[3] Interview in The Evening Post, New York, 1922 (3 March ?)
[4] "E. Phillips Oppenheim," by Himself. Brentano's Book Chat, April, 1921.
[5] The New York Times, New York Herald, and The World, New York, 5 March 1922, reporting a Lotos Club dinner to Mr. Oppenheim.

think of some dramatic situation in which he or she might be placed, and use that as the opening of a nebulous chain of events."

What he said of himself at 55 is still, two years later, true without abatement. "Even if, like one of the heroes of fiction, I should make a million dollars out of a ten-cent piece in Wall Street, I should still continue to write stories so long as I can sit in an easy chair and my voice will carry as far as my secretary before a typewriter." Which is reminiscent of Hugh Walpole's remark in conversation the same year, that he was perfectly sure if a beam fell on his head and made him imbecile, he would continue to write novels for the pleasure of writing them.

iii

Mr. Oppenheim was born in 1866 and went from school into his father's leather business at Leicester— but he had started writing stories before that. He began to write them at fifteen, and showed his first to the headmaster of the school, "who, instead of giving me the birching I deserved, wished me luck and encouraged me to persevere." The leather business was successful and was bought up by Blumenthals, a large American and Paris leather firm, who appointed young Oppenheim their director at Leicester. "His experience in that trade," asserts Mr. A. St. John Adcock in his *Gods of Modern Grub Street*,[6] "has proved immensely useful to him. It has not only helped him to material for his tales, but it was through the American head of Blumenthals that he had his chief incentive to the writing of the type of story that has brought him such success as a novelist. This gentle-

⁶Page 266.

man introduced him to the proprietor of the Café de Rat Mort, the once famous Montmartre haunt, for Oppenheim was frequently in Paris on the affairs of his leather company, and at the Café he acquired his taste for the mysteries of those international intriguings and rascalities that figure so largely in several of his books, for the proprietor used to tell him all manner of thrilling yarns about political and international adventurers, some of whom had been among his customers, and his listener formed a habit of weaving stories around the more striking personalities in the cosmopolitan crowd that he met in the Dead Rat."

He was eighteen years old when his first short story was published, and only twenty when his first novel appeared. Before he was thirty he married Miss Elsie Hopkins, of Chelsea, Massachusetts. Mr. Oppenheim and his wife called their cottage in Sheringham, Norfolk, "Winnisimmet," which was the Indian name of her Massachusetts home town. The house overlooked the North Sea. Perhaps this detail, as much as another, led the author to the construction in the years before the world war of that series of stories in which, as an element of his plots, Mr. Oppenheim kept repeating Germany in the rôle of the villain. Legend has it that during the war itself his name was on the list of Britons to be shot if captured, although lists of that sort are usually myths. "There was one period," he has commented since, "in the autumn of 1918, when a well-directed bomb upon the Ministry of Information might have cleared the way for the younger novelists at the expense of Arnold Bennett, John Buchan, Dion Calthrop, E. Temple Thurston, Hugh Walpole and myself." [7] He visited America in 1911 and again

[7] "E. Phillips Oppenheim," by Himself. Brentano's Book Chat, April, 1921.

in 1922, when Mrs. Oppenheim came with him. On the latter occasion he made by far the wittiest comment of any visitor in reply to the usual question: what he thought of prohibition. "My only fear," with a smile, "is that it may make me a drunkard." [8] Those who met the victim of this reasonable dread saw a sturdy, broad-shouldered figure developed by air and outdoor exercise; and those who played golf with him respected his handicap of seven strokes only. His large, florid face seemed to kindle into laughter from the constant humorous gleam in his blue eyes. Among his own titles he confessed to a fondness for *A Maker of History*, *The Double Life of Mr. Alfred Burton*, *The Great Impersonation* and—perhaps influenced a little by its then impending publication—*The Great Prince Shan*. At this time he was subjected to one of those sets of questions from the answers to which one may construct a totally wrong picture of the person. However, we may note that his idea of happiness was tied up with his work, and that he gave as his notion of unhappiness, "No ideas." His particular aversion, he said, was fog.[9] Fog? Yet he has said: "I would be perfectly content to spend the rest of my days in London. Half a dozen thoroughfares and squares in London, a handful of restaurants, the people whom one meets in a single morning, are quite sufficient for the production of more and greater stories than I shall ever write." [10] He describes himself as no great traveller; he has, though, been in most European countries, and he pretty regularly spends his winters at his villa in Cagnes on the Riviera. He divides his time in

[8] In Boston Evening Transcript for 23 February 1922.

[9] "Mental Photo of E. Phillips Oppenheim," in The New York American for 6 March 1922.

[10] "E. Philips Oppenheim," by Himself, in Brentano's Book Chat for April, 1921.

England between the house in Norfolk and his rooms in London.

iv

Mr. Oppenheim does not take himself seriously in the rôle of prophet. "Large numbers of people have noted the fact that in certain of my earlier novels I prophesied wars and world events that actually did come to pass. In *The Mysterious Mr. Sabin*, I pictured the South African Boer war seven years before it occurred. In *The Mischief Maker*, *The Great Secret*, and *A Maker of History* I based plots upon the German menace and the great war that did actually occur. The romance of secret diplomacy has enthralled me for years. In writing my novels I have had no particular advance knowledge of world affairs. I have reasoned to myself, 'This nation is aiming toward this,' and 'That nation is aiming toward that'; then I have invented my puppets representing these conflicting ambitions and set them in action. It was the story first of all that appealed to me, and not any burning desire to express political convictions and lay bare great conspiracies." [11]

He takes himself seriously only in the rôle of entertainer, of storyteller. "If you tell him you like his books," says Gerald Cumberland, in *Written in Friendship*, "he is frankly pleased; but if you pay him high-flown compliments he will begin to yawn." There need be no paying of compliments in a consideration of Mr. Oppenheim's work, but no analysis of his method could fairly withhold considerable praise. We have spoken of his confidential, easy manner with the reader as a secret of his toward establishing plausi-

[11] "Fiction and Prophecy," by E. Phillips Oppenheim, in The New York Times, Sunday book or magazine section (March, 1922 ?)

bility for the things he is about to tell. But there is more to be noted. Like the best writers of his sort among his countrymen—and like far too few Americans in the same field—he is unhurried. He is never afraid to pause for the amplification of sentiment, the communication of the moment's feeling, a bit of characterization or a passage of pure description. And these are the matters which give an effect of rondure, and not infrequently touches of charm, to a story of whatever sort. At the moment I can think of only one American—Hulbert Footner—who has had the wisdom, or perhaps the temperament, to follow British practice in this by no means negligible affair of workmanship; and it is significant that Mr. Footner, an American, has so far had a better reception in England than in his own country. Apparently we value this certain leisureliness when it comes to us from abroad, for Mr. Footner, re-exported to us, is making distinct headway. What the American writer generally does is to accelerate his action to the pitch of implausibility (if he only knew it). This does very well, and may be indispensable, for all I know, with the readers of a certain type of American magazines; unfortunately the habitual buyers and readers of books demand something more careful.

The other interesting point of excellence in Oppenheim's work derives from his method of spontaneity. He once said: "The lure of creation never loses its hold. Personally I cannot account for the fact. Perhaps it springs from the inextinguishable hope that one day there will be born the most wonderful idea that has ever found its way into the brain of a writer of fiction." [12] For the creator, the superlative never

[12] "E. Phillips Oppenheim," by Himself, in Brentano's Book Chat, April, 1921.

arrives; but certainly for the reader Mr. Oppenheim has materialized more than one wonderful idea. *The Great Impersonation*, deservedly one of his most successful books, is a fairly recent illustration. But I would like to call particularly to attention an earlier story, both for what seems to me to be its astonishing merit and for its interesting light on the method of spontaneity which is Oppenheim's special technique. This is *The Way of These Women*, now ten years old. That it still sells is evidence that its merit is recognized; that one never hears mention of it in any offhand mention of its author's work shows that the recognition is by no means wide enough.

Sir Jermyn Annerley, a young man of fine taste and high honor, though certainly inclined toward priggishness, is a playwright of the intellectual type. Sybil Cluley, the actress who has aroused London by her performance in Jermyn's drama, comes to Annerley Court as his weekend guest. They are to discuss his new play in which Sybil is to appear. Aynesworth, Marquis of Lakenham and Jermyn's second cousin, chances to pay a visit at the same time. Another distant cousin of Jermyn's, Lucille, who has divorced a French nobleman, is Jermyn's hostess. Lucille is in love with Jermyn. During the visit Jermyn surrenders to his love for Sybil; they announce their engagement to the others. Sybil is obviously afraid of Lakenham to a degree not to be accounted for by his reputation for excesses, and after some time Lakenham confirms and shares with Lucille his knowledge of a discreditable episode in Sybil's career before her success on the stage.

Lakenham is murdered at Annerley Court. Suspicion points directly to Sybil, but Lucille has aided Sybil and Jermyn in the removal of very incriminating evidence. As the price for protecting Sybil, Lucille requires Jermyn to marry her within two months.

The story is developed with admirable intervals and suspense. The point of the first quarter of the book is Lakenham's knowledge of something in Sybil's past, and Lucille's determination to fight Sybil for Jermyn. Then Lakenham is killed. Almost half the book lies between the murder and its solution. It is evident that as he wrote Mr. Oppenheim saw (what he may not have grasped at the beginning) that Lucille was his most striking character. As the novel proceeded he became absorbed in the possibilities Lucille offered; if, as may well be the case, he vaguely contemplated solving the murder and bringing Sybil and Jermyn happily together for a quick "curtain," he deliberately abandoned so conventional and easy an ending. Jermyn and Lucille are married under the hateful terms Lucille has imposed as the price of Sybil's safety.

It is this that lifts *The Way of These Women* out of the run of Mr. Oppenheim's work. Did Sybil kill Lakenham? If she did not, who did she think killed him? If Lucille used fraud with Jermyn, why not annul the marriage for fraud and bring down the curtain? (And in putting these questions I decline responsibility for your wrong inferences as to the answers.) In any case, the solution of the murder would seem to end the story. But something larger and more fateful, something of very near universal significance, had by this time lodged in Mr. Oppenheim's mind. The "wonderful idea" had come. The last quarter of *The Way of These Women* is the material, intrinsically, for a very great novel. And Mr. Oppenheim handles it with touches of greatness. He could, of course, by slashing off most he had already written, by adopting some such technical device as W.

B. Maxwell used in *The Devil's Garden*, have made
it a masterpiece, for his knowledge of his theme and
his appreciation of its character are plain to be seen.
I do not know whether this novel has ever been dramatized, but it is incredible that it should not have been
dramatized; the possibilities of Lucille are greater than
those of Camille, for they are less artificial and they
are not either sentimental or cheap. Why did Mr.
Oppenheim not rework it; why did he let it go as the
book is, a mixture? Of several possible extenuations,
I think the best is that by leaving it alone he probably was able to take the reader who sought merely
to be entertained into a very high place whither that
reader could not have been lured directly. And it is
an elevation to which the writer of ready-made plots
never leads.

BOOKS BY E. PHILLIPS OPPENHEIM

NOTE: The reader is referred to the bibliography by Mr.
Hulings C. Brown appearing in the Boston Evening Transcript
for 5 May 1923. Mr. Brown's arrangement of the titles is
alphabetical (including both English and American titles).
His list includes Mr. Oppenheim's five serials of book length,
not given below because not published in book form. Mr.
Brown also gives the publisher (except in a few cases where
no record exists). In the list below books that have been
published in America are starred; those that have been published in America and were recorded by Mr. Brown as in
print are double-starred. Books written under the pseudonym
"Anthony Partridge" are so indicated.

1887   *Expiation*
1894   *A Monk of Cruta*
1895   **A Daughter of the Marionis*. First title in Amer-
      ica was *To Win the Love He Sought*.
1895   *The Peer and the Woman*

E. PHILLIPS OPPENHEIM

1896 *False Evidence*

1896 *A Modern Prometheus*

1896 **The Mystery of Mr. Bernard Brown*

1896 *The Wooing of Fortune*

1897 *The Amazing Judgment*

1898 **As a Man Lives*. First title in America was *The Yellow House.*

1898 *A Daughter of Astrea*

1898 **Mysterious Mr. Sabin*

1899 **Mr. Marx's Secret*

1899 *The Postmaster of Market Deighton*

1899 ***The Man and His Kingdom*

1900 **A Millionaire of Yesterday*

1900 **The World's Great Snare*

1901 ***The Survivor*

1902 ***A Sleeping Memory*
In England: *The Great Awakening*

1902 **Enoch Strone*
In England: *Master of Men*

1903 **The Traitors*

1903 ***A Prince of Sinners*

1903 ***The Yellow Crayon*

1904 ***Anna the Adventuress*

1904 ***The Betrayal*

1905 ***A Maker of History*

1905 ***The Master Mummer*

1906 **A Lost Leader*

1906 *The Tragedy of Andrea*

1907 ***The Malefactor*
In England: *Mr. Wingrave, Millionaire*

1907 **Berenice*

1908 **The Avenger*
In England: *The Conspirators*

1908 ***The Great Secret*
In England: *The Secret*

1908 **The Distributors*, "by Anthony Partridge"
In England: *Ghosts of Society*. Another title in America was *The Plunderers*

1908   *Passers-By*, "by Anthony Partridge"
1909   *The Governors*
1909   ***The Missioner*
1909   ***Jeanne of the Marshes*
1909   *The Kingdom of Earth*, "by Anthony Partridge"
      In England: *The Black Watcher*
1910   *The Long Arm of Manister*
      In England: *The Long Arm*
1910   ***The Illustrious Prince*
1910   ***The Lost Ambassador*
      In England: *The Missing Delora*
1911   *The Moving Finger*
      In England: *A Falling Star*
1911   *The Golden Web*, "by Anthony Partridge"
1911   ***Havoc*
1912   ***Peter Ruff and the Double Four*
      In England: *The Double Four*
1912   ***The Lighted Way*
1912   *Those Other Days* (short stories)
1912   *The Court of St. Simon*, "by Anthony Partridge"
1913   ***The Mischief Maker*
1913   *For the Queen* (short stories)
1913   *Mr. Laxworthy's Adventures*
1913   ***The Tempting of Tavernake*
      In England: *The Temptation of Tavernake*
1914   *The Amazing Partnership*
1914   *The Double Life of Mr. Alfred Burton*
1914   ***The Way of These Women*
1915   *An Amiable Charlatan*
      In England, *The Game of Liberty*
1915   ***Mr. Grex of Monte Carlo*
1915   *The Black Box*
1915   ***A People's Man*
1916   *The Mysteries of the Riviera*
1916   ***The Vanished Messenger*
1917   ***The Hillman*
1917   ***The Kingdom of the Blind*
1918   ***The Double Traitor*

E. PHILLIPS OPPENHEIM

1918   ***The Cinema Murder*
        In England: *The Other Romilly*
1918   **The Pawns Count
1918   ***The Zeppelin's Passenger*
        In England: *Mr. Lessingham Goes Home*
1919   ***The Wicked Marquis*
1919   ***The Curious Quest*
1920   ***The Great Impersonation*
1920   ***The Box with the Broken Seals*
        In England: *The Strange Case of Mr. Jocelyn*
        Thew
1920   ***The Devil's Paw*
1920   *Aaron Rod, Diviner*
1920   *Ambrose Lavendale, Diplomat*
1920   *Hon. Algernon Knox, Detective*
1921   ***Jacob's Ladder*
1921   **The Profiteers
1921   ***Nobody's Man*
1922   ***The Great Prince Shan*
1922   ***The Evil Shepherd*
1923   ***The Seven Conundrums*
1923   **The Mystery Road
1923   ***Michael's Evil Deeds*
1924   ***The Wrath to Come*
1924   ***The Passionate Quest*

SOURCES ON E. PHILLIPS OPPENHEIM

In addition to those referred to in the text and in footnotes, the reader is urged to consult the full-page interview and account appearing in the Boston Evening Transcript for 8 March 1924 ("Oppenheim the Master Maker of Plots," by James Walter Smith). This is by all odds the best and most interesting single article. It quotes Mr. Oppenheim's amanuensis as saying that he dictates 5,000 words a day on good days and about 4,000 words on an average day—a phenomenal speed. "In summer he dictates out of doors and I take it down in my note-book. In winter, he dictates direct to the machine. He likes a low easy-chair while working. It's amazing to me how sure he is in his dictation, and what a grip he has on his plots. Occasionally he has two or more stories moving at the same time, but no matter what the number of characters or of the places where the action occurs, he rarely becomes confused. When he is held up, sometimes by a trifling detail, or by the more important one of getting a character out of a difficulty, he simply says: 'Three dots' . . . like that, and moves on. This may happen several times in the course of a sitting, and I usually can divine, as the story proceeds, when I'm going to hear that 'three dots.' When the dictation is finished, he goes out for a game of golf, perhaps. Then next day he takes up the typescript where the suspension points appear and unerringly fills in the bits which bothered him. This would be easy if the case were single, but where there are several 'three dot' cases it demands skill and concentration to get out of the bunker."

9. G. Stanley Hall, Psychologist

i

IN describing a novel course he gave at Clark University and which he called psychogenesis—the birth and evolution of the soul—G. Stanley Hall remarks in his autobiography, *Life and Confessions of a Psychologist*: "Interest, like steam in an engine, must be developed over a large surface, although when put to work it has to be applied to a small one." That is true of this chapter. The large surfaces of Dr. Hall's long and unusual career can be depended on, I think, to develop interest in my reader; although whether that interest will apply itself to psychology, methods of teaching, child study, or the central figure of the Christian faith is uncertain and perhaps immaterial. A developed interest, before passing on to any of these things, does well to linger for some time on the man himself, who had so many vicissitudes and whose account of his life, outside and inside, is the best of a certain type since Benjamin Franklin's, which it most nearly resembles.

Both Franklin and Dr. Hall were Yankees; both were much abroad and transcended their Puritan beginnings on the intellectual side, though in the sphere of conduct each was a tree inclined as the twig had been bent. Both were zestful of every human experience; each alike, though for a somewhat differing purpose, has gone far and deep in the matter of self-examination, writing down his confessions and conclusions for the world to read. If Franklin is more clear and practical and personal, Dr. Hall takes the reader to greater levels and to vistas of

"fresh woods and pastures new."

His *Life and Confessions of a Psychologist* is a book of more than ordinary account simply for this reason. It has distinct faults. Its material is a little diffuse and not too well organized; it is far from lucid in places and lapses into technical language where it need not do so. In addition, Dr. Hall's particular interests are allowed to override the literary, and sometimes the human, interest. The introductory chapter perplexes and dismays the ordinary reader with a series of conclusions couched in scientific lingo; the second chapter repels him with its dullness. Yet, if he persist, he will soon find himself unable to stop until the book is finished; certain chapters and parts of chapters will absorb his whole attention; and in the end he will have a sense of having had glimpses into many mansions, all spacious; of having come in touch with largeness and nobility of soul.

ii

Granville Stanley Hall, who died on 24 April 1924, was born 1 February 1846 in Ashfield, Massachusetts. His father was of impetuous temperament, his mother a rather submissive and devoutly pious woman. There were three children, all brought up on a farm. From the first, Stanley Hall was keenly interested in animals. But he was also one of those boys whose imagination is strongly exercised by the figures of frost on a windowpane, the broken march of clouds across the sky, the shapes and images seen in dancing fire-

light and the visions excited by musical sounds. He
was sensitive and both brave and timid; pacifistic by
temper, he could persist in a course once taken. He
was essentially a lonely child, as such children often
are, and this loneliness was to become more pronounced as he grew older, developing a habit of isola-
tion which was to be his salvation in the greatest crisis
in his career.

His schooling culminated in Williams College,
which gave him his A. B. in 1867. He was a class-
mate of Hamilton Wright Mabie. Mark Hopkins—
he of whom it was said that "a university was Mark
Hopkins on one end of a log and a student on the
other"—was president of the college and also "professor of moral and intellectual philosophy." An important friendship of this time was with Charles Eliot
Norton.

A single year in New York followed. Young Hall
was a student at the Union Theological Seminary, but
he was also twenty-one, in New York for the first
time, full of a healthy curiosity and bound to satisfy
it. He went to the theatre as well as all manner of
churches and was one of a number employed by the
City Missionary Society to invite women of the street
to attend the midnight mission. Through the friendly
act of Henry Ward Beecher money was provided for
Hall to go abroad and study, the lender being Henry
Sage, the benefactor of Cornell University. It was
already apparent that Hall had no vocation to the
ministry. He dreamed of becoming a professor. Darwin, Spencer and Tyndall, Renan, Strauss, Emerson
and Carlyle had profoundly influenced him. In the
summer of 1868 he went to Germany, first to the
University of Bonn and then to that of Berlin. Here
he dabbled in all manner of subjects, from theology

to surgery and mental clinics. On his return to America he wished to teach the history of philosophy but was unable to lest he should, in the opinion of a college president, "unsettle men and teach them to hold no opinions."

Private tutoring was followed by a spell of teaching at Antioch College, Yellow Springs, Ohio. It was at this time that the first volume of Wundt's *Physiological Psychology* was published. In a sense, psychology as we know it began with this work, so definite in its experiments and conclusions. Here was something one could lay hold of! Hall read it, was amply fascinated, and left Antioch, resolved to go to Leipzig and study under Wundt. But at Cambridge he was met by the offer of an instructorship at Harvard and stopped to teach for a year, going on to Leipzig in 1876. He spent a year in Berlin, some time in Paris and England, and came home to resume his friendship with William James and others, to lecture on education under Harvard auspices, and to cast about. He was much in debt and had no prospects. He had married. Having spent three years in Germany between the ages of 22 and 25, and three more from 32 to 35, "the narrow, inflexible orthodoxy, the Puritan eviction of the joy that comes from amusements, from life, the provincialism of our interests, our prejudice against continental ways of living and thinking, the crudeness of our school system, the elementary character of the education imparted in our higher institutions of learning—all these seemed to me depressing, almost exasperating. I fairly loathed and hated so much that I saw about me that I now realize more clearly than ever how possible it would have been for me to have drifted into some, perhaps almost any, camp of radicals and to have come into such open rupture

[146]

with the scheme of things as they were that I should have been stigmatized as dangerous, at least for any academic career, where the motto was Safety First." But he must teach or go back to the farm.

iii

Luck was with him. In 1881 he was invited to lecture on psychology at the Johns Hopkins University, toward which all ambitious young professors were looking wistfully. He was then asked to teach a half year after which he was appointed full professor for five years at a salary then very generous. The seven fat years—for he remained until 1888—had begun. The great Gilman was president of the university, Gildersleeve taught Greek and Rowland taught physics; Simon Newcomb, astronomy; Spencer, Huxley, Kelvin, Matthew Arnold, James Bryce, Freeman the historian, James Russell Lowell, Dr. S. Weir Mitchell, and William James were visitors and, for the most part, lecturers. Among Dr. Hall's pupils were John Dewey, J. McKeen Cattell, Joseph Jastrow, James H. Hyslop and one young man who took a long Sunday afternoon walk with the professor "in which he debated with me the question of majoring in psychology, although I felt that his mind was already made up not to do so, for his previous studies and his Southern instincts and family traditions already inclined him too strongly toward the historical and political field." This was Woodrow Wilson. "Had he chosen psychology," comments Dr. Hall, "he might never have been President; but, on the other hand, if he had, he might have learned to do better teamwork and have been more ready to compromise and concede."

When he was just forty-two Dr. Hall's lean years

began—lean in the sense that he gave up highly congenial work and surroundings and a maximum salary which was offered him to embark on a new and untried enterprise, in which he was to endure a degree of distress and anxiety and an amount of difficulty and odium hard to describe. The history of his relations with Clark University, first publicly told in Chapter VII of his *Life and Confessions of a Psychologist*, is likely without a parallel. Certainly it throws more light on human nature than any psychologist could hope to do by a lifetime of experiment and reasoning. Briefly, this was what happened:

Jonas Gilman Clark (1815-1900), a successful wagonmaker, had made a fortune in California in 1849 by selling mining implements. He was one of the active Vigilantes and a friend of Leland Stanford. After attaining importance in San Francisco he moved to New York and increased his wealth by dealing in real estate; but with the passage of years he returned to his native county in Massachusetts. The example of Leland Stanford, his own childlessness, and a desire to do something for his native county led him to resolve to found Clark University in Worcester, Massachusetts. Dr. Hall was asked to be president and accepted the post.

Mr. Clark immediately gave a building and grounds and his note for $600,000 for the university, with a note of $100,000 for a library. This, a total value of something like $1,000,000, was the largest single gift that had ever been made to education in New England. The outlook was of unprecedented brilliance, for Mr. Clark's expressed intention was to leave all his wealth to the institution, and his fortune was variously estimated at from $8,000,000 to $18,000,-000 or even $20,000,000. The founder readily agreed to Dr. Hall's suggestion that he, Dr. Hall, spend a year abroad studying the universities of the world.

Surely no one has ever had an opportunity equalling the year which followed. Dr. Hall omitted to visit no university of importance in Europe. The mere recital of the places he saw is impressive enough; when the imagination tries to take in the educational panorama unrolled before his eyes the task becomes impossible. One small cloud darkened the horizon. Mr. Clark had instructed him to bring to this side several of the best German professors. Dr. Hall was put in a painful situation by engaging Von Holst of Freiburg and then having his act disowned. He did not suspect that it was to be only the first of a series of bitter and terrible disappointments.

Clark was opened as a university for graduate students only with few pupils but high hopes and splendid prospects on 2 October 1889. A few simple figures, as Dr. Hall remarks, give the key to the near-tragedy that followed. "During the first year we spent for salaries and equipment, $135,000; the second year, Mr. Clark contributed $50,000 above the income of the $600,000 that had actually been transferred to the board of trustees, making a total income of $92,000; the third year, he gave $26,000, making it $68,000; the fourth year, $12,000, making it $54,000; and the fifth and subsequent years of his life he gave nothing, so that the whole institution subsisted upon the income of its funds, namely, the $600,000 for the University and $100,000 for the library." What was wrong?

Mr. Clark couldn't or wouldn't say. He seems to have been a singularly inarticulate individual. Whether he lost heavily in the misfortunes that overtook the British firm of Baring Brothers, or on his own account, remains uncertain. It may be that he had, all along, much less money than was supposed; or it may be that a university cost more than he expected. There was consternation over his dwindling annual gifts and a deeper anxiety over his failure to add to the permanent endowment. Collectively and individually the trustees implored him to say what the university might expect; at least, they would know where they stood; but Mr. Clark remained silent. "He sanctioned every engagement and knew exactly the liabilities we were incurring, and the optimistic view," says Dr. Hall, "was that he could not possibly bring men here or start departments and then fail to sustain them." It was too optimistic. Men were let go because there was no money to keep them. After a personal quarrel with a professor, Clark compelled the board to request the man's resignation, which they did. The founder would smilingly listen to instructors who asked for supplies, refer them to Dr. Hall, and then order Dr. Hall to deny the requests. A personal tragedy at the beginning of this time befell Dr. Hall as he was convalescent from an attack of diphtheria so severe that for weeks he could not speak, but had to write on a slate. He had been sent to the country when, one night, through an accident in a gas fixture, his wife and the younger of his two children, aged six, were smothered to death.

"As the second year drew to a close and the trustees fully realized that Mr. Clark would almost certainly not maintain expenditures on the basis on which they had been begun, and as there was already much discontent in the faculty, their anxiety focused on the future, and I was instructed to do everything possible not to alienate Mr. Clark to such a degree that he would bestow elsewhere the remainder of his fortune, still believed to be very large. To this end I must, with what grace and tact I could, accept the situation; and when asked, as I often was when I was trying to get his wishes carried through with the faculty as a whole or individually, whether it was my will or the founder's that I was trying to enforce, must give them to understand it was my own and thus shield Mr. Clark. This was most humiliating to my honor and even to my conscience but the situation demanded nothing less, for the entire future of the institution seemed to hang upon this." The foreseen result was a faculty revolt; a majority of the staff offered their resignations because they had lost confidence in Dr. Hall. The trustees left the affair in Dr. Hall's hands, but as those hands were tied by the necessity of keeping a close secret the financial situation and by the necessity of "shielding" Clark from censure, he could explain but lamely.

At this point President Harper of the new University of Chicago came to Worcester, secretly engaged a majority of the faculty at double the Clark salaries, and then tried to hire Dr. Hall for a salary larger than he was receiving. Under Dr. Hall's threat to make the facts public and to appeal to John D. Rockefeller himself—Mr. Rockefeller being Chicago's backer—Harper receded a little. Dr. Hall managed to salvage a few of his men from the raid. Clark University was now reduced to living on the four per cent. income from its $600,000 and waiting for its founder to die, "when it would be clear to us whether we must close up, live along feebly, or enter upon the realization of our large and high initial hopes by finding that, after all, he had vast means and had not diverted them to other sources."

Andrew Carnegie promised $100,000 if an equal amount were raised; when only $37,000 could be raised and Mr. Carnegie was told why he dropped the condition and gave his $100,000 outright. Somehow, the next half dozen years were got through. There was a continuous false position for Dr. Hall and continuous and heavy censure to be borne. He had to suppose that the end would justify the means; and the end, when it came, gave him only partial satisfaction. Clark had got to spend a good deal of time in Europe, perhaps as an aid to his disgusting reticence. He was at outs with the trustees, all men of distinction and all sustaining Dr. Hall as well as they could. The founder was also in disagreement with Dr. Hall over a collegiate department, which he wanted and which Dr. Hall—one would think, very naturally, in the acutely trying circumstances—didn't want. The tenth anniversary of Clark was celebrated with a brave spirit in 1899. It was that darkest hour before the dawn. The perverse Clark died the year following leaving a nasty will with five codicils and expensive litigious possibilities, most of which were realized. In the last of the codicils Clark revoked certain strictures upon Dr. Hall contained in the will itself. However, a collegiate department was provided and university and college came at once into possession of nearly the whole estate, the rest to follow at Mrs. Clark's death. Dr. Hall, who had been teaching and lecturing and worrying, was free at last from his scapegoat rôle. Four years later he was to publish in two volumes his masterly study of *Adolescence;* and every few years after that were to see an important book come from his hands. He was in his fifties and at last comparatively free and unhampered. Not only his interest in child study but his wide knowledge of methods of teaching (pedagogy), of psychology and philosophy, of the vast amount of experimental work in hand everywhere and his novel conceptions of the soul's progress were to bear fruit.

iv

He had always been interested in genetics—beginnings. His psychology, as it matured in a long lifetime of study and reflection, is different from the psychology of other men chiefly in this respect. The one word of science which always had the power to fire Dr. Hall's imagination is "evolution." Let not the fundamentalist rage, at this point of this chapter, nor the reader imagine a vain thing. It is greatly doubtful if, deep in his heart, G. Stanley Hall cared two sticks about Darwinian evolution as such. But evolution as an idea was to him a psychic reality.

Let me explain, as well as I can, in the simplest terms.

A psychic reality is something in which one's faith is so strong that one neither needs nor wishes proofs. It is what you firmly believe; what you believe in so firmly that, so far as you are concerned, it exists. The thing may not exist, but if it did you would order your life just as you do now. Those who live under the shadow of such a belief need no umbrella of evidence spread over them.

To take an important and timely instance: One of the main points in Dr. Hall's work, *Jesus, the Christ, in the Light of Psychology* (1917) bears directly on the controversy now active between the fundamentalists and the liberals. That dispute has been hottest on two points: the virgin birth of Christ and the Resurrection. Dr. Hall holds that both sides are living and disputing in a pre-psychological age; that they are both right in all that they affirm, wish and

[153]

mean, and are both wrong in all that they deny. He says that both the virgin birth and the Resurrection are psychic realities to great numbers of people. He believed in both himself. As a scientist familiar with physiology, the issues offered as many obstacles to his mind as they can possibly offer to any human mind. Nevertheless, he believed; to him the virgin birth and the Resurrection are both psychic realities. "There are psychic realities that are truer than fact, and I wonder if it would not degrade rather than spiritualize faith if we were to discover a motion picture of the Resurrection."

Now whether Darwin was right or not, whether the law of natural selection is true, false or meaningless, "evolution" is the word to cover Dr. Hall's idea of what has happened and what is happening to the spirit of man. Although he studied under Wundt, he thought it unfortunate that one whose influence has been so farreaching was trained in physics and physiology chiefly. Biology, says Dr. Hall, would have given Wundt and his disciples less positiveness; they would have been less set on explaining all things of the spirit by occurrences in and to the body; and the idea of growth and change would have been more elastic and more hopeful. Again, Dr. Hall was one of the few American psychologists of standing who had gone deeply and impartially into the discoveries of Freud and the whole field of modern psychoanalysis. What are his conclusions on this fascinating development of science?

Freud has himself said that there are three great culture epochs marked for us, so far, by what we call science. The first dawned with Copernicus's discovery that the sun, not the earth, was the center of our universe. The second was initiated by Darwin. The third is Freud's own work. Dr. Hall was by no means an extreme or convinced Freudian, but seemed inclined to believe that Freud's estimate of his work may not be much out of the way. Copernicus revolutionized our ideas of space; Darwin transformed the concept of time; Freud is dealing with our idea of eternity. For the world that Freud may be said to have discovered, the world of the unconscious, is a piece of eternity and the only piece that science can lay claim to having captured. If it exists at all, it exists and has existed forever.

In the main the Freudian theories seemed to Dr. Hall "genetic and vital." They put beginnings farther back than we have been used to put them; many of the explanations really do explain, and Dr. Hall was convinced that they saved several of the most gifted of his pupils from mental wreck. "If the Freudian claims of the all-dominance of sex were excessive, as they certainly seem to me to be, it was only a natural reaction to the long taboo and prudery that would not look facts in the face. If the gross and morbid phenomena here were taken as the point of departure, the conclusions here drawn were from a solid and wide basis of clinical facts which no one could dispute, however much they might criticize the methods and interpretations." There was, however, always the danger of measuring the normal mind and spirit by standards got from studying abnormal minds. And Dr. Hall did not believe in the methods of healing practised by Freudian physicians. Such psychoanalytic treatment, he thought, leaves the patient often unduly sexually-minded. Where a cure or real benefit results, he believed, it is not the result of a confession of dreams, etc., tortured into this or that meaning. It is because the patient has come to the conclu-

[155]

sion that he is a dead giveaway, that everybody sees in him what the psychoanalyst sees; shame, dread, and modesty assert themselves and make him do better.

But the emphasis of Freud's teachings is on feeling. It is not a psychology of muscular twitchings as that of Wundt and his followers tended to be. There is a theory, brilliantly expounded by William James and called the Lange-James theory, which explained that we feel sorry because we cry. There is also what is called the psychophysic law, which says that a sensation is increased by a constant amount when the stimulus is increased by a constant multiplication. But the psychophysic law broke down at extremes. For example, a very slight increase in tickling doubles and redoubles the sensation felt; it almost seems as if the law were then the other way about. And the sorry-because-we-cry theory cannot be proved where thoughts only are in question. A. murders B. Very likely he murders him in thought before he does so in fact. Now possibly the murder-in-thought is preceded by some microscopic or passing changes in A.'s brain. But it is yet to prove, and it is very likely unprovable. In the same way, men are now engrossed with their dawning discoveries about the glands of the human body. As Dr. Hall pointed out, the attempt is now well under way to make psychology a mere matter of secretions. The thyroid gland does this, the pituitary gland controls that. The thing will be carried too far and we shall have to retrace many of our steps and, to some extent, start all over again toward fresh conclusions.

We make these mistakes, said Dr. Hall, because we are too eager to find a solution for the mystery of the soul. We want to believe that the mind can be understood from the body. But the explanation of the mind must be sought in the things of the mind. It is likely that history, for example, with its record of human institutions, throws at least as much light on the human mind that made the institutions as anything we can get in a dissecting room. Like James Harvey Robinson, Dr. Hall was unhappy over the increasing tendency of psychologists and other students to go off in a corner and never thereafter to relate what they are doing to the rest of knowledge. The genetic nature of everything bearing on the mind is constantly overlooked. Why? Well, men have fallen into a habit of thinking that psychology must be handled as fossil bones are handled. From a thigh bone found in the ground we can reconstruct, perhaps, the entire skeleton of some prehistoric animal. It is not possible, however, from this experiment or that to reconstruct, infer or measure the mind. This is because the mind is creative, or, at least, reproductive. It can only be studied from what it begets. The child's revolt from the parent both explains and is explained by the historic revolutions and revolts against authority. Hysteria is an escape from some intolerable reality. Certain men have a dread of being shut in by beliefs and opinions because earliest man had a dread of being shut in his cave in the rocks. But every man must have something to believe in, though it change from time to time, because his remote ancestor, when challenged, sought a wall at his back. What, then, is the hope of being exact or final in psychology? None. Would it be desirable to be exact or final? No.

The reader may inquire: What about the tests that are increasingly popular for everything from marriage to hunting the proper job? Dr. Hall refrained from using the short and ugly word. I will use it for him: they are bunk. But I will quote his own recorded experience with them.

[157]

"Some fifty years ago as an impecunious student I paid $5 to have my bumps charted at the Fowler and Wells phrenological institute, then on lower Broadway. Mr. Sizer, who did the job, told me that he would rather feel for five minutes through a cat-hole the skull of a girl he thought of marrying than court her five years. His findings were so pleasing to my self-esteem that two or three years later I went again, with even more satisfaction, so that I had the exhilarating sense that in the interim I had 'every day and in every way' been growing wiser and abler.

"Some thirty years later I chanced to meet the great Cheiro, handsome, magnetic, and in his day the pet of the New York 'Four Hundred,' and I submitted my palm to him. But this time with very depressing results. He found my life-line so broken that I should have been dead about that time; the line of intellect was very faint, indicating low mentality; by my wealth line I ought to be rich (and from his fee he probably thought me so). I was an incorrigible bachelor [1] and my character was a complex of incongruities. In a word, my hand gave the flat lie to what my bumps had said.

"Lombroso has several score of physical and psychic traits which he deems characteristic of criminals, and of these I was found to have seven more or less well developed. At the Bernheim Institute in Paris I had my finger-tips taken and interpreted. Later yet a Blackfordist tested me on all the, I think, twenty-one points in that system and at the close asked me if it was worth $10. It was. In Portland, Oregon, I found an expert who had worked years with the MacAuliffe-Sorel group of anthropologists. I began to psychoanalyze myself but, finding the task too hard, called in

[1] Dr. Hall married twice.

[158]

an expert to finish the work, with results which nothing would ever tempt me to tell.

"Still far too ignorant of the one I ought to know best, I took all the Yerkes army tests and the dozen or so shorter series devised for adults, and even put myself through the Binet-Simon series and their modifications by Terman; also the de Sanctis fool-finding series and at least a score of the tests for special avocations. In fact my friends have spoken rather slightingly of my passion for collecting and trying out tests, of which I have some hundreds. Judged by the Edison stunts, I was a near-moron, and in the Stenquist series much below the average; while I cannot even yet understand the Royce Ring. Some college entrance tests would bar me from entering the freshman class, while in many of the simpler ones my intelligence quotient indicated a mental age of at least 100.

"In Harman's test of the higher mental processes and the Bonser reasoning test, for example, I was surpassed by a girl of eleven. The results of all seem, thus, so confusing that I recall the chameleon which, when placed on a red cloth turned red, on blue, green and yellow, turned these colors, but when placed on a bit of Scotch plaid died trying to make good."

Time-limit tests are not only the hardest but tend to discredit the slow-but-sure type of person who really does so much of the world's best work. The tests merely test a kind of superficial mental quickness. They do not, and cannot be made to, exclude accidental advantages due to special experience or special knowledge. We have no way of testing the testers, some of whom have only enough brains to ask questions and write down other people's answers. There is no way of testing native ability. Persons old enough to take the tests have acquired much of their abilities from experience; and there is no way of separating what they were born with from what they have learned or acquired.

Dr. Hall says, on the other hand, that the tests he found trustworthy in estimating a young man's chances for success are these:

1.   Health.   It is true that Darwin fought neurasthenia all his life, that Nietzsche was always fighting megalomania, that Spencer was everlastingly coddling himself, that Stevenson contended with tuberculosis. But health was required to make the fight—great, excessive vital force—and particularly was the psychic health exceptional and the psychic force strong so to have held off the bodily enemy while great work was done. "The study of 200 biographies shows that the list of great original minds who were supernormal in health is about fourteen times as large as the list of great invalids."

2.   Second breath.   Corresponds to "second wind" in athletics. A state of mental exaltation, inspiration or ease, often coming after we have worked long and hard and past our usual hour of sleep at night. No one is likely to succeed who does not learn while young to tap this mental reservoir.

3.   The ability to pass quickly and easily from one extreme of feeling to the other. What is called the "pleasure-pain scale" extends all the way from despair and suicide up to the most transcendent happiness. Settled moods of long duration are bad. If the soul cannot run up and down the scale frequently, swiftly and flexibly it will have its pressures relieved in some other way, usually by setting up a dual personality—jekyll-hydeism, insanity, etc.

4.   Sympathy.   Confucius called it "reciprocity"; Buddha, pity; Aristotle, friendship; Plato, friend-

ship; Jesus, love; Paul, charity; Adam Smith and Darwin, sympathy; Comte, altruism; Renan, the enthusiasm of humanity; Kropotkin, mutual aid; Matthew Arnold, humanism; Giddings, consciousness of mankind; Trotter, the herd instinct. It is a power to feel for others and must be sufficiently strong to influence action at times.

5. Love of nature. This is the root. There are many flowers—poetry, music, literature, art of whatever form, religion. The mind first feels love and awe, then worship, then a desire for cold, outward study—the order is always the same. But in spite of the mind's insistence on going to extremes, the feeling must be kept alive and must be adequately fed.

6. Sublimation. Teeth, lips and tongue were created or developed to eat with; we have made them serve us to speak with, also. The senses first served to warn us of danger and to find and test food; we now use them in a thousand ways. Anger began as blind rage, but we have gone some way to control and direct it. We cannot be too angry if we are angry aright. As for love, which began on the physical plane, "every real interest sets a back-fire to lust."

7. Activity as against passivity. Although a given person or nation may be predominantly active or passive, doers or knowers, leaders or led, the two forces must be controlled and balanced for success. Do not make the mistake of thinking that activity is all to the good; energy without intelligence is worthless.

8. Loyalty or fidelity. In the first instance, this is loyalty to oneself, creating self-respect. The various loyalties to parents, husband or wife, children, friends, country, etc., follow.

These tests cannot be applied to large groups. They are tests of the individual. They cannot be made within set time limits. They cannot be made by asking a man or woman questions and writing down the answers. They require observation in favorable circumstances and these cannot always be secured by pre-arrangement. But they are the only tests worth making. They require in the tester something which psychology requires very much, in Dr. Hall's estimation, in many psychologists—common sense.

v

Dr. Hall's attitude toward educational theory and practice was derived from his special interest in child study. "In the nature of childhood itself and its different stages of development," he says, "must be found the norm for all the method and matter of teaching." One very general defect of our schools is that the teacher does not teach enough, but gives, or is required to give, too much attention to setting, hearing, and marking lessons. He thought the weakest spot in the American system to be from about the fourth to the ninth grades. Drill and authority can really do most with the child just at this stage. Whatever may be the possibilities eugenics offers in the future, it is a far-off future; for a long time to come we must depend on education to make the best of our child-material. Although it was necessary to exclude religious teaching from the schools, it should be restored as soon as a gradually widening tolerance makes that possible. Education without it lacks heart and soul. "Protestant though I am, I would far rather a child of mine should be trained to be a good Catholic, Jew, or even Buddhist, Confucianist, or Mohammedan than allowed to grow up with no religion at all and made an early skeptic toward all faiths. Not absolute truth but efficiency for the conduct of life is the supreme criterion of all values here. The highest interpretation of the most vital human experiences must always take the religious form."

Motion pictures have more cultural possibilities, wrote Dr. Hall, than anything since the invention of printing; but we have not learned to develop them. Broadcasting may have similar possibilities; but the educational value of our newspapers has deteriorated.

The general problem of education as stated by Dr. Hall is somewhat as follows:

Over-population and a use of the earth's resources so wasteful that we can now date the exhaustion of many of them are the first term of the problem. There is not now in the world one one-hundredth of the wealth necessary to satisfy the demand for it. "As civilization advances, it costs not only more money but more time and effort to keep people happy." And "the average individual wants all that is coming to him now and here, and uses every means in his power (fair and sometimes foul) to get it. Thus he plunges on toward the bankruptcy of his hopes in their present form." Wise minds realize that either men must restrict their desires, which is not likely, or must transform and redirect them—in technical language, must sublimate them, or find more internal surrogates for their gratification. Our industrial system is less than 200 years old. Our political institutions are only a few thousand years old. The mind of man is far, far older. Such men as James Harvey Robinson would adapt the mind of man to these juvenile institutions or phases of knowledge. Dr. Hall said the adjustment will have to be the other way about. It does seem likely. If it is to be made, psychology must make it.

"I know," he wrote, "no class of men quite so hard-boiled and uninteresting and, indeed, unintelligent outside the hard and fast and often narrow limits of their own interests as the American millionaires. Each man has a normal amount of wealth as he has a normal weight of body on which he can best thrive. If I were sentenced to be rich now I should grow neurotic over insurance risks, problems of competition, fluctuation of prices and markets, labor problems, anxieties about special legislation, tariff rates, new fields of fruitful investment, and perhaps efforts to reform our present industrial system."

In his own case, Dr. Hall found happiness through his work, which has never included that "curse of the industrial world today," having to do, for pay, work that he hated. For it must be remembered that the false situation at Clark University was more than off-set by the delight he had as a teacher of graduate students. But, work aside, perhaps the next greatest source of happiness and satisfaction to him has been the trait which Walt Whitman perfectly phrased when he exclaimed:

"In me the caresser of life, wherever moving."

For this psychologist and teacher, who was also for some time president of the New England Watch and Ward Society, a voluntary censorship which asserts itself chiefly over books and plays and in opposition to the social evil, always had "a love for glimpsing at first hand the raw side of life. I have never missed an opportunity to attend a prize fight if I could do so unknown and away from home. Thrice I have taken dancing lessons from experts sworn to secrecy, and tried to learn the steps of ancient and some of the tabooed modern dances—just enough to know the feel of them —up to some six years ago, although I have always been known as a non-dancer." In Paris, London, Vienna, Berlin, New York and San Francisco he found guides to take him through the underworld by night. In an institution for the blind, he blindfolded himself for an entire day; he learned the deaf mute alphabet; he had seen three executions, visited morgues, revival meetings, anarchist meetings. Paupers, criminals, wayward children, circus freaks were among his hobbies. "I believe that such zests and their indulgence are a necessary part of the preparation of a psychologist or moralist who seeks to understand human nature as it is." And as, probably, it will continue to be for a while to come.

BOOKS BY G. STANLEY HALL

1874 *Hegel as the National Philosopher of Germany.* Translated from the German of Dr. Karl Rosenkrans

1881 *Aspects of German Culture*

1883 *Methods of Teaching History*

1886 *Hints Towards a Select and Descriptive Bibliography of Education* (with John M. Mansfield)

1904 *Adolescence: Its Psychology, and Its Relations to Physiology, Anthropology, Sociology, Sex, Crime, Religion and Education.* Two volumes

1906 *Youth, Its Education, Regimen, and Hygiene.* An abridgement of *Adolescence*

1907 *Aspects of Child Life and Education*

1911 *Educational Problems.* Two volumes

1912 *Founders of Modern Psychology*

1917 *Jesus, the Christ, in the Light of Psychology.* Two volumes

1920 *Morale: The Supreme Standard of Life and Conduct*

1920 *Recreations of a Psychologist.* Stories, reminiscences and sketches

1922   *Senescence: The Last Half of Life*
1923   *Life and Confessions of a Psychologist*
1923   *Jesus, the Christ, in the Light of Psychology.*   One
          volume edition

NOTE: An extended list of articles, some of them popularly-
written, will be found in the bibliography appended to *Life
and Confessions of a Psychologist*

SOURCES ON G. STANLEY HALL

His autobiographical *Life and Confessions of a Psychologist*
is of the first importance.

How You Can DO More and BE More, by Bruce Barton.
An interview with G. Stanley Hall. In the American Magazine for November, 1923.

"Stanley Hall: A Memory," by A. E. Hamilton in the
American Mercury for July, 1924.

Aritcle by Dr. Joseph Jastrow on Dr. Hall in the Literary
Review of The Evening Post, New York, 28 June 1924.

10. The Mode in New Fiction

i

IF only books were like hats and gowns it would simplify matters a good deal. I could say: "Ostrich
feathers are being much used," or "Egotism is usually
the center of the design." But although there is an
observable tendency to buy books like clothes, because
some novel or other is all the rage, the tendency grows
weaker from year to year, I think; and if in the title
of this chapter I use the word "mode" it is phrasemaking.

Phrasemaking has its excuse in convenience, but it
must be abandoned in the discussion of some of the
fiction I am going to talk about. Among these books
just one is a first novel. Because it has this distinction,
because of its human quality, and because it borders a
theme of great significance, I want to speak at once
of Marjorie Barkley McClure's *High Fires*. Mrs.
McClure, the daughter of a Detroit clergyman, has laid
her story principally in that city, in the period from
1905 to about the present. Angus Stevenson is a minister of the gospel who sticks by the letter of a somewhat rigid, old-fashioned creed. His sons and his
daughter are young people of today. They cannot see
why they should not do what other boys and girls
of their age are doing. But their father will not for
one moment countenance such things as dancing and
card-playing and Sunday baseball.

The struggle is tempered and made human by Angus

Stevenson's goodness. He loves his children; especially is his daughter the apple of his eye. But he cannot sacrifice one inch of his principles. They are just as effectual in one direction as another. He voluntarily reduces his own salary when it seems to him that the act is called for. If he is intolerant, he is Christlike.

Of several crises, the one that cuts into him most deeply is his daughter's falling in love with a young man whom Angus Stevenson is constrained to regard as an atheist and an infidel. I have said that he loves his children; I should add that even when they are most rebellious against their father, they love him no less. The intensity and depth of Mrs. McClure's portrait of Angus Stevenson fully realizes the feeling on all sides. You are made to see and to acknowledge the claim to justice of conflicting creeds, the rare courage and noble faith and lifelong devotion of the father, the right to happiness and a certain self-fulfillment of the children. I know scarcely a novel of this year in which the human element is so strong; none in which it is stronger; none in which the lessons of a right feeling are more clearly conveyed or are more capable of a direct application in the lives of ordinary Americans.

> Here lies the flesh that tried
> To follow the spirit's leading;
> Fallen at last, it died,
> Broken, bruised and bleeding,
> Burned by the high fires
> Of the spirit's desires.

Mrs. McClure's novel is of interest, too, for its evidence that religion is quickening in the American mind. I am using "religion" in the sense of personal faith, which is at the present hour having a difficult time with established creeds, on the one hand, and life's machinery of motion on the other. There were evidences before *High Fires* was published, in the huge sale of a new life of Christ and in the fundamentalist-liberal controversy in the churches, that something deeply disquieting was coming to the surface. Almost simultaneously with the publication of *High Fires*, a first novel by Lyon Montross, *Half Gods*, by means of the highly realistic presentation of American small town life, tried to disclose the trouble. Mr. Montross's story implied what is probably true: the wine of a strong belief in anything is no longer fermented in most of us; we half-worship, or, at best, only worship half-heartedly.

Now the business of a novelist, or his art, is, as Joseph Conrad said, "a form of imagined life clearer than reality." It is to show you something more plainly than life shows it you; a good novel is a beacon, not a bonfire. Thus in the new novel by Margaret Culkin Banning (the most ambitious work she has so far done), the heroine, after a life of vicissitudes, comes to realize that she is, in the Scriptural phrase of the title, but a "handmaid of the Lord." Veronica is a sensitive girl brought up in depressing though scarcely unusual circumstances. She marries a man whose business career takes her to a social height, both in America and, for a time, in England. Her church, which should mean so much to her constantly, affects her life only at intervals. When the crash comes she finds herself separated from her husband by his struggle to keep afloat. She goes back to her home town. It seems as though she were back where she had started, with little difference except in the perplexity of an uncomprehended experience. So it is that finally she comes to a measure of understanding, to an unquiet peace. She sees that things will go on, though not in her way nor in any way of her choosing. *A Handmaid of the Lord*, like *High Fires* and *Half Gods*, does something to get at the trouble that is in us.

To show what is, including what is wrong, is the novelist's object; to show what came right is also sometimes possible. Dealing with the subject of religion, it has taken that very able novelist, Compton Mackenzie, three books in sequence to show the history of Mark Lidderdale. *The Altar Steps* gave the young man's background and the story of his life up to his ordination in the Church of England. In *The Parson's Progress* we see him as a priest of the English Church constantly beset by doubts and difficulties. These are by no means solved when the third novel of the trilogy, *The Heavenly Ladder*, opens; but they find their solution as it ends. Mark, as a convert in Rome, finds a happiness that Mr. Mackenzie has expressed with the utmost simplicity and with a restrained but lofty fervor.

With a simplicity different but equally honest, Ralph Connor writes his novels of men in a newer country. "Imagine," he said, when asked to tell briefly about his new book, "a man of vitality and power who has given and taken heavy blows in the struggle of human life, who finds himself cornered by forces he cannot subdue. Suddenly he realizes that his back is against the wall, that no further retreat is possible. Spiritually, mentally, physically there is a last stand to be made—a hold on the essentials of life to be groped for and seized. It is this last stand, this fighting chance that I have made the theme of *Treading the Winepress*." The scenes of the story are laid in Nova Scotia.

[170]

THE MODE IN NEW FICTION

If there is no single preoccupation common to the new fiction of other authors, readers will be highly content to find thoroughly characteristic new work by such favorites as Joseph C. Lincoln, Hugh Walpole, Mary Roberts Rinehart, Arnold Bennett, Bertrand W. Sinclair, Susan Ertz, Robert Hichens, and Ruth Comfort Mitchell.

Both Joseph C. Lincoln and Hugh Walpole—and different as they are—seem to me to have surpassed themselves. Mr. Lincoln's *Rugged Water* is not basically different from his other Cape Cod novels. Perhaps in the loose chronology of his stories it is more nearly contemporaneous with *Cap'n Eri* than with his more recent books. It is a story of a Coast Guard Station in the days when the Coast Guard was the Life Saving Service. The chief character is Calvin Homer, Number One man of the crew, brave, honest, and shy of women. In temporary command of the Station, he does gallant rescue work which should place him in line for promotion to Keeper of the Station. But in the same storm, Benoni Bartlett, of a nearby Station, stands out more conspicuously as the sole survivor of a brave crew. Benoni is made Keeper over Homer.

These two men, Benoni Bartlett and Homer; Myra Fuller, to whom Homer became engaged before he quite knew what was happening; Norma Bartlett, daughter of the former Keeper and the young woman with whom Homer eventually discovers himself to be in love, are the main persons of the novel. It is difficult to regard them as Mr. Lincoln's real subject, for the life of the Station and the drama of shipwreck asserts itself constantly in pages that teem with humor and with other qualities of human nature less easy of superficial exhibition.

In other words, the largeness of what he is essentially dealing with has seized upon Mr. Lincoln, and without the sacrifice of his lesser drama, or any of the picturesqueness that has made him so beloved, he has caught something of the loneliness of the Station, the whisper and thunder of the surf, the struggle of men in an "overmatched littleness" under a black sky in the tempest of waters. To me, these captures make *Rugged Water* the best novel he has written.

As for Mr. Walpole in *The Old Ladies*, my verdict, arrived at on different grounds, is equally affirmative and emphatic. Here is a short novel to stand beside Edith Wharton's *Ethan Frome*. There is bleakness as well as sunniness about the story; no haze; no sentimentality, though sentiment a-plenty and a deep, clear feeling. Three women, Lucy Amorest, May Beringer, and Agatha Payne, all seventy, live together in the top of a "rain-bitten" old house in Polchester. All are very poor. Lucy has a cousin who *may* leave her money, and a son in America from whom she has not heard for a couple of years. May Beringer, close to penury, is a weak, stupid, kind creature always terrified of life. Agatha Payne is sensual and strong. There has never, in my knowledge, been a picture more honest or more terribly pathetic of what old age sometimes means. Mr. Walpole has not evaded an inch of the truth or the tragedy; and the measured happiness accorded at last to Lucy Amorest comes not in the least as a concession toward a "happy ending" but solely as a reprieve of pity for her—and for the reader also.

The stories in Mary Roberts Rinehart's *Temperamental People* represent her most recent work and have a unity as interesting as their wide range. Each shows the force of temperament—that quality in people which makes the drama of life. But who are the temperamental people? A queen, a cowboy, a famous singer, a wife, a great sculptor and a business man's secretary are some of them. People as diverse as life; but all of them have temperament, and each story is a revelation of human emotion in action. As one of the characters says (it is the opening of the story of the sculptor, "Cynara") : "I suppose once in every creative life there comes the sublime moment, the consecrated hour when, not from within but from without there comes the onrush of true greatness." These records of that moment and that hour are among the best things Mrs. Rinehart has done.

The title of Arnold Bennett's new collection, *Elsie and the Child and Other Stories*, should be notice enough to the thousands who revelled in *Riceyman Steps* that the new book is one they may not miss. Yes, it is Elsie, the humble but lovable heroine of Clerkenwell, who figures again in this volume. It will be remembered that at the close of *Riceyman Steps*, Elsie, about to marry Joe, weakly consented to go to work as a servant for Mrs. Raste, while Joe (it was arranged) should resume his rôle as Dr. Raste's handy man. This was due to the pleading of young Miss Raste; Elsie was never one to resist children. And so "Elsie and the Child" begins approximately where *Riceyman Steps* left off. It is a novelette in length, a most satisfactory morsel left over from the novel's feast. With the very first page the feeling of *Riceyman Steps* in its more blissful moments is restored to the reader. The dozen shorter tales in the book are all from Mr. Bennett's most recent work.

Bertrand W. Sinclair's *The Inverted Pyramid* is

work of such proportions and of a sufficient dignity to take him quite out of the group of "Western" writers. This is not to rate down the cowboy story, but it is to recognize that such work as Mr. Sinclair's is something far more consequential. The inverted pyramid of the title is the social structure of a family set up by entailed wealth. Hawk's Nest, on Big Dent, just off the coast of Vancouver Island, is the home of the Norquay family, founded in 1809 by a roving pioneer fur trader who obtained the immense tract of land from the Indians for a pittance. He held it intact and it has come down unspoiled to the fifth generation of Norquays—Dorothy, Roderick, Phil and Grove. Luck and ability has aggregated a huge fortune from the natural resources of the estate, which Roderick's grandfather converted into a corporation, seventy per cent. of income going to the oldest son, the rest being divided among the others.

In the fifth generation various destinies open before the three brothers. Money, in the sense of finance (money plus power); love; the call of adventure; the quest of romance exert themselves on the three. The very structure of the family, however, makes it quite impossible that the destinies of one should not react in an exceptional degree upon the others. The responsibility for the maintenance of family standing, financial, social, moral, is interlocking. The old question: "Am I my brother's keeper?" was never asked under a colder compulsion to return an affirmative answer: yes, because he is a fellow director on the board.

I have said nothing about the daughter, Dorothy, and will only say that her rôle in the novel is important. It is enough, I think, to indicate the largeness and the serious character of *The Inverted Pyramid*, and to hail it as a sign that Mr. Sinclair will give us

[174]

other books as good or even better, to stand with this, his finest so far.

Susan Ertz's *Nina* is at once more brilliant and more profound than her *Madame Claire* (a novel which sells better today than when it was first published). *Nina* is the study of a girl whose love, once given, cannot be revoked by any act or will of her own. Brought up by her aunt, Nina Wadsworth falls in love with Morton Caldwell, adopted as a boy by that same aunt. Morton is extraordinarily handsome, good-hearted, and hopelessly susceptible to women. Tony Fielding has the qualities of fidelity and devotion which Morton lacks. Henri Bouvier, the son of a French family in England, is a playmate in childhood. Miss Ertz deals directly only with Nina and Morton after their marriage; what has gone before is cleverly reflected in the scenes put before the reader. As in *Madame Claire*, a delightful feature is the points of view from which the story is told. Much of it is seen through the eyes of Henri, grown to manhood, French in his ideas, sophisticated, and almost equally sympathetic and discreet. His comments, both spoken and unspoken, are delicious. They do much to enliven a situation at bottom profoundly tragic by reason of Morton's limitations as a husband and Nina's tenacious love.

The novel is as unusual as it is competent, and the unusualness springs from the author's competence. And when I say competence, I am not thinking only of the writing, which is admirable, but of the wisdom in human nature which underlies the tale. Every woman will be charmed with this novel because it is veracious in its feminine psychology, as most novels by men are not—and as most novels by women would be if women could avoid sentimentality as cleanly as Miss Ertz

[175]

does. Yes, women will be engrossed by *Nina* because they will find in it those accents and indications which are their tests of the reality of men and women in intimate relation to each other, especially in the relations of love and marriage.

The depths of feminine psychology have been delicately sounded many times by Robert Hichens, whose new novel, *After the Verdict*, is of great length and painstaking detail. Here also we have an extremely dramatic story. Clive Baratrie, as the story opens, is on trial for the murder of Mrs. Sabine, a woman older than himself with whom he had a prolonged affair that began when Clive was a patient in her nursing home after the war. The young man is engaged to marry Vivian Denys, a girl of his own age, a splendid, fresh, outdoor person and one of the best tennis players in England. Miss Denys has stuck to Clive through his ordeal, and after his acquittal they are married. Clive's mother, who lives to see him acquitted and for some time afterward, is the only other person of first importance in the 500-odd pages.

Is Clive guilty or innocent? He has been acquitted, true. And if innocent, of what avail to him? Must not his whole life be lived under the dark shadow of the crime? Must he not suffer as surely one way as the other? One goes four-fifths of the way through this novel in a state of tortured suspense. One does not know what to think as to Clive's guilt or innocence, nor is there a definite clue in his uncertain behavior. The fact, when revealed, stuns by its impact. Mr. Hichens tells me that he had long had it in mind to study a man resting under the cloud of a murder charge; but he had another and greater thing in mind. "I wanted," he says, "to show that in such a marriage as Clive's and Vivian's an absolute sincerity must exist between the

[176]

SUSAN ERTZ

two people." But it is the studies of the women in *After the Verdict* which will impress and entrance the reader.

Ruth Comfort Mitchell, whose popular novels have been of a light character, has also been led to a study of a woman capable of ordering her world and ruling it. The title of her new novel, *A White Stone*, is from the second half of the seventeenth verse in the Book of Revelation: "To him that overcometh will I give to eat of the hidden manna, and will give him a white stone, and in the stone a new name written, which no man knoweth saving he that receiveth it." To Joyce Evers, the white stone at first was her diamond engagement ring. Later it is the great rock on the mountain where she takes her woes for quieting and consolation. It is long before she finds the unseen, intangible white stone of the mystical passage. A homely little girl, she had been the center of a marvelous romance when Duval, one of the world's great pianists, asked her to marry him. In the chapters which show the gradual increase in Joyce of that power which is to be her salvation, Ruth Comfort Mitchell has done much abler work than in any story of hers before. Two somewhat unusual characters—Hannah Hills Blade, a novelist, and Chung, a Chinese servant—do a good deal to differentiate *A White Stone* from the run of novels. Chung is picturesque and is an excellent example of a certain fresh invention which is felt throughout the book. There is a strongly-written love story.

iii

In an interesting article on the work of Concha Espina,[1] Mr. James Fletcher Smith speaks of *Dulce*

[1] "The Foremost Woman Novelist in Spain," in The Boston Evening Transcript for 12 April 1924.

Nombre as "such a notable novel that it cried for instant translation." The translation has been accomplished and under the title, *The Red Beacon*, this impressive story is now available to English readers. (The Spanish title is the name of the heroine, simply— Dulce Nombre de Maria, Sweet Name of Mary, which was shortened by use to Sweet Name.)

Who is Concha Espina? The question does us no credit, but our general lack of information about European writers makes a brief answer necessary. Concha Espina was born at Santander, Spain, in 1877. She is therefore of the Northern seaboard and the mountain country. *The Red Beacon*, for instance, is laid in the Cantabrian Mountains. Concha Espina's title to be considered the foremost living woman novelist of her country seems to be undisputed. Possibly her two finest works are *The Red Beacon* and an earlier novel, *La Esfinga Maragata* (*The Maragatan Sphinx;* it was brought out in English as *Mariflor*). Although she has lived for some years in Madrid, Concha Espina remains unmistakably a Northerner. She married very young and went to South America (Chile) where affairs went badly and where she began writing as a newspaper correspondent to earn money.

The Red Beacon is a dramatic and somewhat tragic story of the people of her native region. Dulce Nombre, the heroine, is the daughter of a miller and the godchild of an hidalgo or nobleman, Nicolas Hornedo. Nicolas's interest serves to educate her above her own station but not up to his; yet when she falls in love with a countryman, a lad named Manuel, Nicolas, distressed, aids a rich man in buying the young fellow off and getting him out of the country. The rich man, much older than Dulce Nombre, succeeds in getting her in marriage. His hope is that she will come to love him, but she does not. The marriage is the beginning of a long ordeal for the girl, an ordeal of waiting which nothing can hasten nor prevent. The story proceeds with well-sustained interest to a crisis supervening some years later, when with her husband's death Dulce Nombre is again confronted with a difficult choice and a situation provocative of final despair. But happiness is in her destiny; Concha Espina shows us how it is realized at last.

A story written with an intimate knowledge of the heroine and with great, though restrained, feeling. It will be of more than ordinary interest to watch its reception by American readers.

NEW AND VARIED FICTION

A Conqueror Passes, by Larry Barretto. An after the war story—perhaps the best of them all—showing the reactions in business and social life of the returned soldier, restless, discontented, missing the excitement and tension of war. Told without either hysterics or despairing cynicism. A noteworthy book and a first novel by a writer who deserves close attention.

The Book of Blanche, by Dorothy Richardson. The love story, half earthly, half spiritual, of a beautiful violinist and a hospital surgeon; unique for its word pictures of the psychic phenomena of anæsthesia, and introducing a new American novelist of brilliance.

Blue Blood, by Owen Johnson. The story of a reckless society girl who sold herself to save her father's honor—then waited in suspense for the order to deliver herself.

Pandora Lifts the Lid, by Christopher Morley and Don Marquis. An extravagant, light romance which opens with the kidnapping of six daughters of the rich from a girl's seminary on Long Island and continues with a dashing yacht.

Semi-Attached, by Anne Parrish. A more serious novel than *A Pocketful of Poses*, but told with the same lively sense of the humorous moments in life. The story of a delightful girl who had to be converted to the idea of marriage.

The Show-Off, by William Almon Wolff, from the play by George Kelly. Aubrey Piper, the show-off, with his wing collar and bow tie, flower in his button-hole and patent leather shoes, is a character who will appeal universally because we all know him and laugh at him in everyday life. A realistic American novel, a satire that is full of humor and pathos.

Rôles, by Elizabeth Alexander. What happened when a discontented wealthy young wife changed places with her double, a hard-working actress—the kind of story one reads at a sitting, anxious to find out "how it will all come out," and very much surprised by the dénouement. Witty.

Deep in the Hearts of Men, by Mary E. Waller. A story of the deeper human interests, especially of a man's coming into spiritual light out of darkness, its scenes laid chiefly in a New Hampshire manufacturing town and the coal fields of West Virginia.

Tomorrow and Tomorrow, by Stephen McKenna. A novel of English inner political circles after the war, in which some of the characters of the author's famous novel, *Sonia*, make their final appearance.

Humdrum House? by Maximilian Foster. An exciting mystery story with both serious and farcical complications. You won't, however, for a considerable time know which is which!

The Brute, by W. Douglas Newton. A mystery-adventure story of rapid movement with scenes in South America and a beautiful and wealthy English girl as the heroine. By a novelist who writes with more than ordinary skill in characterization.

The Thirteenth Letter, by Natalie Sumner Lincoln. Opens with a strange midnight marriage followed soon by a mysterious murder, and centers around the disappearance of a famous diamond worth $250,000. The author is an experienced hand in stories of this type, and the final solution depends upon a remarkable cipher.

The Laughing Rider, by Laurie Yorke Erskine. William O'Brien Argent, otherwise Smiling Billy Argent, is the central figure of this romantic adventure story which runs from the Texas plains to the Canadian Northwest.

A City Out of the Sea, by Alfred Stanford. The story of Michael Ballard, who is a lawyer for the people of New York's waterfront, and who is attached to them because he finds them "hard and fair and wild." His growth through certain violent episodes until the love of a beautiful woman matures his personality and power as an artist is the theme. The novel is the work of a young writer whose work is stamped with distinction. The story suggests Jack London, but is written with more finesse if with no less power.

Cuddy of the White Tops, by Earl Chapin May. An exhilarating tale of a college boy who discovers, on his father's death, that the family fortune is all invested in a circus. He quits college and takes charge of the show—and finds he has a three-ring performance on his hands. Good love story.

After Harvest, by Charles Fielding Marsh. An English love story of the wind-swept Norfolk country, contrasting with, but of the same type as, Sheila Kaye-Smith's Sussex stories. In Priscilla, John Thirtle of Brent Fen Farm, and the shepherd, Reuben Gladden, the author exhibits something common to all humanity and clearly expressed in the simple lives and deep passions of country folk.

Many Waters, by Elinor Chipp. A love story of present-day New England which begins when Marian Pritchard, Mark Wetherell, and Donald Callender are playmates. Marian, however, and Mark as well have a great ordeal to undergo before achieving mutual happiness.

The Quenchless Light, by Agnes C. Laut. A novel based on the lives of the Christian Apostles, vividly written, and of the general type of Sienkiewicz's *Quo Vadis* and F. Marion Crawford's *Via Crucis*.

Low Bridge and Punk Pungs, by Sam Hellman. Mirth-provoking stories for bridge fiends and mah-jongg fans by the newest popular American humorist. With pictures by Tony Sarg.

11. Cosmo Hamilton's Unwritten History

i

Cosmo! He meets 'em one and all,
The Douglas Fairbanks in his hall,
   The Lloyd George in his den!
Cosmo! He meets 'em low and high;
He holds 'em with his glittering eye
   And draws 'em with his pen.

.   .   .   .   .   .

Cosmo! He meets 'em in the flesh!
All his celebrities are fresh!
   No has-been like Frank Harris!
He keeps his contacts up to date!
Cosmo! The great and the near-great
   From Hollywood to Paris!
     —*Keith Preston in the Chicago Daily News.*

HE was the brother to whose early literary success Philip Gibbs looked up with admiration; while Philip Gibbs grew more and more to look like an ascetic, "a tired Savonarola," Cosmo Hamilton (Gibbs) continued to be impressively good-looking, so that today he is not infrequently called the handsomest of male authors. And his looks are no deception, for in ease, urbanity, savoir faire few authors excel him—perhaps none. He can make an agreeable speech, talk interestingly, write a play or a novel with dexterity and a finished effect. It is true that in his lively memoirs, *Unwritten History*, he has embedded

[182]

an occasional groan about the labors of authorship, and tells of one instance in which an indolent writer was led back to the paths of virtuous industry. But for all that, in his own case, it has probably never been as hard work as sometimes it seemed to himself; while as for anyone else, the association of Cosmo Hamilton with toil must forever be an act of mental violence.

No! No photograph exists showing him with the dampened towel binding his brows, the cup of strong black coffee at his lips. It is even doubtful if, were one produced, any but Sir Arthur Conan Doyle would accept its authenticity.

The fact that he made a success so young—he was scarcely twenty-one when his first novel was published —and the fact that this success was immediately followed by others more marked is, no doubt, as much responsible as anything. But the feeling that he managed easily what most men contrive with the most desperate struggle is not lessened by such words as these of his brother's:

"Among my literary friends as a young man," writes Philip Gibbs in his *Adventures in Journalism*,[1] "was, first and foremost—after my father, who was always inspiring and encouraging—my own brother, who reached the heights of success (dazzling and marvelous to my youthful eyes) under the name of Cosmo Hamilton.[2] After various flights and adventures, including a brief career on the stage, he wrote a book called *Which Is Absurd*, and after it had been rejected by many publishers, placed it on the worst possible terms with Fisher Unwin. It made an immediate hit,

[1] Pages 153-154.
[2] "In a spirit of youthful independence, I had lopped off my father's patronymic."—*Unwritten History*, by Cosmo Hamilton, page 8. The father, Mr. Gibbs, had opposed Cosmo's literary ambitions. See also the chapter on Philip Gibbs in this book.

and refused to stop selling. After that success he went straight on without a check, writing novels, short stories, and dramatic sketches which established him as a new humorist, and then, achieving fortune as well as fame, entered the musical comedy world with 'The Catch of the Season,' 'The Beauty of Bath,' and other great successes, which he is still maintaining with unabated industry and invention. He and I were close 'pals,' as we still remain, and, bad form as it may seem to write about my brother, I honestly think there are few men who have his prodigality of imagination, his overflowing storehouse of plots, ideas, and dramatic situations, his eternal boyishness of heart—which has led him into many scrapes, given him hard knocks, but never taught him the caution of age, or moderated his sense of humor—his wildness of exaggeration, his generous good nature, or the sentiment and romance which he hides under the laughing mask of a cynic. In character he and I are poles apart, but I owe him much in the way of encouragement, and his praise has always been first and overwhelming when I have made any small success. As a young man I used to think him the handsomest fellow in England, and I fancy I was not far wrong."

ii

When Cosmo Hamilton was eighteen, he hid himself in Dieppe, France, for a month. It was necessary to convince his family, and most particularly his father, that he meant to write and could make some kind of figure at writing. There, in the Hotel of the Chariot of Gold, he did the story, *Which Is Absurd*, and saw occasionally Edward VII., then Prince of Wales, who was enjoying a vacation as plain Mr. Smith. After

Photograph by Lewis Smith, Chicago.

COSMO HAMILTON

he had lost money he could ill spare one night, a dazzling person with large violet eyes told him to follow her, and he did with a five-franc piece, winning back all he had lost and 100 francs besides. She was Lily Langtry. Back in London and waiting for the publication of his story, he seized on a novel of Robert Barr's and made it into a four-act play. Compton Mackenzie's father, the actor, Edward Compton, played it in the English provinces for a year (after drastic alterations) and it made enough money to enable Hamilton to take rooms in London. Whereupon, for a while, everything he wrote came back with a rejection slip.

Which Is Absurd, whatever its demerits, had the quality of provocation. An evening paper, reviewing it, asked: "Who is Cosmo Hamilton?" and answered: "Either a very bitter old man who is bankrupt of every hope, or an unkissed girl in a boarding school who ought to be spanked with a brush." Now with the fewest exceptions, book reviews do not sell books; but this is the type of review that infallibly sells a book. And shortly Mr. Hamilton found himself writing for the Pall Mall Gazette, along with Mrs. Humphry Ward, Alice Meynell, and others well-known and doing a syndicated London letter which required his presence in the high places.

His play, "The Wisdom of Folly," lived two weeks, and after a spell as editor of a short-lived weekly paper he became one of a brilliant company of contributors to the World. William Archer as dramatic critic, Richard Dehan as fictionist, Robert Hichens as dialogist, Gilbert Frankau, Philip Gibbs and Max Beerbohm were some of the staff. Before Cosmo Hamilton was thirty he was to become editor of this paper. But meanwhile a variety of fates awaited him. He dra-

matized Kipling's *The Story of the Gadsbys* in a
fashion satisfactory to the author; had a close shave
from dishonor as one of the directors of a speculative
mineral exploration enterprise which had trapped various well-known names to aid it; and faced bankruptcy. This last adventure resulted from the failure
of his first wife, the actress, Beryl Faber, in a theatrical season; and after Mr. Hamilton had taken on the
debts he retired to the country to cope with them by
writing.

What then occurred was dramatic enough, as life has
a fashion of being. A telegram came from a man
Hamilton didn't know. It read: "Kindly see me tomorrow twelve o'clock Savoy Hotel Charles Frohman." Mr. Hamilton kept the appointment, which
marked the beginning of a long association with the
famous American theatrical manager. In five consecutive years there was no time when one or more of his
plays was not running in London. Probably the best-
remembered is "The Belle of Mayfair," in which Edna
May was succeeded by Billie Burke, and which ran for
three years.

iii

At a time when he most urgently needed money,
Mr. Hamilton had had a series of conversations with
an actor manager known on both sides of the Atlantic.
This man needed a new play and Hamilton had the
necessary idea, but there was a difficulty. "If I were
prepared to give him all the best scenes, all the best
lines and build the play not round the boy and girl but
all about himself, make him suffer as the boy was to
suffer, love as the girl was to love, and, as he was to be
a clergyman, undergo a momentary shattering of faith
which would give him a first-class opportunity to show

how supremely he could touch the tragic note, a check on account of royalties would be paid at once and a contract signed." Mr. Hamilton refused, thereby sacrificing all future chances in this quarter, but "when that play was offered to the public in 1911 word for word as I had described it to the man who subsequently forgot my face, it was called 'The Blindness of Virtue.' Can't you imagine how I love to say that it has been running ever since?" [3]

It was first written as a novel, however, under that title. The novel was well-received and when Mr. Hamilton's younger brother, Arthur Hamilton Gibbs, came down from Oxford for some golf he suggested that a play be done from the novel. Cosmo's reply can be imagined, but the old idea took instant hold, and the manuscript of the play was ready precisely when an actor who had taken the lease of the Adelphi Theatre, meeting Hamilton on the street, asked: "Why don't you make a play of *The Blindness of Virtue?*" C. H.'s reply was to hand him the typed play.

This novel and play mark a decisive point in the author's career. It appeared in 1911 and the following year Mr. Hamilton made his first visit to America. On his return he was inevitably asked: "Are you going to use your novels for the ventilation of vital questions or are you going to revert to the entertaining novel of society life?" He answered: "I believe that I have now lived long enough, suffered enough, observed enough and studied enough to try and rise a little above the level of a merely entertaining writer,—one content to give his readers satirical pictures of men and women of the world, their surroundings, their little quarrels and their little love affairs. I believe that I have it in me to put into my work something that is

[3] *Unwritten History,* by Cosmo Hamilton, page 89.

[187]

of value apart from any pretensions to literary merit that it may have; that will cause the people who read it to ask themselves whether the world and the social system is as perfect as they imagined it to be, if they ever thought about these things. I don't think I can better describe my intentions than by saying that I am going to write human stories for human beings and no longer light sketches of people who are afraid to think and do not desire to remember their great and grave responsibilities."

Book, play and motion picture must have made everyone familiar with *The Blindness of Virtue* as a sermon on sex education powerfully implied by the engrossing story of an innocence that was merely ignorance. A glance at Mr. Hamilton's succeeding novels will show how consistently he has stuck to his determination not to write mere light fiction.

The Door That Has No Key (1913) is a story of married life. A man has given a woman his name but has never found the key to her mind. *The Miracle of Love* (1915) is the story of an English duke with a conscience and a sense of duty. He faces the necessity of marrying for money in order to restore family fortunes, although he is already in love with a girl whom it is quite impossible for him to marry, even though he sacrifice, for her sake, title and estates. *The Sins of the Children* (1916) is more strictly in succession to *The Blindness of Virtue*. This is a novel of American family life illustrating the danger to young people coming from ignorance of sex truths, and showing that the children's sins are principally due to the failure of parents to tell them what they should know.

Scandal (1917) is an exceptionally good illustration of Cosmo Hamilton's ability to write a dramatically interesting story, freighted with moral and ethical

[188]

teachings, but fictionally buoyant, and with the story uppermost all the time. Beatrix Vanderdyke is the beautiful daughter of wealthy parents. She is also the typical American spoiled child. A flirtation in which she throws conventions aside gives the occasion for scandalous talk; and to enable her to cope with the situation she asks Pelham Franklin, an acquaintance, not to show her up when she announces that he and she have been secretly married. Franklin has his own idea as to the lesson she needs; he at once acknowledges her as his wife and proceeds to treat her as if she were. It is the way, with such a girl, to a happy ending.

Who Cares (1919) is the story of a boy and girl, high-spirited, healthy, normal and imaginative, flung suddenly upon their own resources, buying their own experiences, and coming finally out of a serious adventure hurt and with a price to pay, but not damaged because of the inherent sense of cleanness that belongs to both. *His Friend and His Wife* (1920) describes the tragic repercussions in tranquil homes of one moral misstep. *The Blue Room* (1920) is the story of a young man whose reformation took place too late to avoid giving a shock of keen mental anguish to his prospective bride on the eve of their marriage. These two people achieve happiness not without scars, and the novel is a sharp stroke at the double standard of morality or sex ethics.

The Rustle of Silk (1922) is a presentation of political and social life in after-war London. Lola Breezy, a reincarnation in a shabby, lower middle class environment of the famous and alluring Madame de Breze of eighteenth century France, lifts herself out of her surroundings by sheer force of personality and becomes the friend and confidante of England's Home Secretary, the "coming" statesman.

Another Scandal (1923) is an extension of *Scandal*
and deals with Beatrix Vanderdyke and Pelham
Franklin after their marriage. Mr. Hamilton, describing the genesis of the novel, explains: "Here was this
astounding creature, Beatrix, not only married but
about to have a baby. Sentimental cynic that I am, I
hoped that she had settled down. At the same time,
I dreaded a tangent. I hadn't long to wait. Hardly
had Franklin II. time enough to open his eyes when
Beatrix suffered the inevitable reaction, finding that
the 'girl stuff,' as she had an irritating way of calling
that pathetic-tragic-romantic thing in her, had not
worked itself out." There is some extremely sound
philosophy on the whole subject of marriage in this
novel.

iv

Scandal, like *The Blindness of Virtue*, made an effective play; the number who will recall Francine
Larrimore in the rôle of Beatrix Vanderdyke is large.
Rather better, except for those who have the empty
prejudice against reading plays, than any of Mr.
Hamilton's novels is his *Four Plays* (1924), containing "The New Poor," "Scandal," "The Silver Fox,"
and "The Mother Woman." It is amusing to read the
note in connection with "The Mother Woman":
"Misproduced in New York under the title of 'Danger' in 1922." Mr. Hamilton, in a long experience
with the theater, has suffered much and most of it with
sportsmanship and cheerfulness; he is entitled to this
calm and rather deadly comment.

"The New Poor" is social satire, a comedy in which
actors impersonate the servants; but the other three
plays are in line with Mr. Hamilton's recent novels.
"The Silver Fox" is a comedy of marriage and divorce;

but unquestionably the most powerful play of the collection is "The Mother Woman." Dealing with the question of children in a marriage which is a social contract rather than a sacrament, at least, from the wife's viewpoint, its strength lies in the hardness and the consistency with which the wife is characterized. In its thesis the play bears wholly in one direction—not a weakness in the theatre, of course; but Mr. Hamilton has the wisdom to give Violet Scorrier good speeches and to let her walk off the stage, at the end of the last act, unchanged, unchanging, and satisfied with her unshared ego.

The history of these plays and various others, together with much of the history of his novels will be found in Mr. Hamilton's extremely readable *Unwritten History*. This, if it must be classed, can only be put into the list of informal and anecdotal autobiographies. It has all the good humor, the respect for human interest and the relative disregard for the claims of mere importance which should pervade a book of its sort. In other words, it has the exhilaration of talk devoted to one's liveliest recollections, with no special regard for chronology and with only the spur of mood. And the mood? It is throughout humorous, even self-humorous, democratic and impartial. Mr. Hamilton does not go out of his way to express his opinions, but neither does he dodge a natural comment when the occasion comes. You gather, for example, his very definite and not favorable view of David Lloyd George. The book is exceptional for its range of portraits. In anything from a sentence or two to several pages there is something about Kipling, Barrie, Conrad, Sinclair Lewis, Coningsby Dawson, Gilbert K. Chesterton, Heywood Broun and W. J. Locke among writers; the King and Queen, Lord Roberts, Colonel E. M. House,

[191]

Mr. Asquith, Admiral Beatty, J. Pierpont Morgan, Lord Balfour, Melville Stone and the Prince of Wales among the figures of public life; John Drew, Owen Davis, Pinero, Augustus Thomas, George Arliss, William Archer, Mary Pickford, Douglas Fairbanks, Charlie Chaplin and Granville Barker among the people of the theater. The twelve caricatures, particularly those of Bernard Shaw, Charles Frohman, George Grossmith, Sir Martin Harvey, Mr. Lloyd George and Lytton Strachey are the first public disclosure of Cosmo Hamilton's decided talent as an artist.

But perhaps the interest and engaging quality of *Unwritten History* can best be shown by quoting, not an anecdote of some personage, but some such incident as that of the first trip Mr. Hamilton made to this side:

"Before the ship had left Southampton I was flattered by the attention of an extremely good-looking, athletic, well-groomed youngish man, who insisted on walking the deck with me. He took the trouble to let me know, very shortly after we had broken the ice, that although that trip was not his maiden one he had only made the Western crossing once. But when, an hour before the bugle sounded for dinner, the purser touched me on the arm as I was following him into the smoking-room and murmured the one word 'card-sharp,' I still went on utterly disbelieving this brutal summing up of a delightful man's profession. Those were the old bad days when America was free, and never dreamed of interfering with the rights of foreign vessels, and so we had a sherry and bitters together in what is now an easy though a criminal way of encouraging an appetite. After which, his hand closing familiarly on a box of dice, he suggested with a naïve smile that we should kill an awkward half an hour by

COSMO HAMILTON

throwing for five pound notes, and I saw, in a disappointed flash, the reason of his flattery. The purser
was right, as pursers have a knack of being. And so
as much to retrieve myself from his obvious assumption
that I was an 'easy mark,' as to be able to continue a
pleasant acquaintanceship without having again to
back out of future invitations of the same expensive
sort, I made ready to dodge a knockout blow and told
him that I not only had no spare fivers to lose but had
a peculiar aversion to losing them to a card-sharp.
After a second or two of extreme surprise at my character reading and temerity he burst out laughing, and
we walked the deck together with perfect affability
during the whole of the rest of the voyage. He was
one of the most interesting men that I have ever met,
a student of Dickens and Thackeray with a strong
penchant for the Brontës, and as devoted a lover of
Italy as Lucas is, with much of the same feeling for its
beauty and its treasures. At no cost at all I greatly
enjoyed his company and when, six months later, I met
him by accident in Delmonico's, with the ruddy color
that comes from sea air and shuffleboard, I was
charmed by his eager acceptance of my invitation to
dine. In the meantime he had read *Duke's Son* and
although he liked my story very much and said so
generously enough, at the same time assuring me that
he was not much of a hand at modern books, he wound
up by regretting that I had not met him before I wrote
about cheating at cards, because he could have put me
right on several points. He died fighting gallantly,
and probably as humorously, in the war."

v

Readers of *Unwritten History* may look upon a photograph of Mr. Hamilton's home, an English cottage of

that idyllic air which seems to be the special property of all English cottages belonging to all English authors. Mr. Hamilton and a young son (now somewhat older) are on the brick steps that lead to the house, for the cottage is on a hill. Beside the steps and in front of the house is what we call an "old-fashioned garden"—flowers and plants in a profuse, unordered growth, with the tall spikes of flowering hollyhocks making the garden three-dimensional. Mr. Hamilton's second marriage, after the death of Beryl Faber, was with a Californian; and he now resides here rather more than abroad, although he endeavors to spend his summers in England and on the Continent. In the war, of course, he was in service, first with the anti-aircraft corps (when he was finally detailed to Sandringham, for the protection of the King and Queen during their stay) and then as a British publicist and propagandist in America. American audiences like him, and he reciprocates.

There is, indeed, about him personally a simplicity, directness and fundamental unsophistication that may be perceived in his fiction but which is missed by the casual reader and auditor and observer and acquaintance. Accident, marked talents and a variety of surface tastes and social interests have constantly brought him into what has been well described as "the world where one bores oneself to death unless one is in mischief." But both boredom and mischief are impossible if one continues, as C. H. has continued, to care only for the same handful of essentials. One thinks of him, for example, as the very antithesis of W. L. George. Less poetic than his brother, Philip Gibbs, he has his share of the same moral earnestness (a family trait) and gifts as great or greater as a storyteller, especially a story of drama all compact.

[194]

BOOKS BY COSMO HAMILTON

Which Is Absurd
Adam's Clay
Brummell
Duke's Son (also adapted as a play in French, written
  with Mme. Pierre Burton, and produced in Paris
  under the title, "Bridge")
Plain Brown—A Summer Story
The Infinite Capacity
Keepers of the House
1911   *The Blindness of Virtue*
1912   *The Outpost of Eternity*
1912   *A Plea for the Younger Generation*
1913   *The Door That Has No Key*
1915   *The Miracle of Love*
1916   *The Sins of the Children*
1917   *Scandal*
1919   *Who Cares?*
1920   *His Friend and His Wife*
1920   *The Blue Room*
1922   *The Rustle of Silk*
1923   *Another Scandal*
1924   *Unwritten History* (autobiographical)
1924   *Four Plays: The New Poor, Scandal, The Silver
        Fox*, and *The Mother Woman*

SOURCES ON COSMO HAMILTON

Unwritten History, by Cosmo Hamilton. Autobiographical
throughout. A list of Mr. Hamilton's plays will be found on
page 351 of his *Four Plays*, to which the plays in the volume
must be added. The history of most of them is given in
Unwritten History.

"Cosmo Hamilton, the Man." Booklet published (1923)
by Little, Brown and Company.

"Cosmo Hamilton: His Ambitions and His Achievements."
Booklet published (1916) by Little, Brown and Company.

Reference is made in a footnote to the text of this chapter
to Philip Gibbs's *Adventures in Journalism*.

12. Lest They Forget

i

IN the short preface to his *Eminent Victorians*, Mr. Lytton Strachey speaks of the great biological tradition of the French, of "their incomparable *éloges*, compressing into a few shining pages the manifold existences of men." And he speaks of biography as "the most delicate and humane of all the branches of the art of writing." The tribute of a distinguished master of biographical literature was recalled to me as I read André Maurois's *Ariel, The Life of Shelley*, so ably translated by Ella D'Arcy. Here are a comparatively few, but gloriously shining pages. This biography has burst upon us with an effect as surprising and luminous as Shelley himself. It is written on gauze and its transparency shows opaline colors. The picture it gives us is of Matthew Arnold's "beautiful and ineffectual angel beating his wings in a luminous void"; but I should delete the word "ineffectual." If Shelley was ineffectual, then the soul goes out of the world.

It needed a Frenchman, perhaps, to do the subject justice. Mr. Strachey, as Aldous Huxley has remarked, is congenitally incapable of penetrating the mystical mind. André Maurois was already known to some English and American readers by the humorous and profound novels studying an inarticulate English army officer. No one who read *The Silences of Colonel Bramble* can have forgotten its delicate portraiture. But such fiction was a pastime beside *Ariel*.

I could, of course, quote the praise of Arnold Bennett

and other acute judges, but it seems to me a lame thing to do. Nor is there space to quote from Maurois's book, and it hurts me not to be able to transcribe some things he has written. Any attempt to convey the quality of his book reduces me to despair; and yet I am used—perhaps too well used—to such attempts. Maurois is gleeful, tender, ironical; he recalls in his delicate but firm art Mr. Strachey more than anyone else, but he is more sympathetic, and so more just, than Strachey. This perhaps is because he has that side which Strachey, with his Voltaire-like intellect, quite lacks. Shelley's pathetic youth, his three-cornered marriage, his elopement with Mary Godwin, his few life-long friendships, his strange contacts with Byron, the brief happiness in Italy and the ultimate, tragic release of the captive soul to its flight in immortality— all these are told with a sense of proportion and an effect unsurpassable. The incidental portrait of Byron is more clear than any—yes, any!—of the ponderous biographies that have saluted his centenary.

ii

Besides the large number of sketches and impressions of Woodrow Wilson embedded in various recent books, there have already been published several biographies; but *The True Story of Woodrow Wilson*, by David Lawrence, seems to me distinctly the best of these, and probably the best immediate life of Wilson we shall have. Mr. Lawrence sat under Mr. Wilson when Wilson was professor of jurisprudence and politics at Princeton; he was with him at the time of nomination for Governor of New Jersey; he knew intimately the dissension at Princeton over the Wilson policies as President of the University; and from the time of Mr.

Wilson's nomination for the Presidency of the United States, Mr. Lawrence saw him continuously and at close range. For the younger man had quickly become one of the most brilliant of the Washington correspondents. His daily despatches then, as now, appeared in newspapers throughout America. He was in Washington, covering the White House, during Mr. Wilson's terms; went with him on his campaign tours; went with him through Europe and watched him at Versailles; and finally was with him on the tour on which Mr. Wilson suffered the physical collapse leading to his death. The result of this prolonged contact is a book in which nothing relevant is omitted or evaded. Mr. Lawrence begins with a striking chapter summarizing the paradoxical qualities of the war President—in some respects the most satisfactory portrait yet painted. He continues with the same impartiality and a frankness which no one else has ventured; and not the least valuable feature is the correspondent's ability to throw light on certain public acts of Wilson which have heretofore gone unexplained.

One or two other volumes in which the political interest is predominant deserve mention while our minds are on recent history. Maurice Paleologue was the last French ambassador to the Russian Court, serving about two years, from 3 July 1914 to mid-1916. The three volumes of his *An Ambassador's Memoirs* constitute the most interesting account we have had of the imperial decline, chiefly because M. Paleologue, with all the genius of French writing, pictures the slow downfall with a kind of terrible fidelity. The despairing vividness of this history is mitigated by many delightful asides on aspects of Russian character and psychology, art and life, written with an equal brilliance and a keen enjoyment.

[199]

Twelve Years at the German Imperial Court, by Count Robert Zedlitz-Trützschler, is by the former controller of the household of William II., then German Emperor. Its predominant interest is its gradually built up character portrait of the ex-Emperor in the days of his power. I say "gradually built up," for the book consists simply of private memoranda made by Zedlitz-Trützschler through the years of his service. It seems that the unhappy Count felt keenly the inability to say what he thought or to express his real feelings with safety to anybody. At first, like every one else, he was fascinated by his royal and imperial master. As he says in his preface: "There is a tendency to-day to underrate the intellect of the Emperor very seriously. There can be no dispute that his personality was a dazzling one. . . . He could, whenever it seemed to him worth while, completely bewitch not only foreign princes and diplomats, but even sober men of business." The spell waned because William lost interest. Zedlitz-Trützschler's book is the soberest and in some respects the frankest book about William that I have seen. Its publication has put the author in hot water with his family and all his class.

Charles Hitchcock Sherrill's *The Purple or the Red*, based on personal interviews with Mussolini of Italy, Horthy of Hungary, Primo de Riveira of Spain and other statesmen, as well as most of the surviving European monarchs, contains much interesting material about after-war Europe. It is ultra-conservative in its political attitude, but General Sherrill makes an effective case for his idea that the Crown, in European countries, has served as a rallying point for patriotism and by its place above factions has been a bulwark against revolution with bloodshed.

iii

Two very exceptional autobiographies are Sir Arthur Conan Doyle's *Memories and Adventures* and Constantin Stanislavsky's *My Life in Art*. Both are ample, lavishly illustrated volumes; and far apart as are the lives they record, I hesitate to say that either exceeds the other in charm.

The creator of Sherlock Holmes is a big, amiable man, a person of great simplicity of manner and almost naïve in his enjoyment of people, places and events. His book is inevitably one of a very wide popular appeal, the more so as Sir Arthur is entirely without conceit. In *Memories and Adventures* he tells of his education at Stoneyhurst, in Germany, and in Edinburgh, where he got his doctor's degree. He relates his early medical experiences and tells of his first attempts at writing. A memorable voyage to West Africa as a ship's surgeon, his earlier religious ideas and beliefs and the changes they underwent, and his marriage are all dealt with.

Then comes the story of his first real success as an author, made with the novel, *A Study in Scarlet*. He had resounding subsequent successes with *Micah Clarke*, *The Sign of the Four*, and *The White Company*. The creation of Sherlock Holmes was a great milestone in Conan Doyle's life. This is without question the most famous character in English fiction. Visits to America and Egypt and political adventures are chronicled. There are reminiscences and anecdotes of Roosevelt, George Meredith, Kitchener, Lloyd George, Balfour, Mr. Asquith, Henry Irving, Kipling, Bernard Shaw, Barrie and many others, living and dead, sprinkled through these extremely readable chapters. The closing chapter is devoted to the author's

amazing experiences in psychical research; and it must
be said for him that he writes more persuasively of his
experiences and beliefs in this affair than anyone else
has ever managed to do. Altogether *Memories and
Adventures* will engross anyone who opens it.

Very different, with its own style and an accent of
enthusiasm throughout, is Constantin Stanislavsky's
My Life in Art. This man has been the stage director
of the Moscow Art Theater since its establishment in
1898; and although that theater is now known throughout the world, and is frequently hailed as the world's
foremost playhouse, Stanislavsky's reputation outside
Russia has naturally been confined to the circles of
dramatic art. His autobiography depended for its
American publication wholly on the intrinsic interest
of what he had to tell. You may infer that that interest is considerable. It is.

I spoke of the book's style. It is peculiar, individual; sincere and unskilled, awkward and yet masterful;
admirable because so evidently a part of the author.
Born in 1863, the son of a wealthy Russian merchant
family and the grandson of a French actress, Stanislavsky as a boy showed stage talents in family theatricals; and though he later slaved over accounts in his
father's counting-house, his nights were nights of feverish absorption in the theater. His birth placed him in
the thick of the social and intellectual life of Moscow,
for he belonged to the class which has created the arts
of Russia. At twenty-five he became director of the
Society of Art and Literature, a group of young people
with serious ideas about the stage and a great dissatis-
faction with the current Russian theater. When
Stanislavsky met Nemirovich-Danchenko, the Moscow
Art Theater was founded.

The first half of *My Life in Art* is therefore chiefly

personal, a rich slice of Russian life with plum-like impressions and reminiscences of Rubinstein, Tolstoy, Tommaso Salvini the elder and other great artists of that time. The second half deals with the Moscow Art Theater, in which Stanislavsky made for himself a reputation as one of Russia's greatest actors, particularly in the rôles of Othello, Brutus, and Ivan the Terrible. This part of *My Life in Art* is crammed with material of interest and value not only to those who follow the theater but to all whose great interest is art. Chekhov, Tolstoy, Maeterlinck and others in person are delightfully mixed with interpretative experience in their plays and in the plays of Shakespeare, Molière, Pushkin and other immortals. The book closes with a description of the present work of the Moscow Art Theater, including the Soviet régime in Russia and the visit to America.

At last we have a biography of Clyde Fitch, achieved in that most satisfactory of ways, by means of his letters. Mr. Montrose J. Moses and Miss Virginia Gerson, who edited the memorial edition of Clyde Fitch's plays, have been engaged for some time in collecting the Fitch letters and the result of their labor is now published in one volume. *Clyde Fitch and His Letters* reflects well a personality which people never forgot, since meeting him was, as some one said, like meeting a figure in fiction. Fitch had a genius for friendship. His letters were always unstudied, without pretension to literary style, and brimful of a strongly impressionist reaction to the place or the event. He dashed them off as the spirit prompted—on board ship, by an open window of a Continental hotel, on the terraces of his country house; notes of appreciation, notes of invitation, long, impulsive descriptions of European festivities (some processional in

Spain or some picturesque account of Venetian gondo-
liering). They breathe, these letters, of his warm association with the novelist, Robert Herrick; they show
a light-hearted friendship with Maude Adams and
Kate Douglas Wiggin; they show interchanges of appreciation between Fitch and William Dean Howells.
Again, the reader sees the evidence of the personal concern and interest Fitch showed in the actors and ac-
tresses engaged for his plays. From the incipient idea
of a plot for a play to the play's first night, the letters
enable the reader to follow breathlessly the climb of
Clyde Fitch to the position of America's most successful
playright. But he remained a simple, unaffected sort
of person.

One cannot say more, I suppose, than that from the
day when Richard Mansfield asked him to write "Beau
Brummell" to the day of Clyde Fitch's death, when
he had taken "The City" abroad for a final polishing
which death prevented, *Clyde Fitch and His Letters* is
full of the live rush of the man. A very sane and
fundamentally enthusiastic attitude was his toward
American life, and those who read the book will not
miss that part of it.

iv

Of two books by women, one, *Sunlight and Song*,
by Maria Jeritza, is the great singer's autobiography;
while Frances Parkinson Keyes's *Letters from a Senator's Wife* is autobiographical only incidentally.

Mme. Jeritza is not only the foremost feminine personality in grand opera in America today, but by her
concert tours she has become known throughout the
United States. Her *Sunlight and Song* is a book
pretty certain to interest everyone who has heard her—
or heard of her. It is written with directness, in a

thoroughly popular vein, and is utterly free from affectations or pose. An Austrian by birth, she sang in Olmütz while in her teens, living on the hope of an engagement in Vienna. At length she came to the capital and waited her turn in the trying-out of voices. She was engaged for the municipal opera and afterward for the Court Opera House. Her rôles from operas by Richard Strauss and Puccini were rehearsed under the personal direction of the composers; she met Caruso and dozens of other musical celebrities; she sang before and met the Emperor; and in 1921 she came to America. One of the most interesting bits of her book concerns a rehearsal of "Tosca" at which she slipped and fell. She sang "Vissi d'arte" where she lay, exciting Puccini's enthusiasm. He exclaimed that always he had needed something to make the aria stand out and command attention; and this did it! When it was announced that Jeritza was to sing in "Tosca" in New York, there was a noticeable wave of hostility from those who associated the rôle exclusively with Geraldine Farrar. It vanished after she had appeared.

Among the photographs with which Jeritza's book is illustrated are many extremely beautiful pictures of the singer in her various rôles. The chapters on "How an Opera Singer Really Lives," "Studying with Sembrich," "Singing for the Phonograph," and "Some Guest Performances" will especially repay students of the voice.

The book by Mrs. Keyes, wife of the United States Senator from New Hampshire, is in a class by itself. *Letters from a Senator's Wife* consists entirely of actual letters written to old friends who were some distance away from Washington and who had a full feminine curiosity about life there. Taken as they stand, Mrs. Keyes's letters form a pretty complete record of social and political life in the capital as seen from the inner official circle. Beginning with her first impressions of Washington, Mrs. Keyes goes on to describe the Harding inauguration, the burial of the Unknown Soldier, the arms conference, the agricultural conference in 1922 and the industrial conference in 1923; the dedication of the Lincoln Memorial; the presentation of a gram of radium to Madame Curie; the diplomatic and New Year's receptions at the White House; the convention of women's organizations at which Lady Astor was conspicuous; dinners, teas, an afternoon cruise as Mrs. Harding's guest on the Mayflower and social affairs innumerable.

The result is a picture of Washington exactly as a woman in Mrs. Keyes's place would be privileged to see it; women readers will have a sense of participating in the things described. It is, I should say, exclusively a woman's book; but no one who appreciates the average woman's enjoyment of social detail will underestimate what Mrs. Keyes has accomplished. But in addition to telling the reader what she would have to do, whom she would meet, and what functions she would attend if she were in the Washington circle, the book does really constitute an attractive record of current history in the making and as made. Women who read it can scarcely fail to become more intelligent than before.

v

Fortunately Maurice Francis Egan, one of the most beloved of Americans, lived to complete for us his *Recollections of a Happy Life*. The author of *Everybody's St. Francis*, *Ten Years Near the German Frontier*, *Confessions of a Book-Lover* and other volumes had a scroll of memories which began in Philadelphia

in the 1850s and which included political and social
Washington in the Civil War period. In *Recollections
of a Happy Life* the New York of the Henry George
era is touched in with delightful anecdotes of Richard
Watson Gilder and the group that surrounded him;
there is a crisp picture of Indiana where Dr. Egan was
professor of English at Notre Dame; and the book
fairly launches itself with a full record of life in Washington and of the author's close association with Presidents McKinley, Roosevelt, Taft and Wilson, under
the last three of whom Dr. Egan held the post of
Minister to Denmark. Scholar, poet, critic, and most
winning of companions, Dr. Egan's autobiography reflects a good deal of America in the past half-century
as well as his own varied experiences here and abroad.

Of even more definitely literary interest is *C. K. S.
An Autobiography*, by Clement K. Shorter. An indefatigable book collector whose library is rich in first
editions, original manuscripts, and autograph letters,
Mr. Shorter is probably best known as an editor and
dramatic critic. He has had thirty years in each rôle,
and still writes weekly causeries which carry, on occasion, a provocative sting. George Meredith, Stevenson,
Andrew Lang, Thomas Hardy, and Gissing each are
the subject of a chapter founded primarily on personal
impressions of the man.

Such personal impressions, mixed with estimates of
the writer's work, form the substance of *The Literary
Spotlight*, edited, with an introduction, by John
Farrar, editor of The Bookman. These anonymous
literary portraits have been aptly called "Mirrors of
Literature." The anonymity has made possible a great
deal of frankness, humor, and penetration worth having, and Mr. Farrar has added bibliographies, biographical facts and such data as make the volume

handy for reference. Edna Ferber, Sinclair Lewis, F. Scott Fitzgerald, Floyd Dell, Mary Johnston, Edwin Arlington Robinson and others of high contemporary interest are presented.

THE TRUTH AT LAST!

Robert Louis Stevenson: A Critical Biography, by John A. Steuart. Two volumes. This new biography, by an English writer, will throw much new light on Stevenson. From unpublished documents in Edinburgh and elsewhere, and from several people who knew Stevenson, Mr. Steuart has obtained facts never before printed—so the portrait he draws is somewhat different from those which have already appeared. This biography will be of much interest to the many admirers of Stevenson's work who are not afraid to see the man as he actually was in his strength and his weakness, his gaiety and his gloom. Photogravure frontispieces.

The Truth at Last, by Charles Hawtrey, edited, with an introduction, by W. Somerset Maugham. The amusing, frankly self-revealing memoirs of a famous English actor, well remembered in America for his tours in "A Message from Mars" and "The Man from Blankley's." Illustrated.

Forty Years in Washington, by David S. Barry. Reminiscences of Presidents, Cabinet members, Senators and Congressmen, by the Sergeant-at-Arms of the Senate, who was Washington correspondent of The Sun, New York, when Charles A. Dana was its editor. Illustrated.

The Life of Olive Schreiner, by S. C. Cronwright-Schreiner. The biography, by her husband, of the brilliant author of *Dreams* and *The Story of an African Farm*, a woman of extraordinary personality who was not only a writer of genius but a pioneer advocate of woman's freedom. Illustrated.

Remembered Yesterdays, by Robert Underwood Johnson. Mr. Johnson's reminiscences are unusually entertaining and novel, and their diversity is exceptional. As a stripling he went to New York to join the staff of Scribner's Monthly, afterward known as the Century Magazine, with which he was connected for forty years, as associate editor and as editor-in-chief. Highly interesting are his touch-and-go reminiscences of famous Americans and foreign visitors, his anecdotes of travel abroad, and the account of his service as Ambassador to Italy in Wilson's second term. The portraits of American men of letters from the Civil War to the present are vividly drawn. No recent volume of American recollections keeps the reader in a more tolerant and gracious atmosphere. Illustrated.

Three Generations, by Maud Howe Elliott. A charming book of reminiscences by the daughter of Julia Ward Howe, covering the life and events of the past six decades. After her marriage to John Elliott, the artist, she lived for long periods in Rome, and to her salon came hosts of travelers and world-famous celebrities. It is a volume of memoirs of international interest and a fascinating account of the most interesting people in the world, in literature, art, drama, diplomacy and society, covering sixty years of "glorious life." Illustrated.

Poincaré: The Man of the Ruhr, by Sisley Huddleston. Raymond Poincaré, twice French Prime Minister and wartime President of the French Republic, has been the storm center of Continental politics in connection with the French occupation of the Ruhr. The author gives a vivid account of his career, his strength and his limitations, brightly written, with a considerable spice of wit. Frontispiece.

A Woman's Quest: The Life of Marie E. Zakrzewska, M.D., edited by Agnes C. Vietor. The story of a woman whose courage and perseverance probably did more than was accomplished by any other single person to open the medical profession to women. Dr. Zakrzewska was born in 1829, of Polish-German ancestry, and came to America when she was twenty-four. She had already, in Germany, made her way against bitter and unceasing opposition; in America she was to find herself without any standing at all. After a period of struggle she met Dr. Elizabeth Blackwell who gave her encouragement and in the face of every imaginable difficulty, Marie Zakrzewska studied medicine at Cleveland. She was refused admission at Harvard, but met Emerson, William Lloyd Garrison, Theodore Parker and other noted men and women. Eventually she founded the New England Hospital for Women and Children. Her autobiography is of profound interest and considerable historical importance.

The Life of Anne Boleyn, by Philip W. Sergeant. A full and carefully documented biography of the mother of Queen Elizabeth, written with charm of style and sincerity, and constituting a vindication of Anne. Its view of her is therefore exactly antithetical to the one advanced in the first essay in *Post Mortem: Essays, Historical and Medical*, by C. MacLaurin.

Robert Owen, by Frank Podmore. The incomparable story of the shop boy who became a rich and famous inventor of machines that revolutionized the cotton mills, a mill owner, and a business builder—but whose eager spirit caused him to found an Utopia in America, to work for labor betterment and world peace, to question religious creeds and to become a spiritualist. Few lives show so well the industrial and intellectual transformation that went on in the nineteenth century.

The Truth About My Father, by Count Leon L. Tolstoi. By the one son who sympathized with his father to the extent of accepting his doctrines and endeavoring to work them out. The author says that his mother was the source of his father's greatest happiness and the real author of his greatness; in old age, a will, secretly made under the influence of Tchertkoff, came between the parents (more as a matter of deceit than of the alienation of property).

The Manuscript of St. Helena, translated by Willard Parker. This is the document mentioned in Napoleon's will. He disavowed it as his work. It must, however, have been inspired if not dictated by him. It reads like a private diary, telling of Napoleon's life and achievements in a terse, clear style and showing him as he saw and judged himself. The document was published in French in 1817 but has never before been translated into English.

The Letters of Madame, 1661-1708, by Elizabeth-Charlotte of Bavaria, edited and translated by Gertrude Scott Stevenson. "Madame" was the usual way of referring to Elizabeth-Charlotte, Princess Palatine, a sturdy, outspoken German girl who, at nineteen, was married to Philippe, Duc d'Orleans, only brother of Louis XIV. of France. Philippe was thirty-one, effeminate, extravagant, and debauched; suspected of complicity in the supposed poisoning of his first wife. "Madame" was the most prodigious letter writer of an age fond of correspondence, a keen observer, and much franker than most others dared to be. Her letters are not only a great source for historians but breath-taking reading in themselves. The picture of the court of Louis XIV. is unmatched except in the pages of Saint-Simon.

David Wilmot, Free Soiler, by Charles Buxton Going. At last we have an adequate account of the author of the Wilmot Proviso, offered in 1846 and barring slavery in territory acquired from Mexico—the chief political issue from then to the Civil War, and the chief instrument in creating the Republican Party. Lincoln wrote that he had voted for the Wilmot Proviso more than forty times while he was in Congress, and on becoming President he offered Wilmot a place in his Cabinet.

Servant of Sahibs, by Ghulam Rassul Galwan, with an introduction by Sir Francis Younghusband. Written in quaint English by a man who accompanied Younghusband and who has worked for many years in the service of English and American travelers in the Himalayas, Central Asia, and Tibet. An adventurous and novel book which will delight everyone who cares for Kipling's fiction or for tales of India.

Nell Gwyn, by Lewis Melville. Her career from orange girl to King's favorite; her youthful troubles, her lovers, her stage success, her rivals in royal favor, her vast popularity and later years in Pall Mall. Illustrated in color.

13. That Literary Wanderer, E. V. Lucas

i

FOR a man whose air is so leisurely—whose literary air, that is, gives every aspect of leisure—Edward Verrall Lucas has written a perplexingly large number of books. Perhaps he is the living witness of the efficacy of making haste slowly. If one were a murderer, for example, one would do well to move away without haste (circumstances at all permitting) from the scene of his crime. How often is haste, or even the appearance of haste, fatal! In the unchanging words of the changing Fire Commissioners of the City of New York, in case of murder, walk, do not run, to the nearest exit.

Mr. Lucas's murder was committed at the outset of his career and he has been traveling from it by easy stages ever since. After close on thirty years, the dark moment may be said to be below the horizon. But in his literary youth he called in and slew his first book, a volume of poems. And although the number and variety of his books since is such that he has had to put them, for the reader's guidance, under eight classifications, he has still to give us a book of his own verse.

What, then, has he given us? What not were more quickly answered. His ten novels, being of a special character, he very fittingly designates as ENTERTAIN-MENTS, his thirteen volumes of ESSAYS slightly outnumber his books in any other class; he has compiled eight ANTHOLOGIES and written eight BOOKS FOR CHILDREN; has four collections of SELECTED WRITINGS, two EDITED WORKS and five works of BIOGRAPHY to his account; and is the author of seven books of TRAVEL, the well-known "Wanderer" series. The most scholarly of his fifty-seven books—total as above —is *The Life of Charles Lamb*, which is definitive. The most popular must be *A Wanderer in London* and *More Wanderings in London*, unless it be his first published book of all, the anthology called *The Open Road*, put forth in 1899 and republished in England and America in 1923. The most amusing—? There could be no agreement, though it is possible that later a majority might decide upon his newest novel, *Advisory Ben*.

(Something is wrong with the reckoning. For the total of fifty-seven and the eight classes do not contain the little treatise on *Vermeer of Delft*, with its charming reproductions of paintings by Vermeer. There is, besides, no way at hand of accounting for at least fifty-seven more books in which Mr. Lucas has had some hand [1]—as, for one instance, the English edition of Christopher Morley's *Chimneysmoke*, where Lucas provided the striking preface. However!)

Very evidently the work of E. V. Lucas must be examined in categories and by considering one or two examples under several of the heads; and then, perhaps, the glimpse of his personality afforded us may be lit from within as well as without. It will per-

[1] As long ago as 1916, writing of Lucas's work, Mr. Llewellyn Jones, literary editor of The Chicago Evening Post, said: "It sounds incredible, but Mr. Lucas has put his name—as author, editor or introducer—on about 108 titlepages." See pamphlet, "E. V. Lucas: Novelist, Essayist, Friendly Wanderer," published at the time by George H. Doran Company, New York.

haps clear the ground if we point out in preliminary
that Mr. Lucas is one of the editors of Punch and has
for long been a publisher's reader and adviser for the
English publishing firm of Methuen & Company, Ltd.
—a house of much distinction. He has done much
journalistic work. As would be inferred from *Vermeer
of Delft*, he is something of a connoisseur of painting,
and as will be shown he is much more distinctly a
connoisseur of literary curiosities.

ii

In providing his "entertainments," as he terms his
novels, Mr. Lucas has had in mind a structure always
consistent, always graceful, generally amusing but of
very real strength. His fictions may be compared to
trellises set up with care to support as a rule no more
serious burden than rambler roses or some other innocent vine. But it has occasionally happened that
the trellis has been climbed upon by a plant of more
rugged growth and heavier weight, and the trellis has
never failed to sustain the spreading story. It might
be apter to say that the plant has sometimes put forth
an unexpected flower—instead of the unpretending
rambler blossom a rose more disdainful—and still the
frame has seemed eminently in keeping with the whole
design. For there is this about such brightly elaborated, cheerfully artificial story structures: like the
trellis they are never concealed, though completely hid,
their outline or form remains exposed to every eye;
yet both the eye and the mind receive them naturally.
The truth is, of course, that their absence or apparent
absence would throw us off. A climbing vine unsup-
ported and unformed, its tendrils thrown about dis-
tractedly and frozen in mid-air, would freeze us with

repulsion. And an ingenious, expanding, flowering tale without its evident slight pretexts, its amiable excuse of ingenuity, would be an equal monstrosity. Even artifice may be an art.

Characteristic is the device employed by Mr. Lucas in his most recent book of this sort, *Advisory Ben*. Benita Stavely is an attractive girl who struggles with cooks and other domestic matters until her father re-marries, when she finds herself free to select an occupation. She starts an advisory bureau to assist harassed householders. The Beck and Call, as her office is styled, soon justifies Ben's venture by its popularity. It is approached through a bookshop below and to it come all manner of persons for counsel as to dogs, cooks, birthday presents and matrimony. The book-shop is kept by two young men. Ben's crowning per-formance before she says "Yes" to one of the young men in the bookshop is the finding and furnishing in three weeks of a large house for a rich American. Now there are present in this engaging novel the two requi-sites of Mr. Lucas's art as a fictioner: first, the ami-able pretext or excuse for the tale, the slight but bright invention, which is of course the notion of The Beck and Call itself, and second, the strength, erectile, ten-sile and otherwise in the elaborated structure. For although the scheme of the story is slender and the design of a gay simplicity, the situations developed by Ben's venture sometimes enable the author to touch considerable depths of human feeling. But the airy scheme, the graceful trellis, does not break. I do not mean that no strength is due to the character portrayal; much is due to it. Obviously, if Ben were a flitter-brain, if Mr. Lucas could give her no depth of feel-ing or not enough personal sincerity, his story would crash. But Ben without The Beck and Call would be Ben without opportunities to enable us to realize her quality. An idea is at the bottom of all.

The same virtue of idea or scheme is the technical triumph of *The Vermilion Box*, in which Mr. Lucas uses the familiar red letter box of England as his device. He says, secretly, Open Sesame, and the mail box opens to give us a series of letters between friends, acquaintances, lovers, relatives who are all entangled in the web of the World War. "Through these documents we meet the boy who will falsify his age, so eager is he to serve his country; the 'slacker' who is eager to serve his country by staying at home and drawing a salary for being secretary to a league to enforce economy—but finds the office routine very irksome to his artistic spirit. We meet the unoccupied clubman who has nothing to do but listen to rumors of spies in the Cabinet and disaffection in the field—and who writes of his discoveries to the papers; the old ladies who work and save, and who wait for war office telegrams telling the fate of the sons they have given to England. And then we meet the young English officer who, jokingly, ran an advertisement asking women to correspond with him: who realized the bad taste of his joke when a bereaved mother sent him the letter she had partly written to her soldier son when the news of his death came, but who thanked the fates for his folly when it brought the acquaintance of Portia Grey. . . . But this is much more than a love tale told in letters; behind that and behind the often occurring and charming humor of the book there is a seriously conceived and accurately painted picture of public opinion and feeling. A correspondent has been telling of a clergyman friend who has enlisted as a combatant, but who intends to resume his clerical duties after the war is over. The writer has composed some verses satirizing the view that Christianity is something thus to be put off or on, as circumstances dictate:

" 'Three or four men to whom I have shown these verses have complimented me on the effort which they make to get at the truth. But none of these men would sign a document calling for a close time for the creeds until the war is over, or suggesting that our archbishops were not at the moment earning their not inconsiderable salaries. That is one of the odd things about England—that private conscience and the public conscience are so different. In France a typical private individual's view of things is, when multiplied indefinitely, also the view of the State. Not so here, where as individuals we practice or subscribe to many liberties which would not be good for the general public.' " [2]

iii

Verena in the Midst also employed effectively the device of interchanged letters to develop the tale, and surely not even the expedient of The Beck and Call in *Advisory Ben* is more well-conceived than the tale of the adventures of Uncle Cavanagh in giving away his wife's property (*Genevra's Money*). There are bits about the Barbizon school of painting and there is a surprising deal about religious concepts in *Genevra's Money*, but I have yet to hear it said that this informative and speculative matter obtrudes itself or over-weights the book. It dwells comfortably alongside the high comedy of Uncle Giles (whose sole intellectual accomplishment is the verdict, general and specific,

[2] See pamphlet, "E. V. Lucas: Novelist, Essayist, Friendly Wanderer," published in 1916, the excerpt being taken from Mr. Llewellyn Jones's article therein.

upon persons he doesn't understand: "He's a nasty feller") because Mr. Lucas had the courage, not of his convictions but of his ingenuity.

That he has convictions can scarcely be doubted by the careful reader; the nature of them can scarcely be missed by the thoughtful one. They may now and then be stated more plainly in his books of essays, for the nature of the essay exacts that, but they cannot be put with more poignancy. In the excellent Introduction to his *Essays of To-Day: An Anthology*, (itself a worthy essay), Mr. F. H. Pritchard reminds us of Montaigne's instruction that an essay must be "consubstantial" with its author, of Mr. Gosse's dictum that its style must be "confidential," and adds—what is true and striking—that the lyric and the essay are both "the most intimate revelations of personality that we have in literature." He adds: "The difference, indeed, is one of temperament." [3] But the material, or at least its base, is identical.

It would not be difficult—it would, in fact, be ignobly easy—to indicate this essay of Mr. Lucas's as typical of his power of pathos, that one as showing the exercise of comedy, another as the evidence of a controlled irony which is his. So one might make a swift and triumphant recapitulation of the gifts and qualities of a literary personality among the most rounded of its time. But I had rather not be facile, for the sake, if possible, of going more surely. "Most of the other essays are exceedingly light in texture," observes

[3] "The metal bar, cold or lukewarm, will do anywhere, but heat it to melting-point and you must confine it within the rigid limits of the mold or see it at length but an amorphous splash at your feet." This vivid metaphor of Mr. Pritchard's is surely one of the most inspired explanations and justifications of poetic form ever set down. It can hardly be cited except by the supporters of traditional verse forms, as in a preceding sentence of his eloquent passage Mr. Pritchard speaks of "rime" and "metre" as well as of rhythm.

[218]

Arnold Bennett, in a comment on *One Day and Another*. "They leave no loophole for criticism, for their accomplishment is always at least as high as their ambition. They are serenely well done." But— "it could not have been without intention that he put first in this new book an essay describing the manufacture of a professional criminal." [4] Nor, I think, was it without intention that *Giving and Receiving* closes with that quietly-expressed but piercing account of a bullfight, "Whenever I See a Grey Horse . . ." The word "whimsical" has come to have a connotation exclusively buoyant or cheerful, although the habit of fancy—it is far more habit than gift—may be indulged in any direction congenial to one's nature. Mr. Lucas is whimsical enough in the series of tiny fables ("Once Upon a Time") composing the last section of *Cloud and Silver*. But one of his "whimsies" is savage in its scorn of the hunters of pheasants, another calmly reckons the totals of five years' expenditure on cloak-room fees for a hat and stick, and a third of the twenty, called "Progress," is so brief it is better quoted than characterized:

"Once upon a time there was a little boy who asked his father if Nero was a bad man.

" 'Thoroughly bad,' said his father.

"Once upon a time, many years later, there was another little boy who asked his father if Nero was a bad man.

" 'I don't know that one should exactly say that,' replied his father: 'we ought not to be quite so sweeping. But he certainly had his less felicitous moments.' "

This, like much of Mr. Lucas's expression in the

[4] *Books and Persons,* page 153. The notice first appeared in The New Age, London, 7 October 1909.

essay, is far too perfect to be spoiled by an embroidery of analytical adjectives. Mr. Llewellyn Jones very properly cites the opening paragraph of the essay, "Of Plans for One More Spring" (*Cloud and Silver*) as a fine illustration of "what an emotional effect Mr. Lucas can achieve from the simplest materials." [5] The essay was written in February, 1915:

"It is much on my mind just now that I must not waste a minute of the spring that is coming. We have waited for it longer than for any before, and the world has grown so strange and unlovely since spring was here last. Life has become so cheap, human nature has become so cruel and wanton, that all sense of security has gone. Hence this spring must be lived, every moment of it."

It will be found that in his moments of most entire abandonment to comedy Mr. Lucas is clearly engrossed in the problem of human nature. "The Battle of the Mothers," in *Giving and Receiving*, is laughable throughout; but the recollection is deepened by the very gentleness of the satire. An Archdeacon enters a Club and explains to friends that he has been on a motor tour with his mother, who is ninety-one and "in the pink of condition" and delights in motoring.

" 'Well,' said the testy man, 'you needn't be so conceited about it. You are not the only person with an elderly mother. I have a mother too.'

"We switched round to this new center of surprise. It was even more incredible that this man should have a mother than the Archdeacon. No one had ever suspected him of anything so extreme, for he had a long white beard and hobbled with a stick."

The highly diverting dialogue ensuing would be

[5] See pamphlet, "E. V. Lucas: Novelist, Essayist, Friendly Wanderer."

forgotten as quickly as read were it not the quintes-
sence of that amiable self-conceit common to us all.
A similar effect is the secret of "The Snowball," in
Luck of the Year, where a man wonders what to do
with a good luck chain letter—poohpoohs it, figures its
rapid and enormous multiplication in a week, ponders
the letter's promise of good fortune, begins to jot
down the names of nine friends, reaches toward the
wastebasket, draws back his hand—. Occasionally,
indeed, these essays of Mr. Lucas's compose themselves perfectly as short stories; if, as I suppose, the
work of Katherine Mansfield and others has taught
us that a short story need not be the jack-in-box plot.
Such, in *Luck of the Year*, is "The Human Touch,"
which deals with a single horse cab driver among the
battalions of taxicabs. "When the express arrived
he galvanized his horse and began to make alluring
signs and sounds as the passengers emerged; but one
and all repulsed him." Equally a short story, and
a very good one, is "A Study in Symmetry," in *Adventures and Enthusiasms*, where the conceit of a painter
of portraits is gently punctured.

I suppose such pieces as "Scents," in *Luck of the
Year;* "Davy Jones," in *Adventures and Enthusiasms;* and "Signs and Avoirdupois," in *Giving and
Receiving* are essays in the strict sense of Mr. Pritchard's definition that I have quoted. Certainly the
catalogue at the close of "Scents" is an "intimate revelation of personality" and it borders on the lyrical:

"What are the most delicious scents? Every one
could make a list. Rupert Brooke made one in one of
his poems; but it was not exhaustive. I know what
mine would contain, even if it failed to include all.
Sweet-briar in the air, so vague and elusive that search
cannot trace the source. Pine trees in the air on a

hot day. Lime blossoms in the air. ('Such a noisy smell!' as a small child said, thinking of the murmur of bees that always accompanies it.) Brake fern crushed. Walnut leaves crushed. Mint sauce. Newly split wood in a copse. Any kind of gardener's rubbish fire. An unsmoked brier pipe. Cinnamon. Ripe apples. Tea just opened. Coffee just ground. A racing stable. A dairy farm. A shrubbery of box. Cedar pencils. Cigars in the box. A hot day on the South Downs when a light wind brings the thyme with it. The under side of a turf. A circus.

"And I have said nothing of flowers!"

iv

Taste. It is underlying quality with Lucas, after all. I do not say "catholicity of taste," for it seems to me redundant. A taste which should allow itself to be fenced in would soon shrivel and die for lack of exercise; for what is taste but the faculty of selection constantly exerted and how can one have it except by its unremitting use? Like all other qualities abstracted into words, such as honor, integrity, virtue, and the rest, taste itself is no abstraction. A man cannot have honor, except as he shows he has it, nor virtue except as he behaves virtuously in this or that situation; and his possession of taste must depend upon what he chooses in thoughts, words, actions and objects. I say *what* he chooses, and leave the *how* to the psychologists, who have still a few years, or perhaps centuries, to spend on investigation of this very nice problem.

His taste, then, distinguishes Mr. Lucas as a connoisseur of literary curiosities, which, when taste is shown, become also human concerns. "The Innocent's Progress," in *Adventures and Enthusiasms*, a description of an obsolete book of manners for the young, is a lesser example of Mr. Lucas's taste; his candid rejection of English slang, because it is undescriptive, and acceptance of American slang because it applies and illustrates is the application of excellent taste to a strictly contemporary point.[6]—and no test of taste is more exacting. The essays on "Breguet," the great French watch-maker, in *Giving and Receiving*, and on Hans Christian Andersen[7] and John Leech[8] are to many readers of more importance than a modern topic, like "Telephonics."[9] For while taste must choose, and help us to choose, among the things of the hour, its service in the rescue of the past is an education in taste as well as an enrichment of the present.

Mr. Lucas (to illustrate) never practised his literary connoisseurship to a more humane and generous end than when he gave us, in 1916, *The Hausfrau Rampant*. This, like his edition of Charles and Mary Lamb, is an edited work. Julius Stinde (1841-1905), a native of Holstein, Germany, was originally a chemist and the author of an elaborate treatise on *Wasser und Seife* (*Water and Soap*), to which he affixed the name of his charwoman, Frau Wilhelmine Buchholz, as author. Later it occurred to Stinde to write a satire on the typical middle-class Berlin family with marriageable daughters; he elevated Frau Wilhelmine to the ranks of the bourgeoisie and began a book, or rather a series of books, which became as

[6] "Of Slang—English and American," in *Cloud and Silver*.
[7] "The True Wizard of the North," in *Adventures and Enthusiasms*.
[8] "Thackeray's Schoolfellow," in *Adventures and Enthusiasms*.
[9] In *Adventures and Enthusiasms*.

popular in Germany as Dickens in England. England, France and America all uttered praise of *The Buchholz Family* in the 1880s, and with good reason. The work, outside of Germany, had been lost sight of for nearly thirty years when Lucas, rendered sleepless by a struggle with mosquitoes one night in Venice, came upon the first volume of the English translation in his landlord's library. The quality was such as to make him hunt up the other three English volumes; and from the work as a whole he selected the most entertaining passages, "joining them together with some explanatory cement." This is *The Hausfrau Rampant*. It was, of course, with a purpose that Mr. Lucas published *The Hausfrau Rampant* at a time when feeling in England and America ran high against the country of Stinde. The purpose will be obvious to anyone reading Lucas's Introduction to the book. No imaginable eloquence could be so effective as the word portrait of Herr Stinde there presented. The possession of taste carries its own courage with it.

V

One could go on, as it were, indefinitely, but with Mr. Lucas as guide never indefinably. Such an anthology as *The Open Road* knows what many an anthology never knows—readers who return to it again and again because it is inclusive without being indiscriminate. The impressions of India, Japan, and America in *Roving East and Roving West* are among the most valuable any traveler has put down because they are single impressions and because, with Mr. Lucas, to see is to choose, as with a painter. It is when he comes to consider work where a fine talent has already seen and chosen, as in his *Vermeer of*

E. V. LUCAS

Delft, that he becomes singularly luminous; with the ground cleared, he can give his enthusiasm rein. His *Wanderer* books on London, Paris, Venice, Florence and Holland are digressive in the sense that the longest way 'round is the shortest way home—in other words, the associations of a scene are the shortest cut to enabling us really to see it. And now Mr. Lucas has united his taste for fine painting with his Wanderer's talent: *Little Wanderings Among the Great Masters*, in six illustrated volumes, and *A Wanderer Among Pictures: A Guide to the Great Galleries of Europe*, with its many reproductions of famous masterpieces, are his new volumes. The set of six, dealing with Michelangelo, Leonardo da Vinci, Frans Hals, Murillo, Chardin and Rembrandt, are the best brief popular accounts I know, blending as they do essential biographical facts and the elements of esthetic enjoyment of the artists' work. One hopes the little volumes may be added to by a similar treatment of other great painters. *A Wanderer Among Pictures* is, of course, a thing far more ambitious, a compact treasure delicately plundered from collections in fifteen of Europe's chief cities. But how delicious to have these great paintings described by one who knows how to write and who has a gift for conveying such beauty with literary art and verbal simplicity!

But a few words must be said about E. V. Lucas, the man.

"A youngish fifty, perhaps," wrote Robert Cortes Holliday, meeting him in 1919 or 1920 in Chicago. "Rather tall. A good weight, not over heavy. Light on his feet, like a man who has taken his share in active field games. Something of a stoop. A smile, good, natural, but sly. Dark hair, shot with gray.

Noble prow of a nose. Most striking note of all, that ruddy complexion, ruddy to a degree which (as I reflect upon the matter) seems to be peculiar to a certain type of Englishman." [10] Mr. Lucas spent several days in Chicago on this visit, but only about four persons knew it at the time. Mr. Holliday noted that Lucas studied his menu card "with deep attention" and was particular about the service of the dinner when it came. He was not on a lecture tour and inquired about recent literary visitors from England, appearing to be "much amused at the number of them." He punned twice, badly, spoke admiringly of American humor and especially of the work of Don Marquis,[11] and spoke of the number of American words "which mean so much, and mean nothing at all, like 'cave-man' and 'mother love.'" It also appeared that Lucas could do no writing in a hotel room.

Like nearly all authors, he has an inexhaustible store of gossip about other authors.

His biographical sketch in *Who's Who* (the information for which is supplied by the subject) omits all the usual personal data, such as the date and place of birth, parentage, schooling, etc. It even omits his recreations, which most Englishmen are careful to give. There are his name and his occupations—"writer and publisher's reader"—followed by a partial list of his books, his address in London and the rich array of his clubs, which include the Athenaeum, the Garrick, the Burlington Fine Arts and the National Sporting Club.

---

[10] *Men and Books and Cities,* by Robert Cortes Holliday, pages 196-197.

[11] See also "Stories and Humorists," in *Roving East and Roving West,* page 136 *et seq.,* and also "Chicago," in the same volume. Mr. Holliday's full account is in *Men and Books and Cities,* pages 196-203, inclusive, and also page 206.

This outdoes Mr. Galsworthy, who mentions the year of his birth, though the Athenaeum is his only club.

"He has a kind of mischievous cruelty in his dissection of humanity," a distinguished novelist once remarked, speaking of Lucas's conversation. "But he is extremely good company," came in the next breath. This observer added: "I always think that the best picture of Lucas's character is to be found in Bennett's *Books and Persons.*" Here it is:

"Mr. Lucas is a highly mysterious man. On the surface he might be mistaken for a mere cricket enthusiast. Dig down, and you will come, with not too much difficulty, to the simple man of letters. Dig further, and, with somewhat more difficulty, you will come to an agreeably ironic critic of human foibles. Try to dig still further, and you will probably encounter rock. Only here and there in his two novels does Mr. Lucas allow us to glimpse a certain powerful and sardonic harshness in him, indicative of a mind that has seen the world and irrevocably judged it in most of its manifestations. I could believe that Mr. Lucas is an ardent politician, who, however, would not deign to mention his passionately held views save with a pencil on a ballot-paper—if then! . . . Immanent in the book is the calm assurance of a man perfectly aware that it will be a passing hard task to get change out of *him!*" [12]

And here is more testimony, to the same general effect:

"E. V. Lucas always reminds me of Kipling's 'cat that walked by itself.' He knows everybody, but I have often wondered whether anybody really knows

[12] *Books and Persons,* pages 153-154. First appeared as a notice of Mr. Lucas's *One Day and Another* in The New Age, London, 7 October 1909.

him. He is an amazingly busy man—the assistant editor of Punch, the literary director of Methuen's, the writer of almost countless charming and distinguished essays, to say nothing of novels and travel books. As a writer he has the appealing urbanity of Charles Lamb, of whom he has written far and away the best biography in the language. But I do not think that there is much of Lamb's urbanity in E. V. Lucas the man, the gentle-voiced, modern, rather weary man of the world. The humor of the Lucas essays is sunny and kindly. The humor of Lucas himself is cynically tolerant.

"I have said that Lucas knows everybody. The only circles into which he never goes are literary circles. Where professional writers are gathered together, there you will never find E. V. Lucas. He prefers actors and prize-fighters. There is a story that Lucas once gave a dinner party at the Athenæum Club to which he invited Georges Carpentier and Harry Tate. I do not altogether disbelieve that story, but a bishop ought to have been included in the dinner party to make it complete.

"Lucas loves cricket, and is a good man to dine with. His talk is stimulating and his taste in wine perfection." [13]

Possibly E. V. Lucas's closest personal friends among writers in America—certainly his closest temperamental affinities—are Don Marquis and Christopher Morley. Occupationally, as the sociologist would say, he is allied with such fellow editors as E. T. Raymond and A. A. Milne and with such publishers' literary advisers as—not to go back to George Meredith, who read for Chapman and Hall—Frank

[13] A writer in John o' London's Weekly, London. Reprinted in the Boston Evening Transcript of 3 March 1923.

[228]

Swinnerton, who reads for Chatto & Windus, and J. D. Beresford, reader for Collins.

BOOKS BY E. V. LUCAS

For a full list of books written, compiled, edited by and contributed to by Mr. Lucas, write to Methuen & Co., Ltd., 36 Essex Street, London, W.C. 2. About 130 titles are comprised.

ANTHOLOGIES:

1899	*The Open Road*
1903	*The Friendly Town*
1907	*The Gentlest Art*
1908	*Her Infinite Variety*
1909	*Good Company*
1910	*The Second Post*
1914	*Remember Louvain*
1923	*The Best of Lamb*

BIOGRAPHY:

1905	*The Life of Charles Lamb*
1907	*A Swan and Her Friends*
1907	*The Hambledon Men*
1913	*The British School*
1921	*The Life and Work of E. A. Abbey, R.A.*
1922	*Vermeer of Delft*
1924	*Little Wanderings Among the Great Masters.* Six volumes

BOOKS FOR CHILDREN:

1897	*A Book of Verses for Children*
1903	*The "Original Verses" of Ann and Jane Taylor*
1906	*Forgotten Tales of Long Ago*
1907	*Another Book of Verses for Children*
1908	*Runaways and Castaways*
1908	*Anne's Terrible Good-Nature*
1910	*The Slowcoach*
——	*More Forgotten Stories*

EDITED WORKS:

1903	*The Works of Charles and Mary Lamb*

[229]

1916   *The Hausfrau Rampant*

ENTERTAINMENTS:

1906   *Listener's Lure*
1908   *Over Bemerton's*
1910   *Mr. Ingleside*
1912   *London Lavender*
1914   *Landmarks*
1916   *The Vermilion Box*
1920   *Verena in the Midst*
1921   *Rose and Rose*
1922   *Genevra's Money*
1924   *Advisory Ben*

ESSAYS:

1906   *Fireside and Sunshine*
1907   *Character and Comedy*
1909   *One Day and Another*
1911   *Old Lamps for New*
1913   *Loiterer's Harvest*
1916   *Cloud and Silver*
1917   *A Boswell of Baghdad*
1918   *Twixt Eagle and Dove*
1919   *The Phantom Journal*
1920   *Adventures and Enthusiasms*
1921   *Roving East and Roving West*
1922   *Giving and Receiving*
1923   *Luck of the Year*

SELECTED WRITINGS:

1911   *A Little of Everything*
1911   *Harvest Home*
1916   *Variety Lane*
1919   *Mixed Vintages*

TRAVEL:

1904   *Highways and Byways in Sussex*
1905   *A Wanderer in Holland*
1906   *A Wanderer in London*
1909   *A Wanderer in Paris*
1912   *A Wanderer in Florence*
1914   *A Wanderer in Venice*

E. V. LUCAS

SOURCES ON E. V. LUCAS

"Unless my judgment is much at fault, there has written in English, since the death of R. L. Stevenson, no one so proficient in the pure art of the essayist as Mr. E. V. Lucas," says Edmund Gosse at the beginning of his "The Essays of Mr. Lucas," in his volume, *Books on the Table*. This essay on an essayist should be consulted either in Mr. Gosse's own volume (page 105) or in F. H. Pritchard's *Essays of To-Day: An Anthology*, in which it is included (page 249). No more authoritative or more charmingly stated estimate of Mr. Lucas as an essayist is known to me.

In addition to the sources referred to in the text of the chapter or in footnotes, the reader should consult the READER'S GUIDE TO PERIODICAL LITERATURE for the years since 1913 and the files of The Bookman (London) for the years since 1908.

14. American History in Fiction

THE use of history in fiction is at once an aid and a handicap to the writer. Where he is using historical persons, he may count upon a certain delight of recognition from some or all of his readers; offset by disappointment if the portrait doesn't closely resemble a preconceived ideal. The use of an historical period is on the whole far more satisfactory, and an exact setting is the most satisfactory of all. For fiction is written to express a sense of meaning and to convey a feeling. Like all forms of faith, it creates its own facts. And, as in some other types of illumination, the most effective treatment of historical figures and occurrences by the fictioner is often—indirect lighting.

The three writers I am going to talk principally about in this chapter have certain resemblances and a marked divergence. Although two of them are no longer alive, their audiences were never greater than now. All three belong to the South and West, and two of them wrote novels which have been transformed into motion pictures of enormous influence and success. The third is usually spoken of as a writer for boys, although the boys who read him are, many of them, long past their teens. Both Emerson Hough and Thomas Dixon wrote books which are partly or mainly propaganda. Joseph A. Altsheler, avoiding any suggestion of such a thing, was remarkable for the accuracy of historical detail in his stories. Perhaps the most striking quality in common among these three writers—I won't undertake to give it a name—is the fact that each, on more than one occasion, has had his huge audience waiting in line to get his book.

I. EMERSON HOUGH

The author of *The Covered Wagon* was born in Newton, Iowa, 28 June 1857, and died 30 April 1923, when the motion picture fashioned from his novel was the sensation of Broadway—indeed, of America. The first class graduated from the little Iowa high school had three members, Hough being one. (It is perhaps not out of place to say that he pronounced his surname "Huff"). After a brief experience teaching a country school, the boy entered Iowa State University and was graduated with the class of 1880. "I had a university education, perfectly good and perfectly worthless," he said in later years. His father, Joseph Bond Hough, had been a Virginia schoolmaster, and saw education in terms of a classical course leading to one of the professions. The young man read law in Newton and was admitted to the bar there.

Life began for him then. He went to White Oaks, New Mexico, half a cow town and half a mining camp, about eighty miles west of Socorro in the mountain region between the Rio Grande and the Pecos Rivers. Mr. Hough's *North of 36* has been attacked as lacking in authenticity because, when he came to White Oaks, "the frontier epoch had ended." To which the novelist William MacLeod Raine has made reply: "Interesting, if true. Particularly interesting to me, because it was in 1881 that my father brought his family into the Southwest from England and went into the cattle business (with side lines of tie-making and lumbering). The nearest village was 30 miles away. I and

[233]

my small brothers used to ride twenty miles to get the mail once a week. That outpost of civilization my memory can make the setting of a score of dramatic incidents. The frontier was not a hard and fast condition which can be defined as having vanished on a specific date. Civilization lapped forward here and there, leaving pockets which did not yield to its influence for many years." And Hough himself said simply: "In this rugged field, among these splendid and sterling men, in an atmsphere not too law-abiding, but always just and broad, I got my first actual impression of life; learned to respect a man for what he really is."

He became a sportsman from the first—the practice of law in White Oaks was not exacting—and all his life he was a great hunter and traveler. His father failed in business and something had to be done to make a living for the family. Journalism seemed to be Emerson Hough's only chance; he had already sold fugitive pieces. After a little time in Des Moines and work on a newspaper in Sandusky, Ohio, he got, in 1889, the job of looking after the Chicago office of Forest and Stream. The job paid $15 a week. But he combined with it work for daily newspapers and for a newspaper syndicate. Most of his writing had to do with sport.

There were some bitter times. But, in fact, nearly all his life until within a few years of his death was to be a mixture of hardships and happiness. The hardships concerned money, except those physical hardships he endured out of doors in what were undoubtedly the happiest hours of his life. Out of doors journalism took him into almost every State of the Union and almost every Province of Canada; to Alaska, also. Sometimes he used to wonder if he had

Photograph by Moffett, Chicago.

EMERSON HOUGH

ever slept thirty consecutive nights under one roof. Desperately worried at times, he would say with a sigh of relief: "It is impossible to fret over things when you are wading a trout stream, following a good dog, or riding a good horse." Within five years of his death intimate friends saw him, suffering from ill health, in tears over uncertainties regarding his work and discouraging certainties regarding his income; yet he lived through the swift, dramatic turn of his fortunes to taste the satisfaction of his very great ambition and to reap a substantial part of the money reward.

In 1895 he explored the Yellowstone Park in winter, going on skis, and an Act of Congress protecting the Park buffalo was due to this adventure. By speech and by his writings he did much all his life to aid the protection and study of wild life and to support the system of national parks. The America he had known in the flush of his youth was really a passion with him. One day after he had finished a series of short stories on the old trails for his out of doors department in the Saturday Evening Post the editor, George Horace Lorimer, suggested that he take either the Overland or the Oregon trail as the subject of a novel. The suggestion was in itself the most magnificent of trails to such a mind as Hough's. He wrote, then, *The Covered Wagon*.

His first book, *The Singing Mouse Stories*, which had to do with out of doors, appeared when he was 38; he was forty when, in 1897, he married Charlotte A. Cheesbro, of Chicago, and published *The Story of the Cowboy*, praised by Theodore Roosevelt. His first novel came three years later, and with his second, *The Mississippi Bubble* (1902), he attracted nationwide attention. It is amusing to recall that he made five copies of *The Mississippi Bubble* and despatched them simultaneously to five publishers, each of whom sent an acceptance.

When he died, Mr. Hough left several completed books. Three of them were novels and the first of these, *Mother of Gold*, has just been published. A story of the present day, woven around the old legend of the lost mine of Montezuma, it has to a curious degree the pioneer zest and spirit of Hough's romances of earlier times.

Of his earlier novels, *The Mississippi Bubble* and *Fifty-four Forty or Fight* are the ones that seem likely to be read longest; of his later novels probably *The Magnificent Adventure* (1915), dealing with the Lewis and Clark expedition and with Aaron Burr's daughter as its heroine, *The Covered Wagon*, and *North of 36*, the story of the Texas cattle trail, have the best chance of permanence—always premising that work as yet unpublished may take its place with these.

II. JOSEPH A. ALTSHELER

To Anne Carroll Moore, supervisor of work with children in the New York Public Library, I am indebted for the best picture of what Joseph A. Altsheler's work signifies. Both at the time of his death and since, he was and has been and is the most popular author of books for boys in America. He is more popular than James Fenimore Cooper, to whose work his own is probably most closely allied. He wrote over again, as Miss Moore has pointed out, the tales of our pioneer life and struggle "with a fresh sense of their reality." His "deep love of nature, the ability to select from historical sources subjects of strong human interest, a natural gift for storytelling, and great modesty" were other qualities which the youthful reader senses and appreciates. "Boys who clamor for Altsheler," says Miss Moore, "read history and biography as a natural and necessary accompaniment. Nor do they neglect *Tom Sawyer* and *Huckleberry Finn*, or *The Boys' Life of Mark Twain*. Never in the history of writing for boys has an author attained universal popularity on so broad a foundation of allied interests in reading." [1]

Cooper wrote when American history was brief; another century and the breadth of a continent unrolled itself before Altsheler, who set about in quiet patience to make all that spaciousness and all those crowding events intelligible for the American boy. And because in modesty and patience he had gone far to achieve just that—taking the average boy into the wilderness, as Miss Moore says, "so that he may realize his heritage in the history of his country and take his place there more intelligently"—his death is a sharp loss. Miss Moore has told how, on 7 June 1919, boys came all day long to the New York Public Library, some with clippings from the newspapers telling of their favorite's death. There they could look upon a full set of all his works, and his picture. Said a 17-year-old:

"He looks young in that picture but he could have lived all through American history—he makes it so true. You couldn't do better than to read his books. You can even answer some of the Regents' questions out of Altsheler's books. I read every one of them and I got an A-1 mark for history."

Eyes roved along the shelves over the volumes of the Young Trailers' Series, the Texan Series, the French and Indian War Series, the Civil War Series, and the

[1] Article by Anne Carroll Moore in The Bookman for November, 1918. Reprinted in her *Roads to Childhood*.

rest. They picked out individual titles—always simple and always touched with the imagination of a man who knew supremely how to kindle the youthful mind. Altsheler, indeed, surpassed himself in the titles of the eight books of his Civil War Series, a beautiful crescendo:

The Guns of Bull Run
The Guns of Shiloh
The Scouts of Stonewall
The Sword of Antietam
The Star of Gettysburg

and then the point of rest, on a great chord, followed by a resolution and a final cadence:

The Rock of Chickamauga
The Shades of the Wilderness
The Tree of Appomattox

—guns, scouts, sword, star, rock! The words sing. Then the shades of anguish, weariness, impending defeat, and at last the peace of the spreading tree. . . .

Joseph Alexander Altsheler was born at Three Springs, Kentucky, 29 April 1862. As a boy he would lie on his back in the woods of the Daniel Boone country and dream of the pioneers until they came to have as strong a fascination for him as the myths of Greece have had for other minds. There were not many books, but he heard over and over again the stories of woodsmen and fighters, for he was descended on his mother's side from Virginia and Kentucky borderers. And as a boy he knew personally Civil War veterans, both blue and gray, such as General Simon Bolivar Buckner, General Don Carlos Buell, and General Frank Wolford. The one writer who captivated him

[238]

completely and to whom he afterward said he owed the most was Francis Parkman.

He was educated at Liberty College, Glasgow, Kentucky, and at Vanderbilt University, Nashville, Tennessee. Then he went to work on the Louisville Evening Post. A year later he moved over to Henry Watterson's Courier-Journal, for which he became the political reporter and legislative correspondent at Frankfort, the State capital.

After service as city editor of the Courier-Journal and as an editorial writer, he joined the staff of the World, New York. He covered the World's Fair in Chicago and the events attending the dethronement of Liliuokalani in Hawaii, and then became editor and manager of the tri-weekly edition of the World, a job he continued to hold until his death. His first book of consequence was *The Sun of Saratoga* (1897), which still sells. The first of his boys' books, so-called, was *The Young Trailers* (1906), written when his own son was eleven or twelve years old. But he made it a practice never to allow thought of the age of his readers to affect his treatment of a subject; and while this accounts for the number of older readers who enjoy his books, it probably also goes far to account for the success of his books with boys. He never wrote down to them.

His accuracy and his sense of reality are beyond praise. But the finest tribute to him is the fact that, as Miss Moore testifies, he is the only author whom older boys absolutely insist on having, for whose books they wait in line in the library, refusing to be put off with other titles.

III. THOMAS DIXON

Although Thomas Dixon's new novel, *The Black Hood* (1924), is a story of the Ku Klux Klan of 1870, and so a companion volume to *The Clansman* (1905), it is customary to speak of *The Leopard's Spots* (1902), *The Clansman*, and *The Traitor* (1907) as a trilogy of the Reconstruction period at the South. Of those who admired this series perhaps the best known and certainly the most unqualifiedly enthusiastic was Max Nordau, who hailed the novels as undoing the work of Harriet Beecher Stowe and giving the deferred answer to *Uncle Tom's Cabin*. Similarly, *The One Woman* (1903), *Comrades* (1909), and *The Root of Evil* (1911) are grouped together as a trilogy of Socialism, pleading for the development of individual character and opposing the Socialistic remedies for the ills of society.

Thomas Dixon was born at Shelby, North Carolina, 11 January 1864, the son of the Reverend Thomas Dixon and Amanda Elizabeth (McAfee) Dixon. The father was a Baptist clergyman. At 19 the son was graduated from Wake Forest College, North Carolina, with a scholarship admitting him as a special student in history and politics at Johns Hopkins University. A year later he became a student at the Greensboro (North Carolina) Law School. About the same time he was elected to the North Carolina legislature. He got his law degree, dabbled in politics, was admitted to practice in the North Carolina and United States courts, including the United States Supreme Court, had a part in two conspicuous murder trials of the day, and then, before he was 23, and some months after marrying Harriet Bussey, of Columbus, Georgia, resigned from the legislature to enter the Baptist ministry.

He held a pastorate for a year in Raleigh, North Carolina, and for a year in Boston before coming to the People's Temple in New York. He preached in New York for ten years, 1889-1899. At the same time he became a lyceum lecturer and he continued to lecture until 1903. His outspokenness in the pulpit was coupled with a certain disregard of clerical custom; for example, he enjoyed going hunting. He began to publish books of sermons at least as early as 1891. He was 35 when he quitted the pulpit and turned to fiction.

Three of his novels are centered upon outstanding figures of the Civil War. *The Southerner* (1913) is constructed about Lincoln, *The Victim* (1914), about Jefferson Davis; *The Man in Gray* (1921), about Robert E. Lee. *A Man of the People* is a Lincoln play; *The Fall of a Nation* depicts the conquest of the United States by the Imperial Nation. Such a novel as *The Way of a Man* is more or less related to the novels dealing with Socialism; *The Sins of the Father*, a study of the results of miscegenation, belongs with *The Clansman* group.

It was in 1915, ten years after the sensational success of *The Clansman*, that David Wark Griffith produced his film based on the novel under the title, "The Birth of a Nation."

The new novel of the Klan, *The Black Hood*, is concerned with the time when the original Ku Klux Klan had accomplished the work for which it was organized and was becoming more or less of a menace to the liberty of the Southerners among whom it flourished. Mr. Dixon's hero opposes the Klan's methods as being false to the spirit in which the Klan was founded. He is successful in his stand after many exciting adventures. There is a romantic interest interwoven in the story.

IV. STEPHEN CRANE

The author of *The Red Badge of Courage* has lately been the subject of a brilliant biography. Mr. Thomas Beer's *Stephen Crane: A Study in American Letters* has the color and the abiding fascination of its subject, if sometimes a trifle too cryptic and oracular. The point of *The Red Badge of Courage* is its record of war as the experience of the individual, any war in any age. The book, a product of purely imaginative experience by a youth of twenty-two to twenty-four, lights up its single theme as completely as a Verrey flare exposes some small corner of a battle. Reading either Crane's work or Mr. Beer's study, one can no more doubt that Crane was a genius. He had the intense, piercing, personal vision of the isolated, unexplained (and unexplainable) artist. Such a figure is not to be produced by any sedulous process of education; it is not a triumphant burbank of literary cultivation. Although people remember, or, at least, generally have heard of, *The Red Badge of Courage*, there is a sharp need for republication of most of Crane's work in a good edition; for *The Open Boat* and *The Bride Comes to Yellow Sky* are of the utmost importance, the first on the evidence of Joseph Conrad, the second on the evidence of Stephen Crane. If one were asked to pick the American authors of most interesting significance to literature at large, one would do well, I think, to let both Poe and Hawthorne wait at one side while one weighed carefully Herman Melville, Walt Whitman, and Stephen Crane.

*　　*　　*　　*　　*　　*　　*　　*

Other authors whose use of American history in fiction has interested huge audiences are Everett T. Tomlinson, Elmer Russell Gregor, Frederick Trevor Hill and Bernard Marshall. It is perhaps natural that their fiction should be spoken of, as Altsheler's is often spoken of, as "stories for boys." There is conclusive evidence, however, that about half of the readers of Altsheler are adults; and the percentage of adult readers for the books by Mr. Tomlinson, Mr. Gregor, Mr. Hill and Mr. Marshall is heavy. This might be inferred easily enough from the simple fact that between 1,250,000 and 1,500,000 copies of Mr. Tomlinson's books have been sold.

Everett T. Tomlinson, born in 1859, had a boyish passion for natural history and another for baseball. From Williams College he went into teaching, becoming headmaster of a boys' school, where he still played ball. For twenty-three years he was pastor of a church in Elizabeth, New Jersey. He was appointed a member of the New Jersey Public Library Commission when it was formed in 1901, and became its chairman in 1921. His first book appeared thirty years ago. Besides many fictions, such as *The Mysterious Rifleman* and *Scouting on the Border*, he is the author of a *Young People's History of the American Revolution* and such books as *Places Young Americans Want to Know* and *Fighters Young Americans Want to Know*. His new book (1924) is called *Pioneer Scouts of Ohio*.

Elmer Russell Gregor, born in 1878, was graduated from a military academy and spent twenty-four hours in the drygoods business, six months in real estate, and more successful periods as a farmer and stock raiser, and in lumbering, quarrying and mining. His real job since 1910 has been writing, but, as he says, his hobbies are Indians (foremost), ornithology, natural history, forestry, hunting and fishing, and breeding prize-winning dogs, chickens and pigeons, so "you see

I don't have much time for work." He lives in South-
port, Connecticut, but has traveled much and "my
circle of intimate acquaintances includes cowboys,
'sour-doughs' (miners), Injuns, mountaineers, and
lumberjacks—all good fellows." The books that have
been most popular with his readers are stories of
young Indian chiefs, divided into two series, the
Western Indian Stories and the Eastern Indian Stories,
and, most recently, the Jim Mason series, which follows the fortunes of a white frontiersman in the days
of the French and Indian wars. *Captain Jim Mason*
(1924) is his latest work.

Frederick Trevor Hill, born in 1866, a graduate of
Yale and a graduate in law at Columbia, on the staff
of General Pershing and cited by Pershing, is the
author of very widely-known books on the law, both
as fact and as material for fiction. His interest in
American history has led him to study the three or four
outstanding figures in such books as *On the Trail of
Grant and Lee*, *On the Trail of Washington*, and
Washington The Man of Action. Why, it may be
asked, two books on the Father of his country? And
the response must be that *On the Trail of Washington*
is, as the subtitle explains, "a narrative of Washington's boyhood and manhood, based on his writings and
other authentic documents," and is concerned with the
growth of early years; whereas *Washington The Man
of Action* is an attempt to portray the mature man as
he really was, not as the plaster saint of his earliest
biographers.

Bernard Marshall was born on a farm twenty miles
south of Boston, one of a family fond of books and
music. Having resolved to be a writer, he thought he
could play in orchestras and make a living until he had
his foothold as an author. Thereupon twenty years

were passed as a musician, a legal stenographer, a writer of technical articles and in advertising work. Then, after trying to help build ships to win the war, Mr. Marshall settled in Berkeley, California, a half mile from the university, and began to write historical romances, *Walter of Tiverton*, *Cedric the Forester*, and *The Torch Bearers*. The last two and his new American historical romance, *Redcoat and Minute Man*, form a Liberty Series, showing three crucial points in the history of the Anglo-Saxon struggle for popular liberties, Magna Charta (*Cedric the Forester*), Oliver Cromwell (*The Torch Bearers*), and the American Revolution (*Redcoat and Minute Man*).

BOOKS BY EMERSON HOUGH

1895	*The Singing Mouse Stories*
1897	*The Story of the Cowboy*
1900	*The Girl at the Half-Way House*
1902	*The Mississippi Bubble*
1903	*The Way to the West*
1904	*The Law of the Land*
1905	*Heart's Desire*
1906	*The King of Gee Whiz*
1906	*The Story of the Outlaw*
1907	*The Way of a Man*
1909	*Fifty-Four Forty or Fight*
1909	*The Sowing*
1910	*The Young Alaskans*
1911	*The Purchase Price*
1912	*John Rawn—Prominent Citizen*
1913	*The Lady and the Pirate*
1913	*The Young Alaskans in the Rockies*
1914	*The Young Alaskans on the Trail*
1915	*The Magnificent Adventure*
1916	*The Man Next Door*
1917	*The Broken Gate*

CARGOES FOR CRUSOES

1918   *The Young Alaskans in the Far North*
1918   *The Way Out*
1919   *The Sagebrusher*
1919   *The Web*
1922   *The Covered Wagon*
1923   *North of 36*
1924   *Mother of Gold*

SOURCES ON EMERSON HOUGH

The Men Who Make Our Novels, by George Gordon. Moffat, Yard and Company. Page 140 *et seq*. This book now published by Dodd, Mead and Company.

Autobiographical article in the American Magazine: 1918 or earlier.

Editorial article in the Saturday Evening Post, April or May, 1923.

"A Defense of the American Tradition," by William MacLeod Raine, in the Author and Journalist, Denver, Colorado, 1923.

BOOKS BY JOSEPH A. ALTSHELER

THE YOUNG TRAILERS SERIES: Frontier Life in the Revolution. Two boys, Henry Ware and Paul Cotter, and three scouts are the chief characters:

> *The Young Trailers*
> *The Forest Runners*
> *The Free Rangers*
> *The Eyes of the Woods*
> *The Keepers of the Trail*
> *The Riflemen of the Ohio*
> *The Scouts of the Valley*
> *The Border Watch*

THE FRENCH AND INDIAN WAR SERIES. The period is from 1754 to 1763 and the central characters are Robert Lennox,

an American boy; Tayoga, an Onondaga Indian; and David
Willet, a hunter:

The Hunters of the Hills
The Shadow of the North
The Rulers of the Lakes
The Masters of the Peaks
The Lords of the Wild
The Sun of Quebec

THE TEXAN SERIES. Three stories of the Texas struggle
for independence, with an American boy, Ned Fulton, in the
foreground:

The Texan Star
The Texan Scouts
The Texan Triumph

THE CIVIL WAR SERIES. The principal battles of the Civil
War are covered. In four of the stories Dick Mason, who
fights for the North, is the leading character; in the other
four his cousin, Harry Kenton, fighting on the Southern side,
is featured:

The Guns of Bull Run
The Guns of Shiloh
The Scouts of Stonewall
The Sword of Antietam
The Star of Gettysburg
The Rock of Chickamauga
The Shades of the Wilderness
The Tree of Appomattox

INDIAN WARS OF THE WEST AND SOUTHWEST. Not a series:

Apache Gold
The Last of the Chiefs (Custer's defeat)
The Quest of the Four (Mexican War)

THE GREAT WEST SERIES:

The Great Sioux Trail
The Lost Hunters

[247]

CARGOES FOR CRUSOES

THE WORLD WAR SERIES. John Scott, a young American in Germany when the war opens, and Phillip Lannes, a young French friend, are the central figures:

> *The Guns of Europe*
> *The Hosts of the Air*
> *The Forest of Swords*

HISTORICAL ROMANCES. More definitely for older readers. Not in series:

> *A Soldier of Manhattan* (French and Indian War)
> *The Sun of Saratoga* (Burgoyne's surrender)
> *The Wilderness Road* (Pioneers west of the Alleghenies)
> *My Captive* (Revolutionary romance)
> *A Herald of the West* (War of 1812)
> *In Circling Camps* (Civil War)
> *The Last Rebel*
> *The Candidate* (the romance of a political campaign)

SOURCES ON JOSEPH A. ALTSHELER

"Joseph A. Altsheler and American History," by Anne Carroll Moore. Pamphlet published by D. Appleton & Company.

Article by Anne Carroll Moore in The Bookman for November, 1918. Reprinted in *Roads to Childhood*, by Anne Carroll Moore.

"Some Worthwhile Books," by Robert Page Lincoln in The Review.

"A Kentucky Writer of Historical Novels," by John Wilson Townsend, in the Lexington (Kentucky) Leader for 18 May 1912.

BOOKS BY THOMAS DIXON

1891   *Living Problems in Religion and Social Science*
1894   *Sermons on Ingersoll*
1897   *The Failure of Protestantism in New York*
1902   *What Is Religion?*

[248]

1902 *The Leopard's Spots*
1903 *The One Woman*
1905 *The Clansman*
1905 *The Life Worth Living*
1907 *The Traitor*
1909 *Comrades*
1911 *The Root of Evil*
1912 *The Sins of the Father*
1913 *The Southerner* (Abraham Lincoln)
1914 *The Victim* (Jefferson Davis)
1915 *The Foolish Virgin*
1916 *The Fall of a Nation*
1918 *The Way of a Man*
1920 *A Man of the People*. Play. (Abraham Lincoln)
1921 *The Man in Gray* (Robert E. Lee)
1924 *The Black Hood*

SOURCES ON THOMAS DIXON

"The Men Who Make Our Novels," by George Gordon, page 249. Moffat, Yard and Company (now published by Dodd, Mead and Company).

Articles on the photoplay, "The Birth of a Nation," made from *The Clansman* are too numerous to be cited. The reader may consult the READERS' GUIDE TO PERIODICAL LITERATURE for 1915-16.

BOOKS BY STEPHEN CRANE

1895 *The Red Badge of Courage*

SOURCES ON STEPHEN CRANE

Stephen Crane: A Study in American Letters, by Thomas Beer. Alfred A. Knopf: 1923.

CARGOES FOR CRUSOES

BOOKS BY EVERETT T. TOMLINSON

(For more complete list, see *Who's Who in America:* 1924-25)

1908	*Scouting with Mad Anthony*
1915	*Places Young Americans Want to Know*
1916	*The Trail of the Mohawk Chief*
1917	*The Story of General Pershing*
1918	*Fighters Young Americans Want to Know*
1920	*The Pursuit of the Apache Chief*
1920	*Scouting on the Border*
1921	*The Mysterious Rifleman*
1921	*Young People's History of the American Revolution*
1923	*Scouting on the Old Frontier*
1923	*Stories of the American Revolution*
1924	*Scouting in the Wilderness*
1924	*The Pioneer Scouts of Ohio*

SOURCES ON EVERETT T. TOMLINSON

"The Historical Story for Boys," by Everett T. Tomlinson. Booklet published by D. Appleton & Company.
Who's Who in America.

BOOKS BY ELMER RUSSELL GREGOR

JIM MASON STORIES. The hero is a young frontiersman.

1923	*Jim Mason, Backwoodsman*
1923	*Jim Mason, Scout*
1924	*Captain Jim Mason*

WESTERN INDIAN STORIES. The hero is White Otter, a young Sioux chief:

1917	*White Otter*
1920	*The War Trail*
1922	*Three Sioux Scouts*

AMERICAN HISTORY IN FICTION

EASTERN INDIAN STORIES. The hero is Running Fox, a young chief of the Delawares:

1918 *Running Fox*
1920 *The White Wolf*
1922 *Spotted Deer*

BOOKS BY FREDERICK TREVOR HILL

(For more complete list, see *Who's Who in America*)
1909 *On the Trail of Washington*
1911 *On the Trail of Grant and Lee*
1914 *Washington the Man of Action*

BOOKS BY BERNARD MARSHALL

1921 *Cedric the Forester*
1923 *The Torch Bearers*
1923 *Walter of Tiverton*
1924 *Redcoat and Minute Man*

15. The Fireside Theatre

AS the cost of the theater mounts up—the price of seats, the price of achieving Broadway productions—the Fireside Theater audience is steadily recruited. If there has existed a prejudice against reading plays, it is melting. The mere force of conditions would tend to destroy such a prejudice. The path to Broadway becomes steadily more difficult and the path away from Broadway narrower—all because it costs too much to produce a play on Broadway, and far too much to take the play, once so produced, on the road. Soon the Broadway theater will survive as the horse survives; and Broadway productions, inspired by the same motives as the production of horse races, will be nobly upheld by the same justificatory excuse— it will be argued that they improve the breed of plays.

It does no harm to have a few horse shows or to have a few Broadway productions; but the truth must be stated that the theater in America no longer depends upon the amusement business in the vicinity of Forty-second Street. To an extent never before equaled, plays are now published in America regardless of their production; are bought and read; are read aloud for an exceptional evening's entertainment; and are acted under license, and with payment of very moderate fees, by people to whom a play is a play and not a pair of high-priced tickets.

For amateur actors, many of them amazingly ca-

[252]

pable, there are now available plays of every length and of every conceivable variety of type, settings, and casts; of extreme, moderate and very slight demands upon the actors' skill; tragic, comedic, farcical. And for readers of plays there are certain immutable advantages that have been pointed out before but will bear stressing again, such as that the performance always begins on time, and at *your* chosen time, and that the actors, being your own creatures, are always ideal.

I shall try to speak first of some anthologies of plays, then of plays by individual authors, and finally of a few books about the drama and the theater.

ii

First I would put Montrose J. Moses's ample works. His *Representative British Dramas: Victorian and Modern* is not only a complete history of the British stage, from the beginning of the nineteenth century to 1914; it presents the complete texts of twenty-one English and Irish plays superbly representative of its century. *Representative Continental Dramas: Revolutionary and Transitional* does much the same thing for Europe as a whole. Eight European countries are represented in this anthology, which contains the complete texts of fifteen plays, with a general survey of the development of Continental drama and individual bibliographies. But the greatest demand is for anthologies of one-act plays; a demand richly met by the following standard works:

Representative One-Act Plays by American Authors, compiled by Margaret G. Mayorga, contains the complete texts of twenty-four, all of which have been produced in Little Theaters. Among the dramatists included are Percy Mackaye, Stuart Walker, Jeannette Marks, George Middleton, Susan Glaspell, Eugene O'Neill, and Beulah Marie Dix.

Fifty Contemporary One-Act Plays edited by Frank Shay and Pierre Loving, is an international selection of astonishing variety and exceptional merit.

Twenty Contemporary One-Act Plays—American, edited by Frank Shay, is an anthology which affords variety of choice for acting and ample variety for the reader.

Barrett H. Clark's *Representative One-Act Plays by British and Irish Authors* contains complete texts of twenty one-act plays. Some of the authors are Pinero, Jones, Arnold Bennett, Yeats, Oscar Wilde, Granville Barker and Lord Dunsany. Mr. Moses is the compiler of *Representative One-Act Plays by Continental Authors.* Maeterlinck, Arthur Schnitzler, Strindberg, Andreyev, Franz Wedekind, Sudermann, von Hofmannsthal, Lavedan are some of the playwrights whose work is included; and the book is equipped with bibliographies.

Frank Shay is the compiler of *Twenty-Five Short Plays: International,* in which is much exotic work—plays from Bengal and Burma, China and Japan and Uruguay, as well as from countries with whose drama we have more contact. But as an example of Mr. Shay's selections we may note, from among the writers whose work is fairly familiar, that Austria is represented by a Schnitzler piece, Italy by one of Robert Bracco's comedies, Hungary by Lajos Biro's "The Bridegroom," Russia by an example of Chekhov and Spain by Echegaray.

I may at this point advantageously call attention to Mr. Shay's *One Thousand and One Plays for the Little Theatre,* and his new *One Thousand and One Longer*

Plays—not anthologies, but exhaustive lists. The plays are listed alphabetically by authors and by organizations, and the title, nature of the work, number of men and women characters, publisher, and price of each play is given.

Certain other books, though offering a number of one-act plays, have too few inclusions to be described as anthologies. Such are *One-Act Plays from the Yiddish*, translated by Etta Block and presenting half a dozen effective pieces; *Three Modern Japanese Plays*, translated by Yozan T. Iwasaki and Glenn Hughes, and showing the direct result of Western influences on the Japanese theatre; and *Double Demon and Other One-Act Plays*, by A. P. Herbert and others, one of the British Drama League series.

Colin Campbell Clements, whose *Plays for a Folding Theatre* is known to most amateurs, has a new book this season called *Plays for Pagans*, containing five entertaining short plays, all easy of stage production. Another such group is to be found in *Garden Varieties*, by Kenyon Nicholson, six plays, most of them farcical and amusing.

Certain other one-act plays I shall speak of later in this chapter. But the record of excellent anthologies is not yet completed. *A Treasury of Plays for Children*, by Mr. Moses, provides fourteen dramas with the abundance of incident and action which young people demand but with considerable literary merit besides. Mr. Shay, again, is the compiler of *A Treasury of Plays for Women*, eighteen in all, requiring only women to cast or containing only such male characters as may easily be enacted by women; and also of *A Treasury of Plays for Men*, twenty-one altogether, which men may stage without feminine help. *A Treasury of Plays for Men* also offers a working library list for the Little Theater and a bibliography of other anthologies.

ii

In coming to the work of individual playwrights, I am afraid the method of conscientious enumeration must to a great extent go on. Granville Barker's work is almost too well-known to require special comment. His plays, some one of which is almost certain to be found in any comprehensive anthology, are published in seven volumes, each a single drama except the *Three Short Plays*. Anatol, to be sure, is simply Mr. Barker's splendid version of Arthur Schnitzler's gay satire on a gilded youth of Vienna. Probably *Waste*, at once intimate in its discussions and intensely serious, is the best-known drama by Barker; but *The Madras House*, with its humors of feminine psychology, and *The Voysey Inheritance*, that fine study of middle-class English family life, are both popular. The others are *The Marrying of Ann Leete*, at once a comedy and a satire, and the three-act play called *The Secret Life*, a play of present-day England touched with philosophy and mysticism and occasional cynicism, but of the same distinctive quality as Barker's other work.

Three plays by Lewis Beach have been published. *A Square Peg* presents the tragic results of a mother's unflinching rule of her family. *The Goose Hangs High* is a comedy of family loyalty and affection which brings the younger generation face to face with its elders; it has been a success of the last New York season. But the one to which I want to direct attention especially is *Ann Vroome*, a play in seven scenes giving the story of a girl's long wait for happiness when she postpones marriage to care for her parents. This play has a very fine acceleration of dramatic interest, of

[256]

emotional intensity; and its literary quality is of a high order. It is evident that Mr. Beach does nothing badly.

The history of Owen Davis has been told many times, but I do not suppose its impression of the extraordinary is ever lessened. He wrote, for years, melodramas of the "Nellie, the Beautiful Cloak Model" order; I am by no means sure he did not write "Nellie." In those days he supplied the theaters of the Bowery and other avenues no better as to art if less notorious. It should be said that however cheap were these works, they were infinitely more respectable and of a better moral character than some pretentious affairs playing uptown. Mr. Davis had two reasonable purposes—to learn play writing and to make necessary money. When he had accomplished both, being still a young man, he turned to work of a different description. His play, *The Detour* (1921), the story of a woman's never-dying aspiration and hope, was one of the finest things of its season. Clear-cut, dramatic, with comedy and pathos interwoven, it depicted mental and spiritual force pitted against solely material ambition in a way that those who saw or read it did not forget. The evidence was clear that a new American dramatist of the first rank had been born. *Icebound* (1922), had immediate attention and very marked critical praise, crowned by the award to it of the Pulitzer Prize by Columbia University as the best American play of the year.

The most successful American playwright of his day, Clyde Fitch was also one of the ablest. The Memorial Edition of the *Plays of Clyde Fitch*, edited, with introductions, by Montrose J. Moses and Virginia Gerson, and published in four volumes is a gallant and important affair. The edition is definitive and contains three plays that were never before in print, "The Woman in the Case," "Lovers' Lane," and that most important of the Fitch plays, "The City." The fourth volume of this edition contains Mr. Fitch's address on "The Play and the Public." [1]

The four volumes of *Representative Plays by Henry Arthur Jones*, edited, with historical, biographical, and critical introductions, by Clayton Hamilton, assemble in a splendid library edition the most interesting work of the British dramatist. Henry Arthur Jones wrote some sixty or seventy plays, printed mainly in pamphlet form—"scrips"—for the use, primarily, of actors, professional and amateur. These Mr. Hamilton sifted, at the same time making an effort to indicate the range and variety of Jones's work. As a consequence, *Representative Plays* opens with a celebrated old-time melodrama, "The Silver King," and illustrates the stages in the author's progress until he arrived, in the composition of "The Liars," at a really great accomplishment as a master of modern English comedy. Mr. Hamilton's introductions carry the reader's attention from play to play along a continuous current of historical, biographical and critical comment. Probably the best-known inclusions are the plays in the third volume: "Michael and His Lost Angel," "The Liars," "Mrs. Dane's Defence," and "The Hypocrites."

Of Cosmo Hamilton's *Four Plays* I have already made mention [2] and perhaps I should have spoken of Percival Wilde when dealing with one-act plays. Mr. Wilde's work is itself an anthology of the one-act play. This New Yorker was for a while in the banking busi-

---

[1] See Chapter 12 for an account of *Clyde Fitch and His Letters,* by Mr. Moses and Miss Gerson.
[2] See Chapter 11.

ness; on the publication of his first story he received so many requests to allow its dramatization that he thought he would investigate the drama himself. That was not more than a dozen years ago; yet now Percival Wilde is commonly said to have had more plays produced—or rather, to have had a greater number of productions—in American Little Theaters than any other playwright.

His books to date (of this sort) are five. *Eight Comedies for Little Theatres* contains "The Previous Engagement," "The Dyspeptic Ogre," "Catesby," "The Sequel," "In the Net," "His Return," "The Embryo," and "A Wonderful Woman." Then there are his other collections—*Dawn, and Other One-Act Plays of Life Today* (six), *A Question of Morality, and Other Plays* (five), and *The Unseen Host, and Other War Plays* (five), and *The Inn of Discontent and Other Fantastic Plays* (five).

George Kelly, a young American born in a suburb of Philadelphia, had the daring to satirize the Little Theater movement in America in "The Torch-Bearers," which had a New York success. In this past season his play, The *Show-Off*, has not only been a memorable success but has perhaps had more unqualified praise than any drama in years. "I might as well begin boldly and say that *The Show-Off* is the best comedy which has yet been written by an American," writes Heywood Broun in his preface to the published play; and this does not much exaggerate the note of the general chorus. The committee named to recommend a play for the award of the annual Pulitzer Prize selected *The Show-Off;* and the overruling of their choice by the Columbia University authorities was the subject of considerable controversy not entirely free from indignant feeling.

What is this play? "A transcript of life, in three acts," the titlepage truthfully calls it. The chief character, Aubrey Piper, liar, braggart, egoist, is almost dreadfully real. It is perhaps possible, however depressing, to regard him as a symbol of all mankind, bringing us to realize the toughness of human fiber, as Mr. Broun suggests. But it seems to me much more likely that the play's great merit and supreme interest lies in another point that Mr. Broun makes: there is no development of character in Aubrey, but only in ourselves, the audience, who come to know him progressively better, and finally to know him to the last inescapable dreg. Most critics have tended, I think, to overlook the splendid characterization of Mrs. Fisher, Aubrey's perspicacious and unrelenting mother-in-law. The play is too true for satire, too serious for comedy, too humanly diverting for tears. It is certainly not to be missed.

The Lilies of the Field, a comedy by John Hastings Turner, author of several novels, including that very engaging story, *Simple Souls*, is one of the British Drama League series and will probably have a New York production this season. The desire of twin daughters of an English village clergyman to become the wives of young men met in London—young men who toil not, neither do they spin except at dances—produces the complications, which are both entertaining and somewhat satirical. Of the other British Drama League plays, *The Prince*, by Gwen John, deals with Queen Elizabeth, and is "a study of character, based on contemporary evidence," while Laurence Binyon's *Ayuli* is drama in verse, telling a picturesque story of Eastern Asia. Mr. Binyon has made studies of Oriental art and his drama is of quite exceptional literary quality.

THE FIRESIDE THEATRE

Of novel interest is *The Sea Woman's Cloak and November Eve*, a volume containing two plays by the American writer, Amelie Rives (Princess Troubetzkoy), that are as Irish as work by Lady Gregory, Yeats, or J. M. Synge. "The Sea Woman's Cloak" is based on an old legend of Ganore's mating with a mortal; "November Eve" tells how Ilva, who is fairy-struck, saves a soul the godly folk won't risk their own souls to save.

Dragon's Glory, a play in four scenes by Gertrude Knevels, is based on an old Chinese legend, and makes very amusing reading and a most actable comedy. Yow Chow has purchased the finest coffin in China ("Dragon's Glory") and the action of the piece centers about this treasure, in which the estimable Yow Chow reposes until a crisis which is the climax of the play.

The two series known respectively as the Modern Series and the Little Theatre Series consist of plays published in pamphlet form at a low price for the convenience of amateur theatrical organizations. Included in these series are separate plays by such authors as Booth Tarkington, Christopher Morley, Edna St. Vincent Millay, Eugene O'Neill, Stuart Walker, Floyd Dell, Rupert Brooke, and others, to a present total of thirty titles. The Modern Series, edited by Frank Shay, has two particularly striking new titles in *Lord Byron* and *Autumn*.

Lord Byron, a play in seven scenes by Maurice Ferber, is of the genre of Drinkwater's *Abraham Lincoln* and Mr. Eaton's and Mr. Carb's *Queen Victoria*. Byron is one of the most dramatic of the possible subjects for a biographical play, and Mr. Ferber's work will undoubtedly be frequently staged and very much read at this time of the Byron centenary.

Autumn, in four acts, by Ilya Surguchev, translated

by David A. Modell, is the picture of jealousy between a young wife and an adopted daughter. "This is one of the strongest plays I have ever read," says Frank Shay. It is our first introduction to the work of the Russian author and part of its novelty consists in the last act, which "achieves a monotony that is real and genuine. It does not bring husband and wife together in happiness, but shows that there is nothing else for them to do but to go on."

But the other new titles in the Modern Series deserve brief mention. *Words and Thoughts*, by Don Marquis, presents John and Mary Speaker, who utter the usual banalities of the world, and John and Mary Thinker, who utter their true and less pleasant thoughts. John L. Balderston's *A Morality Play for the Leisure Class* pictures a rich collector's boredom in heaven when he finds that his treasures there have no monetary value. There is an O. Henry twist to the ending. Walter McClellan's *The Delta Wife* is a genre play of the Mississippi River mouth, in type resembling *Hell-Bent fer Heaven*. *The Lion's Mouth*, by George Madden Martin and Harriet L. Kennedy, deals with the relations of blacks and whites. A white doctor ignores a black child in his efforts to save a white baby. An old mammy has an invaluable herb cure; but finding that the doctor cares nothing for her grandson's life, she refuses to save the white infant. Wilbur Daniel Steele's *The Giant's Stair* is a study in mood and atmosphere, like many of his short stories. Before the play opens a man has been murdered. A terrific storm is raging. The scene is between the widow and her demented sister and the sheriff. *Action!* by Holland Hudson is a swift-moving, melodramatic comedy. The son of a silk dealer returns from selling airplanes to protest that the life of a silk salesman is dull. His objections are interrupted by the entry of two silk loft burglars and two bootleggers—followed by Federal officers and policemen with drawn weapons.

The new titles in the Little Theatre Series, edited by Grace Adams, include Edna St. Vincent Millay's *Aria da Capo* and her *The Lamp and the Bell*.

Edna St. Vincent Millay's work is known throughout America. *The Lamp and the Bell*, a Shakespearean play written for a Vassar College anniversary, has for its theme woman's friendship, and is very nearly unique among compositions for an occasion in having solid literary and dramatic merit. Its fresh, vigorous, creative quality is enriched by some lovely lyrical inclusions. *Aria da Capo*, Miss Millay's bitterly ironic, beautiful and interesting one-act fantasy, has been played, one is tempted to believe, everywhere; and will for years be played again and again. No contemporary Pierrot and Columbine composition excels it, if, indeed, any matches it.

Mary MacMillen's *Pan or Pierrot* is a play for children, to be acted out of doors. And I must again call attention to John Farrar's charming plays for children in *The Magic Sea Shell*.

iii

Books about the theater are various, of course, ranging from æsthetic studies down to the most practical handbook for amateurs. Of the latter, I should certainly put first Barrett H. Clark's *How to Produce Amateur Plays*, now in a new and revised edition. This manual is as nearly indispensable to amateur actors as anything can be. It tells how to choose a play, how to organize, the principles of casting, and the methods of rehearsing. It gives very necessary information about the stage itself, lighting, scenery and costumes, and makeup. There is also a list of good amateur plays and information about copyright and royalty.

Another book that will be particularly welcomed by schools and social organizations is Claude Merton Wise's *Dramatics for School and Community*, which covers much the same fields as Mr. Clark's work.

I have already spoken of Percival Wilde's astonishing success as an author of one-act plays; it makes his book on *The Craftsmanship of the One-Act Play* the last word on the subject. But the special value of Mr. Wilde's book is that it considers everything having to do with the construction of the one-act play from the point of view of the stage director as well as that of the author.

Granville Barker's *The Exemplary Theatre*, though by one of the best-known men of the group interested in and influencing modern dramatic theory and esthetics, is preëminently a practical book. It considers the theater as a civic institution and has a valuable chapter on the inner and outer organization of a repertory theater; but the chapters on a director's duties, choosing the best plays, training the company, scenery and lighting, and audiences are of widespread applicability.

A mention of books about the theater is fated to omit many excellent volumes, but can scarcely fail to include a series of books which give a complete circumspection of contemporary drama. The most recent volume in the series is *The Contemporary Drama of Russia*, by Leo Wiener, professor of Slavic languages and literature at Harvard. This entirely new study is likely to create a commotion, for it belies utterly the conclusions generally arrived at as to the relative value of the work of such playwrights as Chekhov, Gorki, Andreyev, Solugub, Evreinov and others, and it brings into prominence many names never heard of before outside of Russia. Its picture of the origin and development of the Moscow Art Theater is not the one of popular legend, and should probably be narrowly compared with that given by Constantin Stanislavsky in his *My Life in Art* [3] and with other accounts. Professor Wiener has relied, however, upon letters, theatrical annals, and other contemporary records. His bibliographies contain fairly full accounts of plays from Ostrovski to the present, lists of books and articles on the contemporary Russian drama, and lists of all English translations of plays.

The Contemporary Drama of England, by Thomas H. Dickinson, covers adequately the history of the English stage since 1866. Ernest Boyd's *The Contemporary Drama of Ireland* presents the Irish literary movement and the work of Irish dramatists. *The Contemporary Drama of Italy*, by Lander MacClintock, traces the development of the modern Italian theater from its inception down to the present day, and has interesting chapters on Gabriele d'Annunzio and the writers now popular in Italy. Frank W. Chandler's *The Contemporary Drama of France*, a longer work than the three preceding, presents a survey and interpretation of French drama for three decades, from the opening of the Theatre-Libre of Antoine to the conclusion of the world war.

[3] See Chapter 12.

16. A Reasonable View of
Michael Arlen

i

THERE is a book called *These Charming People*.
In making this statement I pause for an uncertain time. It is necessary to allow a little interval for
readers—quite as necessary as it is for the orator to
give his audience its innings. Readers do not create
the same interruption for a writer, and that is in itself
a pity. That fact defeats much writing; for the writer
has rushed on before the reader's mind has had a
chance to seethe a little and settle, passing on to a
comparatively calm acceptance of the next assertion.

But you can take anybody's word for *These Charming People*—anybody's, that is, who has read it; and
the number of persons who have read it is very large
and increases steadily. The truth is, this book and its
author have become fashionable; and when a book
and an author have become fashionable, some persons
will go to any length. Now it is known that Michael
Arlen is the author of *These Charming People*, but
who knows who Michael Arlen may be? Is there a
View of Michael Arlen? In the favorite adjective of
one of Mr. Arlen's characters, is there a reasonable
view of the presumptively charming person?

Yes.

The main perspective is before us. Looking down
it, we discern that two years (and less than two years)
ago, nobody in America who was anybody in America

A VIEW OF MICHAEL ARLEN

(or anywhere else) had heard of Michael Arlen. I will not conceal the dark fact that two books of his, entitled *A London Venture* and *The Romantic Lady*, had been published in America.

However, two years ago (as I write) there was published in America a novel called "*Piracy*." No reason existed why people should buy it and read it, apart from the usual totally inadequate one of the book's merits. Yet people did buy it and read it. People said: "This is rather nice!" "*Piracy*" sold. It had absolutely nothing to do with the Spanish Main. If it took life—and perhaps it did take a life or two, socially speaking—it did so, in Mrs. Wharton's words describing the methods of old New York society, "without effusion of blood."

And early this year (1924) there was published a book called *These Charm*— Exactly.

Well, it was so gay, so well-mannered, so witty, so far more than so-so that women of the most varied taste (and even strong prejudices) raved over it, and men of the most invariable taste bought as many as six to a dozen copies to give away to their friends.

The success of Michael Arlen's new novel, *The Green Hat*, has thus been rendered a mere matter of dispersing the good news. It will not do to broadcast it; one must be a little particular in matters of this sort. At the most, it is permitted casually to mention the fact that a new novel by Michael Arlen is about. Quite of course, one cannot decently say more than that *The Green Hat* is a well-polished affair; for still more of course, it isn't the hat but the head beneath it which counts.

The head belongs to Michael Arlen.

(As far as *The Green Hat* goes, the woman of the green hat was Iris March, "enchanting, unshakeably

true in friendship, incorrigibly loose in love," as the
disturbed reviewer for the *London Times* puts it.
"Everything she does has an unnatural elegance and
audacity," he went on.   But what had she done?   She
had broken a good many hearts before marriage and
one afterward; she had turned a lover into a husband
and then into a cynic; and what she did to Napier
Harpenden and his young wife should have been un-
pardonable.   *Should.*   "It is with a sense of having
been cheated that we witness her final whitewashing."
You see how upset he is, though one cannot say he is
outraged, can one, when he talks about a lady like
that? . . .)

ii

Londoners apparently know him as a dark, handsome, suave person who circulates in Mayfair.   Travel-
lers away from London report his presence at the
correct season in Paris, Monte Carlo, and Biskra (not
to mention the Riviera).   He is outwardly one of the
gay rout.   He is inwardly——   Well, I don't know
whether he would want me to mention.

Librarians (some librarians) are relentless persons,
however charming.   They ferret.   They discover
things, and then they root them out.   Or at any rate,
they make Records.   Among other things of which
they make Records are the True Names of Authors.
Was Mr. Tarkington, in infancy, Newton Booth Tarkington?   Then it goes on the librarian's card.   Was
Joseph Conrad born Teodor Jozef Kónrad Kor-
zeniowski?   Then no well-trained librarian ever completely ignores the fact.   An author, in the circumstances, cannot take too much pains to be born and
christened aright.

Occasionally the librarians make a grievous mistake

—as when they identified Rebecca West as Regina Miriam Bloch. Caught in this astounding error, I believe they have now insisted that she is Cecily Fairfield. Yet they must be aware that both in England and America the law permits anyone to change his name at will. If he be consistent in the change, and if he use the new name and induce those who know him to use it, it becomes his lawful name. The sole purpose of going to court about a change of name is to make it a matter of public record—important when the title to property comes up for search. Rebecca West is—simply Rebecca West.

All this is to a point, for already the librarians have rushed to affix to Michael Arlen the name Dikran Kuyumjian. Not only do they tack this name on him, they give it preference. I have before me a clipping from a periodical which is widely relied upon by librarians in making their records and buying their books. And this periodical begins a notice of *These Charming People* as follows:

KUYUMJIAN, DIKRAN (MICHAEL ARLEN, pseud.)

Where they got it, goodness, or rather badness, only knows. I suppose they chanced to learn that Michael Arlen is of Armenian blood. I have nothing to say against Dikran Kuyumjian as an excellent Armenian name. But I imagine Mr. Arlen may have something to say to the founders, editors and reporters of this periodical. I can only hope that, as his English is polite and polished, and as they appear to be versed in a foreign tongue, he will say it in Armenian.

iii

Of course, the fact that he *is* an Armenian lends a joyous piquancy to one of the tales in *These Charming*

[269]

People. You remember the one where Mr. Michael Wagstaffe impersonated greatly? It is called "The Man With the Broken Nose," and as your copy of the book has been borrowed and never returned, I will quote it for you:

"The dark stranger walked silently but firmly. He was a tall young man of slight but powerful build; his nose, which was of the patrician sort, would have been shapely had it not once been broken in such a way that forever after it must noticeably incline to one side; and, though his appearance was that of a gentleman, he carried himself with an air of determination and assurance which would, I thought, make any conversation with him rather a business. There was any amount of back-chat in his dark eyes. His hat, which was soft and had the elegance of the well-worn, he wore cavalierly. Shoes by Lobb.

"At last a picture rose before our eyes, a large picture, very blue. Now who shall describe that picture which was so blue, blue even to the grass under the soldiers' feet, the complexions of the soldiers' faces and the rifles in the soldiers' hands? Over against a blue tree stood a man, and miserably blue was his face, while the soldiers stood very stiffly with their backs to us, holding their rifles in a position which gave one no room to doubt but that they were about to shoot the solitary man for some misdemeanor. He was the loneliest looking man I have ever seen.

" 'Manet,' said Tarlyon.

"The dark young stranger was absorbed; he pulled his hat a little lower over his left eye, so that the light should not obtrude on his vision. . . .

" 'Come on,' I whispered to Tarlyon, for we seemed to be intruding—so that I was quite startled when the stranger suddenly turned from the picture to me.

" 'You see, sir,' he said gravely, 'I know all about killing. I have killed many men. . . .'

" 'Army Service Corps?' inquired Tarlyon.

" 'No, sir,' snapped the stranger. 'I know nothing of your Corps. I am a Zeytounli.'

" 'Please have patience with me,' I begged the stranger. 'What is a Zeytounli?'

"He regarded me with those smoldering dark eyes; and I realized vividly that his nose had been broken in some argument which had cost the other man more than a broken nose.

" 'Zeytoun,' he said, 'is a fortress in Armenia. For five hundred years Zeytoun has not laid down her arms, but now she is burnt stones on the ground. The Zeytounlis, sir, are the hill-men of Armenia. I am an Armenian.'

" 'Oh, I'm so sorry,' Tarlyon murmured.

" 'Why?' snarled the Armenian.

" 'Well, you've been treated pretty badly, haven't you?' said Tarlyon. 'All these massacres and things. . . .'

"The stranger glared at him, and then he laughed at him. I shall remember that laugh. So will Tarlyon. Then the stranger raised a finger and, very gently, he tapped Tarlyon's shoulder.

" 'Listen,' said he. 'Your manner of speaking bores me. Turks have slain many Armenians. Wherefore Armenians have slain many Turks. You may take it from me that, by sticking to it year in and year out for five hundred years, Armenians have in a tactful way slain more Turks than Turks have slain Armenians. That is why I am proud of being an Armenian. And you would oblige me, gentlemen, by informing your countrymen that we have no use for their discarded trousers, which are anyway not so good in quality as they were, but would be grateful for some guns.'

"He left us.

" 'I didn't know,' I murmured, 'that Armenians were like that. I have been misled about Armenians. And he speaks English very well. . . .'

" 'Hum,' said Tarlyon thoughtfully. 'But no one would say he was Armenian if he wasn't, would he?' "

iv

One of the six most famous American men novelists wrote about Michael Arlen a year or so ago, as follows:

"He is one of the phenomena of our time. You may or may not like phenomena"—this seems a little gratuitous. "But anyway, you probably like an original story, so in Michael Arlen's case you can compromise on that. He himself does not compromise on anything, though he did once say that 'discretion is the better part of literature.' Since then, however, his novel, 'Piracy,' in which half London society figures, has run into many editions. The other half is no doubt wondering what he will say next.

"Michael Arlen is 25 years old; and, having served the usual terms at an English public school and University he is, so he says, entirely self-educated. There was also a war. And yet, though no human eye has ever seen him at work, he has written four successful books.

"The first, which he published at the age of twenty, was his memoirs and confessions, for he thought that he would be done with them at the beginning. Many people thought that the book, *A London Venture*, was by George Moore under a pseudonym; some papers

Photograph by Maurice Beck and Helen Macgregor, London.

MICHAEL ARLEN

A VIEW OF MICHAEL ARLEN

stated the fact with authority. Since then he has
been more frequently compared to Guy de Maupassant.

"Michael Arlen believes in working hard and living
hard. He lives in Mayfair. Most of the summer he
spends between Deauville and Biarritz, and most of
the winter he may be found on the Riviera. The
spring he spends in Venice. He also likes dancing and
baccarat, and is a tournament tennis player.

"It is his considered opinion that if one had no
enemies one would have no time to do any writing at
all. So he has collected quite a number, whom he
embitters by the amount of good work he does, while
he amuses himself and his friends by never appearing
to do any at all. That is, of course, a pose; but it is
not a pose that everyone has the ability to wear. Try
it and see.

"The New Statesman has called him 'the romantic
comedian of our time'; adding that he has no present
equal in 'the *dandysme* of the soul.' While the Daily
Telegraph has said of him: 'He concerns himself
with people who are bored to death unless they are in
some sort of mischief. The ladies carry their frailty
as the gentlemen carry their drink—like gentlemen.
Michael Arlen writes with the truculence of a Mohawk
and the suavity of a Beau Nash. . . .'

"This young man is among the last of those who
believe that manners are worth while as manners. The
chivalry of daily life is to him the king of indoor
sports. And he has written that 'a gentleman is a
man who is never *unintentionally* rude to anyone.' " [1]

Now who is the famous American novelist who
could have written thus and thus of Mr. Arlen? Tell

[1] Yes, in *These Charming People;* but it is a remarkable coincidence
that the identical *mot* appeared conspicuously in Donald Ogden
Stewart's *Perfect Behavior,* published in America in autumn, 1922.
(*These Charming People* appeared in England in early summer, 1923.)

it not in Gath; publish it not in Main Street, Ascalon. We are not allowed to reveal his chaste identity. If he had an Armenian name, perhaps. . . .

As a matter of fact, Michael Arlen was born in a Bulgarian village on the Danube. When he was five years old his parents decided to move to England. After he had been at an English public school the usual term of years he went to Switzerland to learn English. He was then seventeen. After he had been seventeen for some months, his parents called him back to Manchester, where they lived. He got as far as London. His parents then abandoned him with rather less than the customary shilling. He started to write. His first book, *A London Venture*, was a book of confessions, as at eighteen he had nothing else to write about. His confessions confessed little except poverty and loneliness.

He was foreign, young, careless of literary cliques, stayed up dancing all night and worked all day. London got to hear about him. He got a name in Fleet Street by never going to see an editor in his office. Michael Arlen always asked the editor to come outside and face him over a cocktail.

The Romantic Lady arrived, greatly disappointing the publishers, as she was a book of short stories. Arlen said she would get on and she did, in moderation.

"*Piracy*" was perhaps the book of a young man who had lived hard and fought hard, with his tailors. It enabled him to pay them; but it was Arlen's opinion that he had not yet begun to write. In an interview he said that so far he had been playing scales in public. *These Charming People* came on, but the author was writing his big novel, *The Dark Angel*, and gave little heed to anything else. *The Dark Angel* took him a year. He destroyed it. He realized that

[274]

it was not the advance on *"Piracy"* which he and the most intelligent part of his public expected. *The Green Hat* more nearly satisfies him.

V

But already there is a word minted. *"These Charming People,"* observes Mr. Philip Page, in some nondescript London newspaper cutting, "is very Arlenesque." Mr. Page preferred it to *"Piracy"*—and it is indeed better work—although he missed the fun which *"Piracy"* afforded "of celebrity spotting, and the satisfaction of being able to say to myself, with a glowing feeling of being in the swim: 'Here is Lady Diana Cooper!' or 'Here is Mr. Eddie Marsh!' " It is to be feared that most Americans cannot have Mr. Page's warm sensation of culture, but in our uncultured way it is quite possible for us to enjoy such a portrait as the following, from *"Piracy"*—for we have him in America, too:

"The poetry Pretty Leyton discovered was often good, for his was a delicate and conservative taste; but it would have been easier to appreciate the good if one could only have discovered it among the bad, for his was also a delicate and kindly nature. While as for the young poets, of whom many called and all were chosen, he was continually begging his women friends, particularly Lois and Virginia, not to be *'too* cruel' to them, for they were so sensitive and worthwhile. To see and speak to Pretty Leyton in a crowded room was really very comforting, sometimes —which was just as well, since he was always in every room that happened to be crowded, saying: 'Isn't it a marvellous party?' He gave all his women friends beautifully bound copies of *Tristram Shandy*, which he said was *the only* book."

And now—what shall I say? I could quote the processional of admiring, envious and rapturous adjectives applied to Mr. Arlen's work. I could quote other notes of his fashionable progress as a person as well as a writer; but it would be repetitious. Besides, you will prefer to form your own adjectives and perfect your own legend; which is right and proper, and ever so charming of you. Kindly note that the correct name and address is Mr. Michael Arlen, 14, Queen Street, Mayfair, London, W. 1. Ask to be put through to Grosvenor 2275. But only in the Season, only in the Season.

BOOKS BY MICHAEL ARLEN

1920   *A London Venture*
1921   *The Romantic Lady*
1923   *"Piracy": A Romantic Chronicle of These Days*
1924   *These Charming People*
1924   *The Green Hat: A Romance for a Few People*

SOURCES ON MICHAEL ARLEN

Review of *These Charming People* by Arthur Waugh in the Daily Telegraph, London, for 6 July 1923.

Curtis Brown, Curtis Brown Ltd., 6, Henrietta Street, Covent Garden, London, W. C. 2.

17. Palettes and Patterns in Prose and Poetry

i

WAS it Emerson who said of the poems by Emily Dickinson that they were "poetry pulled up by the roots, with the earth and dew clinging to them"? I can't be sure, for someone has culpably made off with my copy of Thomas Bailey Aldrich's *Ponkapog Papers*, in which there is a pleasant essay on Emily Dickinson. Aldrich, of course, said in his meticulous way that poetry should not be pulled up by the roots; but modern feeling does not agree with him, holding the bit of earth and the sparkle of dewy freshness evidence incontrovertible that the flower is authentic and not mere paper or wax. Emily Dickinson lived from 1830 to 1886, a recluse who in her lifetime wrote over 600 poems, hardly any of which were published until after her death. And then?

Ah, but the estimation in which she is held, and a sequence of fame, steadily grows. Almost forty years after her death, she is more read and more delighted in than ever. "A mystic akin only to Emerson," W. P. Dawson, the English critic, says in his own anthology. "Among American poets I have named two—Poe and Emily Dickinson." And a reviewer for the London Spectator said not long ago: "Mr. Conrad Aiken in his recent anthology of American poets calls Emily Dickinson's poetry 'perhaps the finest by a woman in the English language.' I quarrel only with his 'perhaps.'"

Splendid news, therefore, that we now have a new one-volume edition of her work! *The Complete Poems of Emily Dickinson* contains all the verse which appeared in *Poems, First Series*, in *Poems, Second Series*, and in *Poems, Third Series*, and also those in the book brought out as recently as 1914, *The Single Hound*. The total body of Emily Dickinson's work is therefore presented, and all in a new and proper arrangement, making the edition definitive. Emily Dickinson's niece and biographer, Martha Dickinson Bianchi, has written an introduction for the work.

Having begun, in spontaneity and pleasure, with poetry, let us stick to it a while. Here are three more volumes by women poets, sisters, the Brontës, no less. Clement K. Shorter has edited them and C. W. Hatfield has provided the bibliographies and notes. They are *The Complete Poems—of Charlotte Brontë, of Anne Brontë, of Emily Jane Brontë*, respectively. Each is a first complete collection, and each contains a large percentage of poems never before published. I need not say anything of the romance investing the lives of these three women. Shut in a lonely parsonage in bleak moorland country, haunted by ill health and destined to die young, they made their lives one of the most extraordinary adventures in the history of the literary spirit. Their verse, of course, shows the Byronic influence.

The indefatigable J. C. Squire has been busy compiling an *A Book of American Verse* with ingratiating results. Himself a poet, an editor who selects new verse and a critic, Mr. Squire has ranged over the whole field of American literature from its beginnings and has been at once personal and catholic in his inclusions. His most recent collection of his own work, *Essays on Poetry*, includes short papers on Matthew

Arnold, Thomas Hardy, A. E. Housman, W. B. Yeats, and some others.

Walter de la Mare: A Biographical and Critical Study, by R. L. Mégroz, is the first book devoted to the life and writings of this poet and prose writer of such marked distinction. Mr. Mégroz says that the purpose of his volume is "to show the poet of dream in a human light and in relation to the rest of society." It is difficult to think of a living writer of more interest for such a study than the author of the *Memoirs of a Midget*, the close friend of Rupert Brooke, and the poet of happiest childhood as well as of soberly reflective and tranquil age. Mr. Mégroz's book has the charm of its subject, and more.

One need not be a professor or scholar in the technical sense to write a good book on English literature, and the proof of it, if a fresh one be needed, is T. Earle Welby's *A Popular History of English Poetry*. Mr. Welby is an amateur, unless his amateur standing may have been impaired by his articles in the London Saturday Review and his other book, a critical study of Swinburne. *A Popular History of English Poetry* is said to be the only one-volume book of its sort, but whether it is or not, it is remarkably welcome. Its survey runs from Chaucer (there is even a prefatory chapter on pre-Chaucer) to Meredith and Hardy and Masefield and de la Mare. And it deserves the adjective in front of the word "History" in its title. Anyone who knows or cares about poetry at all can read with delighted ease and will learn something in every chapter. Mr. Welby has both a fertile knowledge and a light touch. His judgments are neither vague characterizations nor conventional utterances; he has taste and he has an opinion, and he gives you each.

ii

To leave the poets for the moment but to keep in the
sense of an exquisite color and form: *Echo de Paris*,
by Laurence Housman, is a bit of severely ornamented
reminiscence which I think of first when now I think
of decorative prose—not so much because of its own
brief perfection as because of its subject. Oscar
Wilde's influence is not a negligible thing in a contemporary literature which embraces Cabell, Hergesheimer, Elinor Wylie, Carl Van Vechten, and others,
both American and English, who value words somewhat as James Huneker valued them, for their sound,
shape, smell and taste. I take from the London Times
a description of *Echo de Paris:*

"At the end of September, 1899, three friends are
sitting in a café near the Place de l'Opera. They are
awaiting a guest for luncheon, and from their amicable
chatter we learn that it is Wilde who is expected.
Presently he appears, and while they take their aperi-
tifs holds his audience with that marvelous conversation which long before had made him legendary. It
is substantially the record of an actual conversation,
Mr. Housman tells us, for he was the host on this
occasion. Apart from the actuality of the setting, he
has imagined a dramatic incident which he believes,
though symbolical, will represent the existing emotional situation. As Wilde talks, with an apparent
indifference to his personal disaster, another man is
seen coming along the street. He advances toward the
group, all of whom he knows well, especially Wilde,
who befriended him before his imprisonment, but,
after clearly recognizing them, passes on without a
sign. Wilde continues to weave his unwritten stories;
but he has been deeply hurt and gracefully disentangles

himself from a luncheon which, faced with the spectators of his pain, would have been more than even he could bear.

"The difficulty of producing a reasonable imitation of Wilde's conversation has been overcome so successfully that we sometimes feel that one of his essays is being read by one of the characters in his comedies— there is that combination of verbal wit and bold intellectual paradox. In these pages we are made to feel something of the reality on which his reputation was built."

Judges so diverse as Sinclair Lewis, James Branch Cabell, and Carl Van Vechten have uttered words of extreme praise for Elinor Wylie's *Jennifer Lorn*. I don't know of a recent work before which one feels an equal impotence of the descriptive faculty. This novel of an eighteenth century exquisite and his bride is as brightly enameled as the period it deals with; every paragraph is lacquered. You have perhaps stood long before some Eastern carpet with old rose, cream, ivory and dark blue in enigmatical patterns, your eye delighting in its intricacy. Have you tried afterward to tell someone about it? Then, precisely, you know the difficulty of reporting *Jennifer Lorn*. It is worth noting, though, that the novel does not merely purvey an eighteenth century story; it seeks to purvey it, with delicate, inner irony in the eighteenth century manner. The adroit printing and binding in simulation of an eighteenth century format was inevitable, perhaps; but it was not so inevitable that it should be so delightfully well-done.

An autobiography would seem to belong in Chapter 12 of this book; I saved out Thomas Burke's autobiographical volume because the spirit of it, and the color of his writing, seemed to place it here. He calls

it *The Wind and the Rain;* it is the most intimate book
he has ever written, and the best since *Limehouse
Nights* (from some standpoints it is better than that
work). In *The Wind and the Rain*, Thomas Burke
returns to Limehouse, telling of his boyhood and
youth, of the squalor of his early years, of the loneliness and hunger of his City days, of the moments of
spiritual exaltation that came to him at night in
London streets. He recalls his friendship with old
Quong Lee, a storekeeper in the Causeway; his one-
room house with an Uncle; his adventures in the
kitchen of the Big House at Greenwich where his
Uncle worked; his rapturous hours in the street; his
four wretched years in an orphanage; his running
away and being sheltered by the queer woman in the
queer house; his first job; his friendship with a girl
of thirteen and its abrupt end; his discovery of literature and pictures and music; his first short story accepted when he was still an office-boy; and then his
first success. This somewhat long recitation speaks
for itself and will kindle the imagination of anyone
who ever read Thomas Burke or saw Griffith's film,
"Broken Blossoms."

Hugh Walpole's critical study of *Anthony Trollope*
is welcome both because a good account of Trollope is
needed and because Walpole's own work used to be
likened to that of the author of *Barchester Towers.*
I believe the comparison is pretty well obsolete—Mr.
Walpole is now rather the object than the subject of
comparisons—but those who know Walpole best have
long known of his very definite interest in Trollope
and his gradual acquisition of materials for a survey of
Trollope's work. The *Anthony Trollope* by Walpole
is a book to set beside Frank Swinnerton's *Gissing* and
R. L. Stevenson; we have a right to hope that the

[282]

fashion will spread among the novelists; and I should like nothing better than to record a similar book by Arnold Bennett, even if, as is very probable, he would consent to do one only on a French subject—in which case he would probably select Stendhal.

But this leads directly to the whole subject of literary discussions. It is too big to deal with here, and yet I can't drop it without some reference to the two most provocative books of the sort in recent memory. Dr. Joseph Collins is a well-known New York neurologist whose literary hobby has been cultivated in private during a number of years. It was the rich pungency of his conversation which first led to insistences that he write a book about authors. He did. *The Doctor Looks at Literature*, with its praise of Proust and its incisiveness regarding D. H. Lawrence, its appreciation of Katherine Mansfield and its penetrating study of James Joyce, was something new, sparkling, resonant and simply not to be missed. Dr. Collins's second book, *Taking the Literary Pulse*, is as strongly brewed and as well-flavored. I find it even more interesting because it deals to a much greater extent with American writers—Sherwood Anderson, Edith Wharton, Amy Lowell and others—and because of the uncompromised utterance in the first chapter on literary censorship, a subject which most discussion merely muddles.

iii

Of collections of essays, I have no hesitation in putting first the anthology by F. H. Pritchard, *Essays of To-Day*. Not only are the inclusions amply representative of the best work by contemporary English essayists, but to my mind Mr. Pritchard has supplied, in his Introduction, one of the most inspiring essays of the lot. He writes, naturally, about the essay as a form of art, and shows quite simply how the essay and the lyric poem are "the most intimate revelations of personality that we have in literature." His wisdom is equaled by a power of expression which can best be intimated by quoting a few of his words regarding the lyric:

"Ordered by the strict limitations of rhythm, and obedient to the recurrences of rime and meter, the unruly ideas are fashioned into a lyric, just as scattered particles, straying here and there, are drawn together and fused into crystalline beauty. The difference, indeed, is one of temperature"—the difference between lyric and essay. "The metal bar, cold or lukewarm, will do anywhere, but heat it to melting-point and you must confine it within the rigid limits of the mold or see it at length but an amorphous splash at your feet."

Then follow thirty-four selections, each prefaced by a short biographical note on its author. Youth and old age, reminiscences, the spirit of place and of holiday, and various interrelations between life and letters are the subjects. Kenneth Grahame, Joseph Conrad, Maurice Hewlett, E. V. Lucas, Robert Lynd, W. B. Yeats, Hilaire Belloc, Rupert Brooke, C. E. Montague, E. Temple Thurston, Alice Meynell, George Santayana, Gilbert K. Chesterton and Edmund Gosse are some of the writers who achieve inclusion; and the variety of the essays is great—irony, humor, romantic feeling, delight in places and sadness all have their moment.

Such a collection, one feels, cannot but lead the reader to books by some of the authors represented; and I hope such readers will not miss Robert Lynd's *The Blue Lion*. Here are some chapters dealing apparently with children, birds, flowers, taverns and the like, but animated by that interest in, sympathy for and appreciation of human nature which is the field of the essay's most fertile cultivation.

It is, to a great extent, the field which Robert Cortes Holliday has occupied himself with since the day of his *Walking-Stick Papers;* and while the title of his new book is *Literary Lanes and Other Byways*, the "other byways" are frequently the most engaging to tread. Mr. Holliday, for example, has been interviewing the ancient waiters on the subject of the golden years at a lost Delmonico's; and he has also become an authority on nightwear. But there is plenty of contact between life and literature in *Literary Lanes*. One essay is devoted to the subject of the vamp in literature; another to books as presents; another harvests *bons mots* from the inner circles of celebrated wits; "and," as Mr. Holliday would say, "and so on."

Stephen McKenna's *By Intervention of Providence* is a felicitous blend of diary, essay and short story, written by this novelist during an extended visit to the West Indies. The atmosphere of the West India islands is conveyed with some care, while the digressions to the essay or the short story are anecdotal, philosophical, and frequently humorous. "From day to day," Mr. McKenna explains, "I set down whatever fancy tempted me to write. The result can only be called 'Essays' in the Johnsonian sense of that word. I desire no more accurate definition of what is in part a series of letters, in part a journal, in part vagrant reminiscences, in part idle reflection, in part stories which I do not ask the reader to believe." But the potpourri, however unusual, will be welcomed alike by the traveler and the arm-chair tourist.

iv

The return to poetry must not be deferred longer. And first let me speak of John Farrar's book of verse, *The Middle Twenties*, which is more than usually interesting because it is the first collection of his serious work in a half dozen years. There has been none since his book, *Forgotten Shrines*. I do not forget *Songs for Parents*, but that is somewhat of a piece with his book of plays for children, *The Magic Sea Shell*, and it is likely it would continue popular for this reason alone. His work as an editor and an anthologist, with many other activities, have tended to obscure Farrar the poet, and have certainly taken time and energy the poet could ill spare. But I know that much of the hardest work Mr. Farrar has done these past few years has been upon the verse in *The Middle Twenties*. The result ought to satisfy him, though probably it won't; he is not easily pleased with his own work. But all the poems in *The Middle Twenties* keep to a high level and the volume has more than variety, it has positive and effective contrast. Whether he is most successful in the "Amaryllis" group, gay and rollicking, or in the savage pain and passion of "The Squaw" is for the reader's own decision. But from the flaming "Ego," the opening poem, to the fine understanding of such work as "War Women" the book affords a range of subject, treatment, and emotional feeling which leaves no reader indifferent.

Nellie Burget Miller's *In Earthen Bowls* explains its title in these lines which open the book:

So here we have our treasure in an earthen bowl,
Distorted, marred, and set to common use:
And some will never see beyond the form of clay,

[286]

And some will stoop to peer within and softly say,
"There is a wondrous radiance prisoned there,
And I heard the stir of an angel's wing."

Such a volume makes its candid appeal to the audience—very large—which asks insistently for poems of a simple sincerity and a direct relation to daily lives. Their lives are the earthen bowls in which they want to be able to see the suggestion of something radiant and feel the stir of something divine. In the fifty-seven poems in her book, Mrs. Miller has not tried to build an imaginary world, but has appealed to the love of nature, and to the feelings of happiness and grief, for her lyrical expression. The evidence of her success has been recorded in several ways. She has, for one thing, been made the chairman of the literary division of the National Federation of Women's Clubs. She has also been chosen poet laureate of her State, Colorado.

Essentially the same qualities of mood and appeal characterize Martha Haskell Clark's book, *The Home Road*. Mrs. Clark has been a contributor of verse to Harper's and Scribner's magazines and to several of the enormously popular women's magazines, so-called. Her poems are concerned, as her title indicates, chiefly with the longing, often wistful and sometimes delightful, for an old home or fireside, old friends and holidays and memories. The language is as simple as the feeling. Curtis Hidden Page, professor of English at Dartmouth and compiler of *English Poets of the Nineteenth Century*, writes the preface to *The Home Road*.

Here is an anthology of recitations! Grace Gaige's *Recitations—Old and New for Boys and Girls* seems to me of more than ordinary interest, because the author is the buyer of books for one of the largest

[287]

stores in the world. It is a store of so widespread
a reputation that one thinks of it as constantly creating book readers from the mere fact of its having
a book department. And certainly Miss Gaige is in
an unequaled position to know what, in the way of a
book, people want. Well, she does. And having
found no present-day book that quite met the problem,
she has made one. Her *Recitations—Old and New
for Boys and Girls* has a foreword by Christopher
Morley and contains poems dealing with every imaginable subject. They are divided into sections in a
natural grouping: poems about and for children, poems
about fairies, about birds and other animals, about
flowers and seasons; humorous poems, patriotic poems,
holiday poems—I can't remember them all. But
despite the classification, the range is so great that
over 200 poems had to go under "Miscellaneous."
You are sure to find it there, if nowhere else!

How were they chosen? With just three things in
mind, (1) their interest, (2) their proved popularity,
and (3) their special fitness for recitation. The triple
crown of the collection is the threefold index, of authors, of titles, and of first lines. And although people want poems for recitation, and though these poems
are for recitation, there is nothing to debar this mam-
moth anthology as a book for reading. As such, it will
be found a work of the utmost satisfaction.

A book that particularly deserves inclusion in this
chapter is the new illustrated edition of Jay William
Hudson's novel, *Abbé Pierre*. The great success of
this charming story is of the kind that goes steadily on,
year after year; and while our present-day taste is
rather against the illustration of novels, a book of this
character (like *David Harum*) can be greatly enhanced by the right pictures. Mr. Hudson has got

exactly the thing, I think, in the sixteen pencil drawings and the endpapers by Mr. Edwin Avery Park. This artist will also become familiar to readers by his work in collaboration with Maitland Belknap in *Princeton Sketches*. Mr. Park traveled in the parts of France where the scenes of *Abbé Pierre* are laid and has caught both the spirit and character of place and tale. His drawings have been rather carefully reproduced as half-tones, and with other details of the book's new dress, make a volume of a sort in entire keeping with the novel's quality.

18. Coming!—Courtney Ryley Cooper
—Coming!

i

WHAT I need at the moment is not a chapter but a billboard on which to paste with great splashy gestures a three-sheet announcement: "Coming!—The Literary Lochinvar—Coming!" Both words and pictures—yes, and muted notes from the steam calliope—are requisite to herald adequately the author of *Under the Big Top*. If I tell the story of Courtney Ryley Cooper, fiction, even his own fiction, will seem colorless beside it. Therefore read no further. The lights are off and a beam flung from the projection room high overhead shows us——

Scene. Large white canvas mushrooms growing closely together and obviously attracting swarms of the human ant. Animals in gaudy cages, the living skeleton, lemonade, spangles and paper hoops. Close-up. Fifteen-year-old boy, at once timid and bold, interviewing the master of destinies. Caption: "Boy, water the elephants!"

Scene. Amphitheatre within the largest of the tents. Several thousand faces that are all one face and that have even less significance than one face and that emit a crackling, collective sound. Clowns, masked by perpetually surprised looks painted on noses, mouths and eyebrows, in ballooning white costumes, rolling and tumbling about the arena. Thwack! Close-up.

[290]

Fifteen-year-old ecstatic over the time of his life, working hard. Caption: "Spare the slap-stick and spoil the child."

Scene. Office of the Denver Post, twelve years later. Enter Buffalo Bill, white hair pigtailed and everything. He strides up to the city editor. Caption: "Whar's that reporter fellow——"

Flash. "Film not broken, but we have just been informed that all motion picture rights in the career of Courtney Ryley Cooper are reserved to Mr. Cooper. Please keep your seats."

ii

He was born in Kansas City, Missouri, 31 October 1886, the son of Baltimore Thomas Cooper and Catherine (Grenolds) Cooper. He is a descendant of the Calverts, Lords of Baltimore, and of other settlers of Maryland and Virginia. He ran away from school in Kansas City to become water-boy and clown in a circus. He also became an actor, bill distributor, property man and song and dance artist with bad repertory companies playing "East Lynne," "In Old Kentucky," "The James Boys in Missouri" and other classics of the road.

He has been a newsboy, a trucker, a glove salesman, a monologist in vaudeville, a circus press agent, a newspaper man, and general manager of the world's second largest circus.

He began writing at 24, a play, "the world's worst play," he says. It was produced in Kansas City "and I had to sit and watch the darned thing for two weeks." Then he began to write magazine stories. So great has been his output that at least five pen names have been necessary. They are Barney Furey, William O. Grenolds, Jack Harlow, Frederick Tierney and Leonard B. Hollister. He has written as much as 45,000 words of fiction in three days—or days and nights. As a newspaper man he has written eight columns (1,200 words to the column) in two hours. For such excesses he naturally pays in an inability to walk, eat or sleep for some immediate time afterward. It might be supposed that the work so turned out would be mere machine-made stuff, but this is not true. However, the ability to write at such speed has necessitated a small staff to gather the writer's material.

There are several reasons why Mr. Cooper could never gather it all himself. He married, in 1916, Genevieve R. Furey, of Los Angeles, and they have a pleasant home in Idaho Springs, Colorado. Mr. Cooper gets his recreation in the mountains round about. But the stuff for the hundreds of stories he has written of circus life and jungle animal life cannot be renewed except from elsewhere. It cannot be renewed and added to sufficiently except—almost literally—from everywhere. After all, Mr. Cooper has contributed stories to more than half a hundred magazines. And if he were to stop writing to gather material——!

"I have a little circus all my own," he explains. He knows nearly everything that is happening in all the big shows. He keeps up an uninterrupted correspondence with circus people and he has five persons on his payroll at all times. One is a man who makes a specialty of circus pictures. Another is a lion trainer who has trained as many as thirty lions in one den. Whenever he has some unusual incident of animal behavior to report, he writes to Cooper. A third member of the little staff is an all-round animal man, menagerie superintendent and "bullman." A fourth is a highly educated woman with ten years' experience in training lions, tigers, leopards and elephants. Mr. Cooper pays her a salary and she takes "assignments," just as if she were a reporter—which, in fact, she is in this work. She is a reporter on animals, their training, and their characteristics. The fifth employee is a circus clown who sends a regular monthly letter reporting things that happen under the big top.

There is, besides, a large number of volunteer correspondents, friends of long standing.

Mr. Cooper has used his material both directly, in the form of articles, and in stories. While he was on his way from clown to general manager of the circus, he became deeply interested in jungle animals and discovered a great many human traits (or traits parallel, if you prefer) in them. He himself, it must be remembered, has been in the training dens with leopards, lions, tigers and pumas; and he has been in with as many as six lions and tigers at one time.

He looks, in certain poses, remarkably like Eric von Stroheim, and the camera sometimes brings out the multitude of his freckles. He is bald and enjoys baldness. Better company is not to be had, and this is only partly due to the innumerable anecdotes at his command. Many of these grow out of his association with Buffalo Bill, whose personal secretary he was for a while and whose biographer (with Buffalo Bill's widow, Mrs. W. F. Cody) he became. There is, for example, the story of the time when Cooper contracted with a clipping bureau for newspaper notices. They were to be ten cents each. They arrived —a bale—and with them a bill for $134.90. With a single exception, they consisted of 1,348 clippings about the Buffalo baseball team, which was much to the fore owing to the temporary existence of the Federal League.

Cooper also told this story at a Dutch Treat Club luncheon in New York:

"Colonel Cody arrived home unexpectedly early one morning. Going to his wife's bedroom window he tapped on the glass, calling: 'It's all right; let me in.' 'Go away,' said Mrs. Cody. 'This is Buffalo Bill's house, and I'm his wife, and I can shoot, too.' Buffalo Bill, sore, remounted his horse and rode off to a neighboring saloon. Eventually he returned home, galloping up the driveway and on to the veranda of the house, letting out whoops the while. As he reached the door a gentle voice greeted him from behind it: 'Is that you, Willie dear?' "

iii

In 1918 Mr. Cooper enlisted as a private in the United States Marines. Very shortly he was commissioned as a second lieutenant and sent to France to collate historical matter for the Marine Corps.

He has a very exceptional talent for handling people in masses, and has sometimes been requisitioned by motion picture people and others who had spectacles to produce. As the talent is coupled with a talent for creative organization at least equal, the life of a writer represents a deliberate sacrifice of money on Cooper's part. For example:

Wild West shows, rodeos and bucking horse contests are one of his hobbies. A few years ago he ran the first Annual Round-up at Colorado Springs. In three days the show took in $19,800 gate money. And the whole show, from the announcement, building of grandstands to seat 8,000 persons, hiring of cowboys, wild horses, bucking broncos, steers for bulldogging, advertising and everything else, was put on in less than three weeks. Overtures piled in on Cooper to go into the business in other places. In the end, he refused contracts for $150,000 for two years' work.

iv

His books have been of two principal kinds, novels of the West and the two volumes, *Under the Big Top* and *Lions 'n' Tigers 'n' Everything!* that spring from the circus. The novels are *The Cross-Cut, The White Desert,* and *The Last Frontier,* in that order. Are they simply the usual "Westerns"? No. There is in *The Cross-Cut* that quality of humor, that enjoyment of a capital hoax, which first cut out from the stampeding herd of Western stories Owen Wister's *The Virginian.* Almost everyone, recalling Mr. Wister's novel, thinks of the opening scene in which the cowboys, like Little Buttercup in Mr. Gilbert's "Pinafore," "mixed those babies up." That affair, so refreshingly different in its realism and sense of scandalous fun from the sentimental heroics of other Western tales, is easily recalled when most other incidents of *The Virginian* are forgotten. Similarly one recalls with fresh amusement the ruse whereby 'Arry 'Arkins got the Blue Poppy mine unwatered. Messrs. Fairchild and 'Arkins had very little capital; but by a convincing effect of drowning in the mine, the whole community was stirred to rescue the presumed corpse of 'Arkins; machinery that the two men could not have hired was set to work pumping, and by the time the hoax was revealed, the mine was dry.

The White Desert has nothing to do with sand and alkali but is a story of the bleak, white stretches of the Continental Divide, where the world is a world of precipices, blue-green ice, and snow-spray carried on the beating wings of never-resting gales. It is the tale of a lumber camp and of a highly dramatic, last ditch struggle. Mr. Cooper admits that the first chapters were from an experience of his own. On the Berthoud Pass, 11,300 feet high, his speedster broke down. Now safety speed on the roads thereabouts is possibly fifteen miles an hour. The grades sometimes run as high as eighteen and twenty per cent. With no windshield, no gears to aid his brakes, no goggles and a sprained steering gear, Mr. Cooper was towed on these mountain roads by a largely liquored gentleman in a truck at a speed of twenty-five miles an hour. Mr. Cooper was bald before this happened. . . .

Essentially, *The Cross-Cut* and *The White Desert* are stories; *The Last Frontier*, with no sacrifice of story interest, can stake a claim of more importance. Like certain novels of Emerson Hough's [1] and Hal G. Evarts's, this is an accurate and alive presentation of American history in the guise of fiction. The period is 1867-68 when, as an aftermath of the Civil War, many impoverished families sought the unsettled frontier lands. The Kansas-Pacific Railway, a link between East and West, was under construction, its every mile contested by the Indians. It was the period when Buffalo Bill made his reputation as a buffalo hunter and Indian scout; when General Custer nearly wore himself out hunting Indians; when the Battle of Beecher's Island aroused the nation. Buffalo Bill, Custer, and the building of the railroad are the true subjects of this fine romance which ends when the great stampede has failed. "The buffalo were gone. Likewise the feathered beings who had striven to use them as a bulwark and had failed—enfiladed by

[1] See Chapter 14.

scouts, volleyed by cavalry, their bodies were strewn in the valley with the carcasses of the buffalo." Within months Custer was to come back, and in triumph. The "golden-haired general" was to ride to the battle of Washita "at the head of the greatest army of troops ever sent against the red man. . . . There would be other frontiers—true. But they would be sectional things, not keystones, such as this had been."

These novels, in their order, mark a growth in the writer's stature; and Mr. Cooper, like others who show growth, has humility as well as ambition. The thing he has in mind to do, possibly in his next novel, is more difficult than anything he has done—an attempt to take a few contemporary lives and view them in the perspective that history affords. This, of course, is very hard to do. Certainly Sinclair Lewis did not do it in *Main Street*, and no amount of exact, faithful, realistic detail accomplishes it. It can only be done by simplifying one's material so that a few humble people are seen as typifying human endeavor. But if the effort is successful, the result will mean as much in one century as in another, and the work will live.

v

Mr. Cooper's two books based on the circus accomplish something that no one else, so far as I know, has even attempted. They make a permanent and fascinating record of a truly American institution. *Under the Big Top* presents the circus as a whole, although five of the eleven chapters are concerned with the circus animals. *Lions 'n' Tigers 'n' Everything* is wholly about the menagerie.

The first of these books is a curious illustration of

the breach ordinarily existing between literature and life. Although, in the complexities of a surface civilization, the circus may hold less significance for Americans today than fifty or forty or even twenty years ago, most of us were brought up to go to the circus. Or, at any rate, went. The formative influence of the circus on American character is incalculably great. Yet neither literature nor formal education took any cognizance of the circus tent. Public officials, as Mr. Cooper points out, very generally took into consideration the educational value of circus animals when fixing license fees. But that was about all the notice of value the circus got. Where were books on the circus? When was the circus reckoned with by the professional analysts of American character? How far has present-day American advertising acknowledged its immense debt to the traveling show? What Matthew Arnold or James Bryce coming to our shores to examine American character and lacking, possibly, the wisdom of the serpent acquired the wisdom of the circus? And our psychologists busied with delicate tests on the nerve-endings of frogs; were they dumb-bells so long? They were. They went not to the circus, the sluggards; they examined not its ways.

Yet it would be true to say that the circus is the one most typical American institution. Between the American circus and the traveling shows of other lands no comparison is possible. In size, in variety, in achievements of audacity, devotion and courage, the American big tent show has no rival. It is, to begin with, playing around in a country which is to most other countries as a ten-acre field is to a city lot. Its self-reliance must be complete. Its morale, especially in the days of its greatest importance, has had to be high and unwavering; for otherwise-excellent people have been its unrelenting foes. At the same time the circus has been something much more than a spectacle; frequently it has been a coöperative enterprise. Mr. Cooper gives some idea of the innumerable occasions on which the American small boy, judiciously and fairly rewarded with a free ticket, has pulled the circus out of some insuperable physical difficulty. The circus was the original discoverer of the most important element in American psychology, the love of bigness and display, the admiration for achievement in size. It was the circus which first put in firm practice the important principle of human nature which time merely refines upon: the desire to be bunked: and the circus drew the correct line between bunk and bunco and with the fewest exceptions steered clear of bunco.

Now in *Under the Big Top*, Mr. Cooper, who natually knows circuses, gayly gives the whole show away—a process which a good show can come out of with colors flying. And the circus does. The gist of the book, the real why of the circus, will be found in that rousing final chapter written upon the text:

RAIN OR SHINE
THE WORLD'S GREATEST SHOW
WILL POSITIVELY APPEAR

Here are stories of that ultimate sheer persistence which is the spirit of the circus and, pretty nearly, the history of the nation to which it belongs.

vi

The chapters on animals in *Under the Big Top* led directly to Mr. Cooper's *Lions 'n' Tigers 'n' Everything*, which is the menagerie inside out. In the course of long study of caged and captive jungle creatures, and aided by the continuous study of his staff-helpers, Mr. Cooper has found no human emotion which these animals do not exhibit at some time or other in appropriate circumstances. "I have seen jealousy, insanity, hallucination, the highest kind of love including mother love, the fiercest brand of hate, trickery, cunning and revenge. I have seen gratitude. The only desire I will exclude as not being common to humans and animals is the desire for money. There is a corresponding animal desire, however. It is horse meat. Horse meat is the currency of the animal kingdom." [2]

The extraordinary instance of Casey, a giant, black-faced chimpanzee [3] captured in infancy in the Cape Lopez district of Africa, has suggested to Mr. Cooper that something most remarkably approaching a man could be bred from a monkey in as few as four generations. Not a physical likeness, but mental, is the prospect. Enough apes of Casey's type would be necessary to avoid inbreeding, and the first generation born in captivity would have to be subjected to wholly human contacts. [4] About 150 years would be required for the experiment.

But *Lions 'n' Tigers 'n' Everything* is a book of fact, not of theories. It is most valuable, perhaps, in its contrast between the old and new methods of an-

[2] "Animals Love, Hate and Become Angry, Just Like Human Beings, Says Expert." Interview by Jane Dixon in The Evening Telegram, New York, 23 January 1922.
[3] W. T. Hornaday, curator of the New York Zoölogical Gardens, is quoted in *Lions 'n' Tigers 'n' Everything* as saying: "Casey was a mystery. I am frank to say that I could not put my finger on his exact classification. Of course, he was an ape. But just what kind—that is the question."
[4] "He'd Make a Man of a Monkey—and in Four Generations." Feature article in The Gazette Times, Pittsburgh, Pennsylvania, 7 May 1922.

imal training. Mr. Cooper shows in the first chapter the transformation that has come about:

"The circus animal trainer of today is not chosen for his brutality, or his cunning, or his so-called bravery. He is hired because he has studied and knows animals—even to talking their various 'languages.' There are few real animal trainers who cannot gain an answer from their charges, talking to them as the ordinary person talks to a dog and receiving as intelligent attention. Animal men have learned that the brute isn't any different from the human; the surest way to make him work is to pay him for his trouble. In the steel arena today . . . the animals are just so many hired hands. When they do their work, they get their pay. . . . The present-day trainer doesn't cow the animal or make it afraid of him. . . . The first thing to be eliminated is not fear on the part of the trainer, but on the part of the animal! . . . Sugar for dogs, carrots for elephants, fish for seals, stale bread for the polar bears, a bit of honey or candy for the ordinary species of bear, pieces of apple or lumps of sugar for horses; every animal has his reward for which he'll work a hundred times harder than ever he did in the old and almost obsolete days of fear." With lions, tigers and leopards the trainer, imitating their own sound that expresses satisfaction, can convey to them his satisfaction with their work. And there is catnip. "To a house cat, catnip is a thing of ecstasy. To a jungle cat it holds as much allurement as morphine to a dope user, or whisky to a drunkard. The great cats roll in it, toss it about their cages, purr and arch their backs, all in a perfect frenzy of delight."

Does this new method of animal training seem to remove from the circus menagerie most of its adven-

ture and romance? Does Mr. Cooper's account of the
"Wallace act," in which a lion impersonates an un-
tameable lion and fights its trainer, seem to sickle
over all such performances a hopeless theatricalism?
The answer may be found in the pages of *Lions 'n'
Tigers 'n' Everything*, a chronicle of breathlessness if
ever there was one. Here are stories of Mabel Stark,
Captain Ricardo, Bob McPherson and many others to
make the hair curl: stories of animals that remembered
and men that forgot, of trained dogs and untrained
leopards, of animal nature and—best of all—of human nature. How much better, this book, than the
fiction which attempts to approach animals from the
imaginative side! With a low bow in the direction
of Mr. Kipling, it may be pointed out that the ordinary child's sole contact with the beasts of the jungle
is through the circus menagerie or the zoo. As captive
animals are utterly different from wild, it is in terms
of the captive existence that the child reasonably
craves to know and appreciate them (I say "child,"
but in this matter we are all children, regardless of
age). But no one who reads *Lions 'n' Tigers 'n'
Everything* will ever see an animal act again without
an observation at least twice as intelligent or an interest at least doubly great.

BOOKS BY COURTNEY RYLEY COOPER

The Eagle's Eye (with William J. Flynn, then Chief
of the U. S. Secret Service)

1919 *Dear Folks at Home* (with Kemper F. Cowing)

1919 *Memories of Buffalo Bill* (with Mrs. William F.
Cody)

1921 *The Cross-Cut*

1922 *The White Desert*

COURTNEY RYLEY COOPER

1923 *The Last Frontier*
1923 *Under the Big Top*
1924 *Lions 'n' Tigers 'n' Everything*

SOURCES ON COURTNEY RYLEY COOPER

Several are referred to in footnotes to the text of the chapter. The usual record will be found in *Who's Who in America,* and there is **Mr.** Cooper himself (address, Idaho Springs, Colorado).

19. Edith Wharton's Old New York

WILLA CATHER once made a significant confession, to the effect that nothing which had happened to her after the age of twenty seemed to matter as material for her fiction. On the whole, the statement is strongly borne out by her work; and there is reason to believe that it is true of other women writers. Dangerous as the path of generalization may be, I am persuaded that in such cases as Miss Cather, Zona Gale, Edna Ferber and Edith Wharton, all or nearly all of the writer's best work is traceable to contacts and impressions in those young years which alone seem to hold an inextinguishable spark for the tinder of imagination. And in the instance of Mrs. Wharton one has only to consider her early life in relation to some of her fiction to feel that she could echo Miss Cather.

For whatever the high merit of much of her fiction, its finished irony, its polished strength, its assurance and ease, where is the work of hers, leaving aside *Ethan Frome*, which has the robust vitality of her pictures of old New York? It is not a question of accuracy in historical detail; various slips have been charged up against *The Age of Innocence*. Well, the fact that Keats confused Cortez with Balboa has never diminished the splendor of a famous sonnet. Vitality has little to do with structure or detail, and everything to do with the artist's feeling for what he is

modelling, painting or writing about. Who can read
The Age of Innocence, or the four novelettes grouped
under the general title *Old New York* (*False Dawn,
The Old Maid, The Spark*, and *New Year's Day*) and
doubt that it is a return to first loves?

As everyone knows, or should know, she was born
in New York in 1862, Edith Newbold Jones; and
her mother was a Rhinelander. One grandparent was
a Stevens, another a Schermerhorn.[1] In the period
before her marriage at the age of twenty-three to Edward Wharton, of Boston, and in spite of much time
spent abroad, she was herself one of those sensitive
souls who "in those days were like muted keyboards,
on which Fate played without a sound," who found
themselves inextricably and by no means unhappily
enmeshed in a "cautious world built up on the fortunes of bankers, India merchants, shipbuilders and
ship-chandlers," a world where everybody "lived in
a genteel monotony of which the surface was never
stirred by the dumb dramas now and then enacted un-
derneath."[2] In this society the girl and young woman
had need of imaginative sympathy as well as sharpened perceptions if she were ultimately to comprehend
what went on. For few can comprehend such things
as the affair of Ellen Olenska and Newland Archer,[3]
or such behavior as Lizzie Hazeldean's[4] at the time.
Innocence of mind is not in question here, nor observations; it is simply that one has to be older, to have had
one's own experiences, and to be able to relate what
one has seen to what one has come to know from life.
Then and only then can comprehension come in terms

[1] See the chapter on Mrs. Wharton either in *Authors of the Day*
or *American Nights Entertainment* (both Grant Overton).
[2] The quotations are from the first two pages of *The Old Maid.*
[3] *The Age of Innocence.*
[4] In *New Year's Day.*

of that sympathy which Mrs. Wharton beautifully defines as a "moved understanding." One is no longer shackled by exact memory and one is animated by the same strong feeling, in the flood-tide of which one takes the past and fashions from it a story serviceable in meaning for mankind.

ii

It is tempting to speculate whether Mrs. Wharton could have written *The Age of Innocence* in present-day New York. The thing seems improbable. Not even in the shelter of the National Arts Club, with a window overlooking Gramercy Park, or in one of the old Chelsea houses, does the feat look the least likely. Living in France she could quite readily cross the Atlantic in recollection, sit in a shabby red and gold box at the old Academy of Music and listen to Christine Nilsson singing in "Faust." "She sang, of course, '*M'ama!*' and not 'He loves me!' since an unalterable and unquestioned law of the musical world required that the German text of French operas sung by Swedish artists should be translated into Italian for the clearer understanding of English-speaking audiences." Newland Archer would be in the club box with other men, of whom Sillerton Jackson would be the undisputed social authority. He would sit at the back but where he could see directly across the house in the box opposite the "young girl in white with eyes ecstatically fixed on the stage-lovers," May Welland. "It was only that afternoon that May Welland had let him guess that she 'cared' (New York's consecrated phrase of maiden avowal)." And then? Mrs. Wharton is not the one to avoid the delicious opening offered to review Newland Archer's confused but hopeful visions. His masculine pride, a tender reverence he felt for her "abysmal purity," the simple vanity which led him to wish May to be as worldly-wise and eager to please as the married woman of his acquaintance ("without, of course, any hint of the frailty which . . . had disarranged his own plans for a whole winter")—these elements of Newland Archer's feeling are pieced together easily enough *now* from dozens of young men one grew up with and dozens of young couples one looked on at. . . .

The infatuation of Newland Archer for Ellen Olenska would be gradual, handicapped by the efforts of his sympathy, unaided by any quality of imagination, "to picture the society in which the Countess Olenska had lived and suffered, and also—perhaps—tasted mysterious joys." The constraint, like an enormous enveloping pressure, as if everyone in the old New York society lived in the remotest depths of the sea, would overcome both Ellen Olenska and Newland Archer. But, as Mrs. Wharton realized—one feels that it is these two moments for which she wrote—the time would come when Newland would look at his wife and wish she were dead, and the time would come when he would sit as the victim of tribal ceremony.

"Archer, who seemed to be assisting at the scene in a state of odd imponderability, as if he floated somewhere between chandelier and ceiling, wondered at nothing so much as his own share in the proceedings. As his glance traveled from one placid well-fed face to another he saw all the harmless-looking people engaged upon May's canvas-backs as a band of dumb conspirators, and himself and the pale woman on his right as the center of their conspiracy. And then it came over him, in a vast flash made up of many broken gleams, that to all of them he and Madame Olenska were lovers, lovers in the extreme sense peculiar to 'foreign' vocabularies. He guessed himself to have been, for months, the center of countless silently observing eyes and patiently listening ears, he understood that, by means as yet unknown to him, the separation between himself and the partner of his guilt had been achieved, and that now the whole tribe had rallied about his wife on the tacit assumption that nobody knew anything, or had ever imagined anything, and that the occasion of the entertainment was simply May Archer's natural desire to take an affectionate leave of her friend and cousin.

"It was the old New York way of taking life 'without effusion of blood': the way of people who dreaded scandal more than disease, who placed decency above courage, and who considered that nothing was more ill-bred than 'scenes,' except the behavior of those who gave rise to them.

"As these thoughts succeeded each other in his mind Archer felt like a prisoner in the center of an armed camp. He looked about the table, and guessed at the inexorableness of his captors from the tone in which, over the asparagus from Florida, they were dealing with Beaufort and his wife. 'It's to show me,' he thought, 'what would happen to *me*—' and a deathly sense of the superiority of implication and analogy over direct action, and of silence over rash words, closed in on him like the doors of the family vault."

Here, indeed, is the novel of character at its finest. One does not have to praise the character novel in a day when the turn of critical taste has caused it to be esteemed above everything. As we know this type of fiction it has passed through several mutations since Jane Austen gave it existence by her novels. Men have seized upon Miss Austen's lesson and have wrought so prodigiously with it, as in *Vanity Fair*, in *The Egoist*, and in *The Old Wives' Tale*, that nothing is easier than to forget that the whole business originated in a woman's mind. But the novel of character is even yet distinctly feminine. It ignores the mysterious and unknown. It says that whatever may be the Unknowable, there is much we do and can explore and know. It baffles the typically masculine effort to reason with the mind, and yields at a touch to the typically feminine approach by sympathy and intuition, by thinking, as it were, not with the mind but with the nervous system. Among the many perversions to which it has been subjected none is more hopeless than a sort of conscientious, wholly masculine realism, a placid apprehension of surfaces, such as triumphed in the work of William Dean Howells. Mr. George Moore said in malice that Henry James went abroad and read the great Europeans, while Mr. Howells stayed at home and read Henry James. It would be at least as true to suggest that Mrs. Wharton, for whatever time she was his "pupil," chose Mr. James to escape from Mr. Howells. At home was dignity and dullness; abroad was the author of *The Portrait of a Lady* busy with highly-disguised melodrama. Who—least of all, a woman like Mrs. Wharton—could hesitate?

iii

The four novelettes grouped under the title, *Old New York*, are doubtless as works of art more perfect than *The Age of Innocence*, for in each case Mrs. Wharton has selected a subject as a painter might, with a feeling for the effect in certain lights and with a wish to avoid so far as possible the air of having "composed" her figures in their background. The extreme artificiality and rigidity of the society she writes about demands that at least one or two persons —the one or two in the foreground—shall possess a movement apparently unstudied. Therefore her task has been finely and ruthlessly to cut away the richly rambling growth of her recollections, the profusion in this direction or that; it has been to isolate a single crucial situation, or to expose behind the dried leaves and the withered roses of mid-century sentimentality and correctitude the reality of a heart that beat in its pathetic moment of terror or of despairing courage. These are exquisite stories; I do not think it an exaggeration to say they are the finest things Mrs. Wharton has ever done with the exception of *Ethan Frome*. Indeed, they have something that no work of hers but *Ethan Frome* has in the same degree, the mood of stirred comprehension and compassionate pity, joined to something that no work of hers but *The Age of Innocence* has, a rapturously perfect setting.

False Dawn (*The 'Forties*) begins at a country house which overlooked Long Island Sound at a point now shabby with cliff-dwellings and gas tanks. "Hay, verbena and mignonette scented the languid July day. Large strawberries, crimsoning through sprigs of mint, floated in a bowl of pale yellow"—and young Lewis Raycie, who has hard work to down his punch ("perfumed fire") is twenty-one and ready for the Grand Tour. The more tender-hearted of his sisters has a habit of going out furtively at daybreak to take comforts to poor Mrs. Poe, the very sick wife of an atheistical poet. The son, secretly in love with an ineligible girl, runs across in his travels John Ruskin, and buys Italian primitives instead of the Raphael and conventional "masters" desired by his father. For this he is cut off from a fortune and left with the collec-

[310]

tion. We have a glimpse of him and his wife and little girl embraced in poverty while the pictures are exhibited to a New York still totally unready for them. Lewis Raycie, his wife and child are dust when the "dawn" comes.

In *The Old Maid* (*The 'Fifties*) Mrs. Wharton deals with a situation so dramatic that I feel the shocking unfairness of disclosing it prematurely to the reader. Although Delia Lovell, wife of James Ralston, and Charlotte Lovell are actually cousins, one comes to think of them as sisters. The faithful but unsparing presentation of what, essentially, is comprised in motherhood grows out of the most intimate glimpses of husband, wife, lover and mistress. "Afterward: why, of course, there was the startled puzzled surrender to the incomprehensible exigencies of the young man to whom one had at most yielded a rosy cheek in return for an engagement ring; there was the large double-bed; the terror of seeing him shaving calmly the next morning, in his shirt-sleeves, through the dressing-room door; the evasions, insinuations, resigned smiles and Bible texts of one's Mamma; the reminder of the phrase 'to obey' in the glittering blur of the Marriage Service; a week or a month of flushed distress, confusion, embarrassed pleasure; then the growth of habit, the insidious lulling of the matter-of-course, the dreamless double slumbers in the big white bed, the early morning discussions and consultations through that dressing-room door which had once seemed to open into a fiery pit scorching the brow of innocence. And then, the babies; the babies who were supposed to 'make up for everything,' and didn't —though they were such darlings, and one had no definite notion as to what it was that one had missed, and that they were to make up for."

CARGOES FOR CRUSOES

Although *The Spark* is subtitled *The 'Sixties*, it is more truly a tale of the 'Sixties reflected in the 'Nineties. Hayley Delane, whose "harsh head stood out like a cliff from a flowery plain," is the supremely good-natured, stupid husband. It is only by slow degrees that the young man who tells the story comes to understand that while Delane is intellectually no different from the other men of his social set, he is morally far in advance of them. Parenthetically, it is interesting to note Mrs. Wharton's use of the young man as narrator not only in this story but in *New Year's Day*, and to compare it with Willa Cather's use of the same device in *My Antonia* and *A Lost Lady*.

The Spark is a story devoted to the exploration of character, an obscure but fascinating task resumed at intervals over the years. The secret of Delane's character leads back, curiously and astonishingly, to his brief contact as a youth with "an old fellow in Washington" who visited the sick in the army hospitals. Otherwise Delane has never heard of Walt Whitman. I withhold the ironic and perfect ending.

A sample of Mrs. Wharton's zestful writing comes in the first sentence of *New Year's Day* (*The 'Seventies*):

" 'She was *bad* . . . always. They used to meet at the Fifth Avenue Hotel,' said my mother, as if the scene of the offense added to the guilt of the couple whose past she was revealing."

Her son's mind flashes back to an incident when he was a boy of twelve watching, with older people, the rapid and unbecoming rush of folk from the Fifth Avenue Hotel, which was on fire. With her admirable technique, Mrs. Wharton at once slips quietly back to the incident itself, and we follow Lizzie Hazeldean in her progress from the scene of so much confusion—a flight, but a controlled flight. This story holds a surprise for the reader, who will not be likely to surmise Mrs. Hazeldean's true feeling any more than Henry Prest did. The scene between these two, meeting for the first time after Charles Hazeldean's death, is incomparably well done.

Surely these four novelettes will be read a half-century hence with as much appreciation as today! For such work, for such New York primitives, one feels there can be no false dawn. I have no doubt that the immediate effect, only partly traceable to the presence in the background of some of the same persons, like Mrs. Manson Mingot and Mr. Sillerton Jackson, will be to set everyone to re-reading *The Age of Innocence*. Which is entirely as it should be, for they will find that novel fresher, livelier, more wistful and even more beautifully satisfactory today than four years ago.

A NOTE ON EDITH WHARTON

For a full list of Edith Wharton's books and for reference to several important discussions of her work, see the chapter on her in either *Authors of the Day* or *American Nights Entertainment*.

The Age of Innocence is a story of New York society in the 'Seventies. It was published in 1920, receiving the Pulitzer Prize, awarded by Columbia University, as the best American novel of its year (over Sinclair Lewis's *Main Street*). The four novelettes called *Old New York* were published in 1924 (separate volumes, or set) and are:

> *False Dawn* (*The 'Forties*)
> *The Old Maid* (*The 'Fifties*)
> *The Spark* (*The 'Sixties*)
> *New Year's Day* (*The 'Seventies*)

20. Not Found Elsewhere

i

CERTAIN books which have seemed not to drop naturally into the scheme of my other chapters are to be discussed in this; but that does not mean an entire lack of relation among them. I shall first say something about books dealing with Europe; then something about books on American subjects. Both these groups are mainly of an historical character. There will then remain for our attention a few books of a somewhat diverse but distinctive character.

Easily the most important of the European studies is promised in a two-volume work by the Earl of Birkenhead with the title, *The Inner History of British Politics, 1906-1922*, to appear early in 1925. The author first came to general attention as Frederick E. Smith, an Ulster lawyer. As Sir Frederick E. Smith he was Attorney-General under Mr. Lloyd George and later, as Viscount Birkenhead, he was Lord High Chancellor. When he retired from office with Lloyd George he was made an Earl. With Sir Andrew Carson, he was generally held to have been responsible for the gun-running in Ulster when an Irish civil war seemed in prospect in 1914; and he does not disclaim the rôle.[1] On this and other accounts he is in some

[1] "I admit most fully that I myself proceeded with Lord Carson to great lengths—and would even have proceeded to greater—in order to prevent the forcible inclusion of the Northern provinces in a Parliament sitting at Dublin."—The Earl of Birkenhead in *America Revisited* (1924) page 40.

quarters one of the best-hated men in British public life.

But he is also one of the most direct, uncompromising and candid. He is also much more open in his disillusion than most English public men have ventured to be—or actually were. None of the rosy colors of Mr. Lloyd George's auroral intellect have any place in Birkenhead's thinking. His literary style is the somewhat encumbered one of the lawyer; but if it is a little tortuous, it is precise, and leaves his meaning not vague. His "Inner History" of events between 1906 and 1922 will be most bitterly attacked, as biased, partial, misrepresentative of men and purposes. But the reader will do well to form his own judgment; and in any event it will be necessary to wring from the attacks, as you wring water from a cloth, the large amount of emotionalism with which they are certain to be saturated.

Birkenhead has, of course, certain advantages in preparing his work. Lloyd George has spoken in one book [2] and Asquith has given his account of the pre-war period.[3] Various other actors in the striking political events that began just before the Asquith Ministry and continued until Mr. Lloyd George's defeat have been heard from. The material at Birkenhead's disposal is far more complete than the record of history so entirely contemporary has ever been.

Arthur Hamilton Gibbs is a brother of Philip Gibbs and of Cosmo Hamilton.[4] At the beginning of the war he was just out of hospital and had gone home to England to recuperate his strength. He was under

[2] *Where Are We Going?* (1923), by the Right Hon. David Lloyd George.
[3] *The Genesis of the War* (1923), by the Right Hon. Herbert H. Asquith.
[4] See Chapters I and II.

a strict injunction not to ride a horse for six months. In one month he had enlisted as a private in the British Army and was training as a cavalryman. After service in France he was commissioned, eventually becoming Major Gibbs. He also saw a long period of that morale-destroying inaction which was the lot of certain units sent to the Bulgarian front. His final period, in France, coincided with the great German drive of March, 1918.

Out of this experience he wrote a book, *Gun Fodder*, published in 1919, when the world, in sheer reaction, wouldn't look at a war book. Yet Arthur Symons called *Gun Fodder* one of the six best books about the war. And people on this side, like Christopher Morley, who have a faculty for personally discovering the exceptional book, read it and talked about it. When *Gun Fodder* was republished this year (1924) it took its place as one of the very few books of war experience that will last—that have lasted—for more than the war's own hour.

It is the only war book I shall bring to your notice; but there are one or two after-war books which deserve your attention. *The Awakening of Italy: The Fascista Regeneration*, by Luigi Villari, will of course actively interest those who may have read the chapter on Italy in Charles H. Sherrill's *The Purple or the Red*[5] but many will go to it directly in an effort to grasp the significance of Mussolini and Fascism. They will find a singularly clear and even luminous account, as little encumbered with unfamiliar detail as a full account can be. But they will also find a story full of drama, yet told without any of the rhetoric or verbal excess and floridity which one might expect in a book on Italian politics written by an Italian. Vil-

[5] See Chapter 12.

lari is frankly an admirer and partisan of Fascism, and his opinion of Mussolini as a great leader is plain-spoken; but he is neither a mere enthusiast nor an indiscriminating historian. The defects of Fascism he records as he sees them. He does not contend that there are not grave problems ahead of Italy. But, as he says, "the mass of the people, both among the educated classes and the ignorant, are more interested in results than in theories, and no one who compares the state of Italy today with that of the days before Fascismo's advent to power can for a moment deny the enormous improvement in every field. 'Ora si vive,' the people say, 'mentre prima non si viveva piu.' ('Now we live, whereas before life was not possible.') . . . One has the feeling that the country is really moving forward rapidly and surely, and shaking off the shackles of the bad traditions by which it had been bound for centuries."

The Prime Ministry of Ramsay MacDonald in Great Britain makes particularly timely *An Outline of the British Labor Movement*, by Paul Blanshard. This is a short history, just what its title states, an "outline" conveying exactly what the American reader desires to know about the British Labor Party. The author is a young American with training in the field of social and political study. His book was written from material gained in England and its authenticity is attested in the introduction provided for it by Arthur Henderson, the Labor leader.

Tons of books have been written about Russia and sovietism; yet I expect there will be general agreement with me when I say that only one other man (now dead) was so qualified to write on the subject as Leon Trotzky. There can certainly be no denying the high interest of Leon Trotzky's *Problems of Life*.

The Soviet Minister of War gives a pretty complete
view of the new Russia from the inside. It will possibly come as a surprise that the new Russia is more
interested in home life, recreations, literature and the
arts than in economics and politics. From the viewpoint of Trotzky, the foundation of the home rests
on the mutual attachment of husband and wife—as
always—but must be secured by the liberation of both
in economic directions. Most especially must the wife
and mother be aided by communal kitchens and relief
from the effective slavery of cooking, washing, and
other ordeals by fire and water. The ten chapters of
Problems of Life are discussions of the problems
deemed vital in Russian reconstruction. Such chapter titles as "Not by Politics Alone Does Man Thrive,"
"Reconstruction Requires Introspection," "From the
Old Family to the New," and "Mind and Little
Things" give the angle of vision.

ii

I might as well confess frankly that I am fascinated
by William A. Ganoe's _The History of the United
States Army_. Therefore, if you feel it necessary, dis-
count by a percentage for enthusiasm what I may say.
These will still remain solid, incontestable merits.
This is the first history of our army ever to have been
written; and it has been written with a strong story
sense, so that it reads like a story. It covers in a single
volume the whole period from 1775 to 1923. Dates
have been placed in the margin, and reference to sources
are omitted so as not to interrupt the reader. There
is a chronological account of a soldier's life in the
American Revolution, and the first picture of the
period of military decadence after the Revolution.

The truth about General von Steuben seems to have been arrived at for the first time. What the army did and did not do in the War of 1812 is told. There is a good picture of the life of the soldier in peace times, when he becomes the nation's most important builder. The view of the Civil War is somewhat new and certainly impartial. For the first time, this book gives us a complete account of our Indian wars in chronological shape.

I think there is a great deal of truth in the assertion that one cannot know American history without having read this book. Much that has heretofore been withheld from general knowledge is told for the first time. And there are picturesque matters which are far from being affairs of general knowledge—for example, the fact that the construction of the Union Pacific Railroad was due to the army and army training, or the fact that General Winfield Scott, single-handed, saved the country three times from war.

Who is William A. Ganoe? A West Pointer commissioned in the regular army in 1907 who has served in Cuba, Hawaii, and various parts of the United States. He was instructor, and afterward assistant professor of English, and finally adjutant for four years at West Point. He was in command of a company in the first series of training camps when we entered the war, and head of a board of officers formed to edit the Infantry Drill Regulations after the war. He is now head of the military history section at the U. S. Infantry School at Fort Benning, Georgia. He has written for the Atlantic Monthly ("Ruggs—R. O.T.C."), Scribner's, and the Yale Review. He has, of course, had access to various records and historical confirmations not available to the non-army writer.

A History of the United States Navy had already

been written by Edgar Stanton Maclay, and readers will welcome Mr. Maclay's *A History of American Privateers*, which truly supplements the earlier work. For during the Revolution the number of privateers was about four times that of regular naval vessels; and the part played by the privateer in the War of 1812 has never been minimized by any historian. From before the Revolution to after the War of 1812 hundreds of respected men made their livings—and their fortunes—by sailing as licensed pirates with full powers to capture any ships of unfriendly countries. Men who were unable to go bought shares in the privateers and often, when a rich prize was captured, reaped an incredible dividend. So slight was the difference in practice between privateering and plain piracy, so enormous was the profit in both, that it is not surprising to learn that every once in a while a privateersman, having waited in vain for a "lawful" prey, attacked a ship of his own nation, or any first comer. The classic instance is that of Captain Kidd, sent out as a privateersman, hung as a pirate.

It goes without saying that Mr. Maclay's book is romantic; it couldn't be anything else. Its interest is equally the interest of authentic history and daring adventure; its value always that of fact. There are plenty of books giving the history of our merchant marine; Mr. Maclay had done a history of the navy; here he has filled the gap between by telling what is perhaps the most exciting story of the three.

iii

If there is one thing more important than the American Constitution, it is the United States Supreme Court. Charles Warren, formerly assistant Attorney-

General of the United States, and author of *A History of the American Bar*, is a person with a remarkable capacity for hard work in research. He has that other priceless gift, the ability to digest what he has learned and to present it clearly but without the sacrifice of opulence. For this double reason his *The Supreme Court in United States History*, occupying to some extent the same field as Beveridge's *Life of John Marshall*, is the only work worthy to be put beside Senator Beveridge's masterpiece. The award of the $2,000 Pulitzer Prize for the year's best book on the history of the United States, made annually or less often by Columbia University, quite naturally fell to Mr. Warren after publication of his three-volume history. "This book," Mr. Warren says in his preface, "is not a law book. It is a narrative of that section of our national history connected with the Supreme Court, and is written for laymen and lawyers alike. As words are but 'the skin of a living thought,' so law cases as they appear in the law reports are but the dry bones of very vital social, political and economic contests. This book is an attempt to restore, in some degree, their contemporary surroundings to the important cases decided by the Supreme Court."

In other words, this is the first history of the one most tremendous factor in American government, and it is written from a non-legal standpoint. After its publication Chief Justice William H. Taft and Justices Day, Van Devanter, McReynolds and Clarke joined by personal letters of praise the great voice of critical commendation which was heard from all over the country. Chief Justice Taft spoke particularly of the enormous labor involved in the reading of early American newspapers, necessary if Mr. Warren were to get the contemporary view and feeling on Supreme Court decisions. "I consider that you have put the profession, and indeed the whole country, under a heavy debt," the Chief Justice concluded. But I submit that Mr. Warren's perfect readability is the chief item of our indebtedness.

I spoke of the Constitution: books upon it are much in demand these days. One which has had a wide sale and praise from high sources is Thomas James Norton's *The Constitution of the United States: Its Sources and Its Application*. Mr. Norton writes for the layman and his book has had a somewhat extensive use in Americanization work. One of those heartiest in praise of it has been the Hon. James M. Beck, Solicitor General of the United States, who says: "I know of no book which so completely and coherently explains our form of government, and I hope, indeed, for the welfare of our country that it may have the wide circulation which it so richly merits." The generosity of this is the more appreciable when we consider that Mr. Beck's own book, *The Constitution of the United States*, appearing about the same time, and founded on his Gray's Inn lectures in London, was in more or less degree a rival for readers' attention. But it is apparent that people read, if they read at all, not one but several books on the Constitution; for Mr. Beck's volume, rewritten and considerably expanded, is just being republished as *The Constitution of the United States: Yesterday, Today—Tomorrow?*

James Myers's *Representative Government in Industry* and Sterling Denhard Spero's *The Labor Movement in a Government Industry* are volumes that, because of their specialized character, are more related to Mr. Blanshard's *An Outline of the British Labor*

Movement. But they are both on American subjects. Mr. Myers is executive secretary of the board of operatives of the Dutchess Bleachery, Inc., at Wappingers Falls, New York. This bleachery is an "industrial democracy," or partnership enterprise, operated by the employees. Mr. Myers's book has therefore a great advantage over most books of its sort: it records an actual experiment in successful operation, not somebody's theories as to what ought to work. Mr. Spero's book is adequately described by its subtitle, "a study of employee organization in the Postal Service." After a short survey of unionism in the civil service, Mr. Spero gives the full record of its history among the United States postal employees. The book is not propaganda for any organization or group, but the work of an impartial historian with no axe to grind.

Are new books on Lincoln justified? Yes. We are only beginning to get those of enduring value, aside from certain contemporary records. "The Lincoln papers, rich in letters to Lincoln, many of them quite as important to the biographer as those written by him, have not yet been released, nor will they be available for a number of years," points out Daniel Kilham Dodge, in the preface to his *Abraham Lincoln—Master of Words*, "and the Hay Diary, a source of the utmost importance, is still in manuscript form, to be consulted only by special permission of the Harvard Library authorities." These are only two of the known important items. Mr. Dodge's own new book is entirely confined to one phase of Lincoln's life, though a phase of the greatest interest. Was he an orator? Was the Gettysburg address composed briefly on the train, in effect an impromptu? Just what was Lincoln's genius for effective utterance?

Mr. Dodge has uncovered some interesting facts,

[323]

and brought others into valuable juxtaposition. Lincoln was no natural born orator. All his life he was unable to make an extempore speech. On the day Richmond fell, Lincoln dispersed an enthusiastic crowd before the White House, telling them to come the next day when he would have a speech ready. He kept his promise. It was his last speech before his assassination.

The young Lincoln modeled himself on Henry Clay. His earliest speeches often contained the purple patches not entirely dissociable from Southern oratory. The Lincoln humor, notorious in conversation, was extremely rare in his speeches; another evidence that when he spoke his words were studied. He simply could not express himself gracefully—or effectively—on short notice. The evidence is that the Gettysburg address was as carefully prepared as anything else. Mr. Dodge has made an onerous examination of contemporary newspapers and sources to find out if anyone really did perceive the speech's classic line and immense stature. Only about three voices were raised in acclaim.

Abraham Lincoln—Master of Words is worth adding to the Lincoln shelf. But its lesson is distinctly that such eloquence as Lincoln had came from toil and care and thought—perhaps was achieved only because, so often, the need for utmost sincerity in expression, the grave consequence of an issue impending, came to his aid.

iv

It was Edmond Rostand who once said that the only vice was inactivity (*l'inertie*), the only virtue, enthusiasm. Douglas Fairbanks long ago adopted this as his watchword. But enthusiasm is peculiarly a trait of youth. How keep this youthful enthusiasm? The answer to this question is the whole subject of Fairbanks's new book, *Youth Points the Way*. "You may have all the machinery for a successful life," says the actor, "education, health, intellect, and still fail to find the true zest in life because your machinery lacks the vital electric spark—enthusiasm." It is necessary to think hard, work hard, play hard and live enthusiastically. Fresh air and exercise are "the only medicine I ever take." Mr. Fairbanks rises in time to see the sun rise and chases his breakfast to the top of a California mountain. "Keep in motion; that is the main thing, and it matters little whether you do stunts on a flying ring or only chin yourself on an upper berth."

How is a young man to get a start in life? That, Douglas Fairbanks says, depends entirely on what sort of a person he is; but one thing he must do, "dive in." Fairbanks himself, on graduating from college, borrowed a thousand dollars and went to Europe. His start in life came through the strenuous way he had to work to pay that money back.

Youth Points the Way is the book of a man who has kept in motion and who believes that to cease moving is to die. Some people stop after failure, some after success. Fairbanks says that either is fatal. Were he writing a scientific treatise, and not a popular, partly autobiographical, inspirational book with many anecdotes and considerable humor, he could find very important evidence in the work of physicists, physiologists, and others to prove that he is right.

Perhaps you think that so much motion will disturb your blood pressure (of which you have heard a good deal, and about which you are secretly worried at times). Well, no; at least, only beneficially. If you would like to know the truth about blood pressure—the subject of much ignorance and much uninformed discussion—you may as well read the new book by Lewellys F. Barker, M.D., LL.D., and Norman Brown Cole, M.D. Although Drs. Barker and Cole are members of the Johns Hopkins faculty, their book is equally serviceable for the physician and the general reader. Technical expressions are avoided, and a very complete glossary helps the ordinary reader where a medical name must be used for exactness. But the book should remove all sorts of misconceptions. Blood pressure is just as normal as breathing. It has certain general averages related to age and condition; marked departures from these are the danger signal. Heredity, the wear and tear of modern life, the use of alcohol, tobacco and coffee may produce exceptional blood pressures. Development of high blood pressure is a process rather than a disease; the symptoms develop rather late in its course; and preventive measures must be taken early. *Blood Pressure* gives, in plain, comprehensible English, the information that anyone interested in longevity, or even in normal length of life, would like to have.

V

About 500 years ago there lived a Turk named Nasr-ed-Din, which means "Victory of the Faith." He became a teacher and a magistrate in the district of Angora. As a teacher he was called "Khoja," which means "Teacher" and is a title of respect and honor. He was the author of a series of Æsop-like fables which have come down as perhaps the most authentic and indigenous piece of Turkish literature. There is not much Turkish literature which is not an imitation of, or a borrowing from, Persian or Arabic

NOT FOUND ELSEWHERE

The Khoja, or Nasr-ed-Din's stories, is today as popular and as universally read and repeated as ever.

The work has finally been translated into English with the title, *The Khoja: Tales of Nasr-ed-Din*. Henry D. Barnham is the translator, and Sir Valentine Chirol, an authority on Turkey and the East, provides an entertaining and instructive foreword. Although the wisdom in these fables is generally for young and old, it can scarcely be illustrated except by quotation. I select for that purpose, and on account of its brevity, a fable for grownups:

"The Khoja had two wives. He gave each of them a blue shell as a keepsake, telling each not to let anyone see it. One day they came in together and asked him, 'Which of us do you love best? Who is your favorite?'

" 'The one,' he answered, 'who has my blue shell.'

"Each of the women took comfort. Each one said in her heart, ' 'Tis I he loves best,' and looked with scornful pity upon the other.

"Clever Khoja! That is the way he managed his wives!"

For contrast, we may pick up *Sixty Years of American Humor: A Prose Anthology*, edited by Joseph Lewis French. Here are selections, and the best selections, from the best American humorous writers, from Artemus Ward to the absolutely contemporary Sam Hellman, of "Low Bridge" reputation. The selections from Josh Billings remind us that he relied for some of his effect on misspelling, just as Ring Lardner does today. Edward Eggleston's "The Spelling-Bee"; Mark Twain's "The Jumping Frog of Calaveras"; Bill Nye's "Skimming the Milky Way"; and Eugene Field's "The Cyclopeedy" are representative inclusions. More recent humorists for whom Mr.

[327]

French has found place are Finley Peter Dunne, George Ade, Thomas L. Masson, George Horace Lorimer, Stephen Leacock, Don Marquis, Irvin S. Cobb, Ellis Parker Butler, George Fitch, Montague Glass, Christopher Ward, Robert C. Benchley and Harry Leon Wilson. *Sixty Years of American Humor* provides considerably more than the ordinary humorous book's quantity of diversion to the square inch.

But I come at last to the two books whose claim to inclusion in this chapter is most undeniable—two books of which it can truthfully be said, not only that they are not found elsewhere, but that they contain a thousand things not to be found elsewhere.

John Bartlett's *Familiar Quotations* is so wonderful in its completeness and its resourcefulness that although it went without revision for twenty-three years, it remained the best book of its kind and no more recent work was able to displace it. It has now been revised and enlarged by Nathan Haskell Dole, so that the new quotations included are from nearly 200 of the more important writers of the last few decades, not included before, among them Stevenson, Swinburne, Kipling and Mark Twain. This, then, is the book without which newspapermen, editors, writers, public speakers, scholars, librarians, and many, many households could not exist—at least, the households could not exist in harmony. It is the book which saves you from saying, "fresh fields and pastures new"; that tells you it should be "fresh *woods*," and that the line is Milton's. Is it possible that in this book of 1,400 pages, citing from nearly 1,000 authors, and with its quotations indexed and cross-indexed under their various outstanding words, so that the index has almost 50,000 entries—is it possible that there is some phrase you half-recall and yet cannot find? It is just possible. If it occurs, there is something left for you yet to do. You may try Frank J. Wilstach's *A Dictionary of Similes* (the new and enlarged edition).

Mr. Wilstach's social register of similes is the only book of reference of its kind. Since its original publication, in 1916, *A Dictionary of Similes*, with its 17,000 quaint figures of speech, has become pretty nigh indispensable for writers, speakers, teachers and students. One hundred pages have been added in the new edition, as Mr. Wilstach says that similes should be kept fresh, like oysters. And the figures of speech themselves? They are drawn from the writings of a great number of authors, from Chaucer and Shakespeare, through English and American literature, to O. Henry and Irvin S. Cobb. The arrangement is alphabetical under subject headings. I have nothing against the 16,999 other comparisons in the book, though personally I shall always maintain that the best simile in the world is Irvin S. Cobb's "no more privacy than a goldfish." I have looked for hours in Mr. Wilstach's masterpiece in search of a suitable comparison for *A Dictionary of Similes*.

Well, I cannot find one.

21. Frank L. Packard
Unlocks a Book

i

FROM his home on the shore of the St. Lawrence, Frank L. Packard sent word that the title was *The Locked Book*. No details. *The Locked Book* remained a locked book until the manuscript arrived. One had a vision of Mr. Packard going to his safe and turning the combination and swinging open the door and taking out the story, complete, released only in its entirety. Knowing his work, one has similar visions of the tales he has written unlocking themselves and stepping, full-statured, into his mind. Mr. Packard, one of the most disconcerting of men, would not be himself disconcerted by such apparitions. His is a personality full of outward contradictions and inward reconcilements. There is something gruff, even ferocious, in his speech and manner on many occasions; it melts every other moment into a really exquisite urbanity. He is alarmingly direct, dreadfully uncompromising—and he is the soul of hospitality and gentleness, a person of stainless honor. He assumes rudeness like a mask and his blue eyes and the look in them give him quite away with an utter transparency. His coat is rough, fuzzy, scratchy, yet his heart is on the sleeve of it. And his fiction? Full half of it moves in the "underworld" and is peopled with criminals; yet the thing that most markedly distinguishes Frank L. Packard from all other writers of mystery-adventure stories is his belief in a moral order. Immanuel Kant and Sherlock Holmes are commingled in him; and though he may invent plots he really believes in miracles.

He is, as everyone must know, the author of *The Miracle Man*, a novel which George M. Cohan made into a successful play and which, as a motion picture, made millions of dollars for various persons *not* including the author. . . . A moral order has some advantages over a money order.

ii

Frank Lucius Packard was born of American parents at Montreal on 2 February 1877 and was graduated from McGill University in 1897. The following year he took a postgraduate course in engineering at L'Institut Montefiore, University of Liege, Belgium. He engaged in engineering work in the United States for a number of years and when, in 1906, he began writing for various magazines, his first tales were railroad stories. *On the Iron at Big Cloud* (1911), *The Wire Devils* (1918), which tells of the work of a band of expert telegraphers and masters of the art of cipher codes, and *The Night Operator* (1919) are best characterized in Mr. Packard's own Foreword to *The Night Operator:*

"Summed up short, the Hill Division is a vicious piece of track; also, it is a classic in its profound contempt for the stereotyped equations and formulæ of engineering. And it is that way for the very simple reason that it could not be any other way. The mountains objected, and objected strenuously, to the process of manhandling. They were there first, the mountains, that was all, and their surrender was a bitter matter.

"So, from Big Cloud, the divisional point, at the

eastern fringe of the Rockies, to where the foothills of the Sierras on the western side merge with the more open, rolling country, the right of way . . . sweeps through the rifts in the range like a freed bird from the open door of its cage; clings to canyon edges where a hissing stream bubbles and boils eighteen hundred feet below; burrows its way into the heart of things in long tunnels and short ones; circles a projecting spur in a dizzy whirl, and swoops from the higher to the lower levels in grades whose percentages the passenger department does not deem it policy to specify in its advertising literature, but before which the men in the cabs and the cabooses shut their teeth and try hard to remember the prayers they learned at their mothers' knees. Some parts of it are worse than others, naturally; but no part of it, to the last inch of its single-tracked mileage, is pretty—leaving out the scenery, which is *grand*. That is the Hill Division."

So much for the setting.

"And the men who man the shops, who pull the throttles on the big, ten-wheel mountain racers, who swing the picks and shovels in the lurching cabs, who do the work about the yards, or from the cupola of a caboose stare out on a string of wriggling flats, boxes and gondolas, and, at night time, watch the high-flung sparks sail heavenward, as the full, deep-chested notes of the exhaust roar an accompaniment in their ears, are men . . . whose hearts are big and right."

The human values of these early stories of Packard's are as sturdy today as when they were first written; whatever their shortcomings, a lack of vitality was not one of them. The man who was to become a chef of plots began by simply pitching the fat of human nature in the fire of dramatic incident. His first stories are like steaks; and if they are hastily and simply cooked, they are not cooked up. Thick, rich cuts from the flanks of actual life, burned a little at the edges, perhaps, they still are tender with juices and flavor. They nourish directly. Their protein is the example of courage, from the story of a train newsboy who averted a wreck to the tale of how Martin Bradley saved the Rat River Special.

iii

In 1910 Mr. Packard married Marguerite Pearl Macintyre, of Montreal, and the next year saw the publication of his first book, *On the Iron at Big Cloud.* In 1912 he wrote his first novel, *Greater Love Hath No Man.* The novel was written in Lachine, a city eight miles from Montreal, where Packard had settled and where his home is now. The outline of the story is as follows:

"Varge, the hero, was a foundling brought up by Dr. and Mrs. Merton as if he had been their own son. Their real son, Harold, kills his father in a quarrel, and begs Varge to disappear so that it will seem that he is the actual murderer. Varge goes further than that. He does not run away, but publicly shoulders the guilt for the sake, not of Harold, but of Mrs. Merton, whose heart would break if she knew that her son had killed his father. Varge believes he owes them this act of sacrifice in return for the life-long kindness of his benefactors. The story thereafter is the story of this sacrifice; his life in prison, where as a trusty he meets the warden's daughter, Janet Rand; his love for Janet which both impels him to escape and to give himself up again—and finally his freedom as Harold Merton, dying, confesses the truth." [1]

[1] Quoted from the article, "Progress of Frank L. Packard," in the *Argosy-Allstory Weekly* for 3 February 1923.

CARGOES FOR CRUSOES

Here was a novel on the theme of sacrifice, a theme which had already been persistent and noticeable in Frank L. Packard's short stories, and a theme which was to recur later, but interwoven with another idea of equal strength and beauty. The discovery of that other idea—its discovery, that is, in the necessary terms of a story—was to come in the same year in which *Greater Love Hath No Man* was published. If you journey directly north from Montreal, you will find yourself after a while in mountainous country with summits of less height than many on the North American continent. Nevertheless the Laurentian Mountains have a distinction more interesting than altitude; they are geologically the oldest formation— older than the Adirondacks, the Alleghanies, the Rockies; older than the plains. They are fundamental and as unchanging as the capacity to wonder and the will to believe in the heart of that higher insect, Man. In 1913 Packard was in the Laurentians and there and at Lachine he was engaged in writing a novel which he purposed calling "The Wrong Right Road." When it was finished it appeared as a complete novel in Munsey's Magazine for February, 1914. A set of advance proofs was sent to George M. Cohan, who bought the dramatic rights and changed the title. The book was arranged to appear immediately and Mr. Cohan at once set to work to fashion the play.

The scene of Packard's story was the village of Needley, Maine. In Needley, says an outline,[2] "lives an old man—deaf, dumb and almost blind—known as the Patriarch. For many years, through the exercise of faith, he has cured the people in the neighborhood of their simple ailments. An article about him finds

[2] See article, "Progress of Frank L. Packard," in the Argosy-All-story Weekly for 3 February 1923.

its way into a New York City newspaper which comes under the eye of the celebrated 'Doc' Madison, a quick-witted and ingenious confidence man, who at once evolves a scheme to make the Patriarch's home a shrine to which Doc will entice all ailing humanity from far and near, and then pluck the golden hoard through his trickery.

"Among Doc's disciples is a clever and beautiful girl named Helena Vail. Another is a dope fiend, Pale Face Harry, an artful dodger with a hacking cough. The faker that Doc Madison selects to take the star part in setting the procession of ailing ones in motion is called the Flopper. The Flopper has an uncanny control over his joints by which he can, with a single gesture, convert himself into a loathsome cripple, twisted and broken, begging in the streets, shattered in body and soul; truly a spectacle to soften the hardest heart. Doc Madison rounds up his little band of efficient scoundrels, takes them to Needley, Maine, and plants them on the sweet-souled Patriarch, whose faith in his own powers to heal is merely his faith in the influence upon man's soul and body of love and goodness and belief in all that is worth while. Helena forces herself upon him as his grandniece, and becomes his trusted confidante. The Flopper crawls from the train through the dust of the street to the Patriarch's threshold. Here the old man, practically blind, surrounded by a crowd of visitors and devotees from all over the country, stretches out his thin hands, and the Flopper rises from the earth a new man. At the same moment a crippled child, helpless from birth and staggering along on crutches, throws his artificial supports from him and cries aloud: 'I can walk!'"

This supreme moment of *The Miracle Man*—book, play and picture—leads to the wreck of Doc Madison's scheme; the crooks are self-defeated by the advent of a power they cannot understand. A valley has been exalted, a mountain and hill have been made low, the crooked has been made straight. . . .

And Mr. Packard had made the discovery of his second idea, the theme of regeneration which is so much the most powerful manifestation known to human lives. In finding it he had unlocked more than a book, or a striking play, or an extraordinary motion picture. The camera version of this simple tale did indeed make lasting reputations for Thomas F. Meighan, Betty Compson and Lon Chaney, as well as enhance the reputation of the late George Loan Tucker, whom Mr. Meighan prodded into directing the picture; money rolled in upon the picture's backers in a tidal wave; the success of "The Birth of a Nation" was outdone, nor has any film since surpassed the record set by Packard's story. These phenomena are picturesque—staggering, if you like. But they came afterward; they had little to do with the author, who, perhaps, could have used some of the money but to whose work these successes could have no true relevance. What Mr. Packard had unlocked was an inwardness in himself, the fullness of his own mind. He was, perhaps, never to write well in the sense of writing with literary distinction; he was to become a master of plot and of incident, and to do stories in which characterization was to suffer from the very rush of action and the galvanization of suspense. But he was never to write a book in which the emotion was cheap or the immanent morality less than uncompromising. And with his themes of sacrifice and regeneration, intertwined, he was to arrest, enthrall and convince the thousands.

[336]

iv

The next book was *The Belovéd Traitor* (1916. And please make three syllables of the adjective). Jean Laparde and Marie-Louise are fisher folk in a French village and are affianced. Jean, who is always modeling little figures in clay, is a genius. A wealthy American named Bliss discovers him. Jean is sent to Paris to study and his great gift ultimately causes a sensation. Bliss's daughter makes him her conquest, for adulation has turned the sculptor's head and he has forgotten Marie-Louise. Jean and Myrna Bliss sail for America where they are to be married at the Bliss home. Marie-Louise in her great loneliness decides to go to America. On shipboard, in the steerage one night, Jean sees Marie-Louise. His love for her returns, and with it repentance for the way he has used her. It is now a question of both sacrifice and regeneration. Regeneration comes first; and the apparent sacrifice is canceled by a far greater success; for on his return to France, Jean's work reflects the new sincerity of his life and love.

Consider *The Sin That Was His* (1917). Here regeneration leads to sacrifice, or willingness to sacrifice, and the story develops with a power which makes Packard's first novel, *Greater Love Hath No Man*, appear weak and insufficiently motivated. Raymond Chapelle, alias Three-Ace Artie, a gambler, is banished from the Yukon. Later, in a little village in French Canada, in order to save himself from the consequences of a murder which he has not done, but in which circumstantial evidence would insure his conviction, he masquerades as Father Aubert, a young priest who had been hurt. The story shows the conditions that force Raymond to continue the rôle of

Father Aubert; tells how he loves Valerie; how he converts an old hag named Mother Blondin and becomes the idol of the parish; how, finally, the real Father Aubert becomes the victim of that same circumstantial evidence which Raymond has tried to escape. When the real priest is tried and sentenced to death Raymond's assumed rôle has so wrought upon him that he confesses the false part he has played—which, in the situation, involves taking the death sentence upon himself. Mother Blondin, his convert, who is really guilty of the murder, in turn saves him.

Again: *From Now On* (1920) tells the story of Dave Henderson, who succumbs to temptation and steals $100,000. He succeeds in hiding the money before he is caught, convicted and sentenced to five years in the penitentiary. When he is released both the bookmaker who had employed him, and who is an inherent crook, and the police take up his trail. But it is a woman's love and his love for her which finally bring Dave Henderson to the point of returning the money. Regeneration. A sacrifice.

In *Pawned* (1921)—a story of pawned people, not pawned things—the father of Claire sacrifices his rights and privileges as a father in the effort toward regeneration. Ultimately he sacrifices his life to free her from a man more dissolute, and far more evil, than himself. Regeneration fails, but redemption takes its place. It is John Bruce, to save whose life Claire has risked everything, who is regenerated. The novel is an extraordinary achievement in plot construction, the precursor of *The Four Stragglers* in that respect; for *Doors of the Night* (1022) was earlier in point of composition.

In order to trace connectedly through a succession of novels the dual themes of sacrifice and regeneration which are Packard's forte, we have omitted mention of his best-known figure, Jimmie Dale. He was introduced with *The Adventures of Jimmie Dale* (1917), carried through *The Further Adventures of Jimmie Dale* (1919) and not necessarily finished with *Jimmie Dale and the Phantom Clue* (1922). Mr. Packard began to write these tales of his gentleman burglar in 1914 and it is a tribute to his skill as a storyteller that, ten years afterward, people read *The Adventures of Jimmie Dale* with a conviction that he will never do better stories.

Jimmie Dale is a rich young man, the inheritor of a fortune made in manufacturing safes. "It had begun really through his connection with his father's business —the business of manufacturing safes that should defy the cleverest criminals. . . . It had begun through that—but at the bottom of it was his own restless, adventurous spirit. He had meant to set the police by the ears." [3] What he had been doing was to force safes as a burglar might force them. The police would find no theft, "in the last analysis they would find only an abortive attempt at crime." Partly "as an added barb," partly "that no innocent bystander of the underworld, innocent for once, might be involved," he had made a habit of pasting conspicuously in sight (on the safe's dial, generally) a diamond- or lozenge-shaped paper wafer, prepared with adhesive on one side and handled with tweezers to avoid leaving a finger print. The succession of crimes without theft became known as the work of the Gray Seal. Then, one night, he had been caught while at work in Maiden Lane, New York. He had wrapped a string of pearls around his wrist in a facetious moment and discovery had compelled him to a desperate dash without time to

[3] *The Adventures of Jimmie Dale,* page 20.

leave the jewelry behind. Not until the next day had he known that his detector was a woman. "The first letter from her had started by detailing his every move of the night before—and it had ended with an ultimatum: 'The cleverness, the originality of the Gray Seal as a crook, lack but one thing,' she had naïvely written, 'and that one thing is a leading string to guide it into channels worthy of his genius.' In a word, *she* would plan the coups, and he would act at her dictation and execute them—or else how did twenty years in Sing Sing for that little Maiden Lane affair appeal to him?"

Cold consideration convinced Jimmie Dale that not even his own father (then alive) would believe in his innocence. "And then had followed those years in which there had been *no* temporizing, in which every plan was carried out to the last detail, those years of curious, unaccountable, bewildering affairs . . . until the Gray Seal had become a name to conjure with." In all this time Jimmie Dale, though communicated with by letter and telephone, had never been able to trace or identify his directress. A year before the book opens she had written: "Things are a little too warm, aren't they Jimmie? Let's let them cool for a year."

Mr. Packard opens, in masterly fashion, at this point; it is the technique of Conan Doyle in the case of Sherlock Holmes (to quote no other examples). One establishes one's detective or criminal—or other exceptional character who tests plausibility—by raising the curtain on him in full career. The way to begin is—not to plunge, but just to slip casually into the middle of things. At first our interest is centered on Jimmie Dale's successive adventures—extremely well-constructed—but as the book develops, the importance and interest of the woman back of Jimmie

Dale asserts itself. Jimmie Dale is led into a series of adventures strictly on her behalf; and what has been in effect a chain of connected short stories becomes virtually a novel. But one characteristic stands out in every chapter. Other writers have shown, though only rarely, an equal ingenuity; no one that I can now recall has shown the same fundamental concerns, the same intense preoccupation under his melodramatic structure. For the exploits of Jimmie Dale, those bizarre and disconnected enterprises to which he is ordered, are Robin Hood exploits, rightings of wrongs, crimes of form and philanthropies of intention. So, later, are the struggles into which Jimmie Dale is precipitated on behalf of the woman whom, no longer mysterious, he deeply loves. Simply, Frank L. Packard is a man who cannot abide the spectacle of a world unless it is the philosopher's world, erected about the steel framework of a moral order. He indulges in crime for morality's sake.

v

In algebra, as you may remember, one equation suffices if you are solving to find a single unknown quantity; two are necessary if two unknown quantities are to be ascertained; and so on. Given three unknown quantities and only two equations, the affair is hopeless. In a perfectly constructed mystery story, the reader is solving for several unknown quantities— for x and for y and possibly for z—but always with one too few equations.

When he came to write *The Four Stragglers* (1923) Mr. Packard had had a considerable experience in handling plots. The first eight pages of the book show three men huddled together under a bombardment in France. Their talk reveals them as former confederates in crime in London. There is a fourth man lying very still on the ground, apparently dead or dying. To make sure, one of the three shoots him. The group is in pitch darkness except for occasional flares. One of these, coming shortly, lights the scene fully. All three look at the spot where a murdered man should be lying. No man is there.

The story opens three years later, in London. We see the three confederates, a varied, effectively contrasted three, reassembled and active. We follow them in a thrilling operation. The main thread now begins to spin. Just as the three have planned to cease operations and take a vacation they come to know of the existence of a treasure hid and watched over by a madman on one of the islands or keys off the Florida coast. The knowledge comes to each one separately, except that B and C each knows that A knows it. And the fourth man, D?

One of the excellences of *The Four Stragglers* is the economy of means; there is not a character in the book who is not indispensable to the action. There is, too, an effect of a Monte Cristo tale, due probably to the treasure quest, the island, and the hiding-place devised by the madman's cunning. The suspense is not only sustained but is steadily intensified; and the book has some scenes very exceptional in their bizarre character. Take this, which is imaginative and not merely inventive. The setting is an aquarium at night, brilliantly lighted, but with the window shades tightly drawn down: ·

"Locke blinked a little in the light as he stepped forward. It reflected bewilderingly from the glass faces of the tanks that were everywhere about. He joined the old man in the center of the aquarium.

Here there was an open space from which the tanks radiated off much after the manner of the spokes of a wheel. A heavy oriental rug was on the tiled floor, and ranged around the table were a number of big easy chairs.

"From under his dressing gown now the old man took a package that was wrapped in oiled silk, and laid it on the table.

" 'Money!' he cried out abruptly. He suddenly commenced to titter again. 'Did I not tell you I was being followed, always being followed? Well, last night they followed a wrong scent. . . . They were there—they are always there—watching—eyes are always watching.' He broke into his insane titter again. . . .

"Subconsciously Locke was aware that the old maniac was still talking, the crazed words rising in shrieks of passionate intensity—but he was no longer paying any attention to the other. He was staring again at the glass tank, behind and a little to one side of the old madman, that contained the sea-horse. It was only a small and diminutive thing, but, unless he were the victim of an hallucination, it had taken on an extraordinary appearance. It seemed to possess *human* eyes; to assume almost the shape of a face—only there was a shadow across it. The water rippled a little. The sea-horse moved to the opposite corner of the tank—but the eyes remained in exactly the same spot."

The reader of *The Four Stragglers* will say, with entire truth: "There is no principal motif of either regeneration or sacrifice here."· No, but there is another motif which Frank L. Packard has reiterated with an equal persistence—punishment for evildoing. The story has, furthermore, a distinctly more ironical quality than Mr. Packard, in his warm indignation at moral disorder, in his determined institution of a moral order, has generally been able to fall back upon. If the wages of sin is death, as his story reminds us, the reward of greed is defeat and the possession of money as money is a grim futility. It is a sharp lesson from one who has learned it—how? I think of the fortunes made by *The Miracle Man* and feel a Jimmie Dale smile on my lips ("his lips thinned"; "a mirthless smile was on his lips") as it occurs to me that Mr. Packard could easily have learned it from simply watching others learn it at his expense. The bill for the lesson, so presented, does not seem unreasonable.

vi

Frank L. Packard and his wife and boys live in a particularly pleasant, and rather a roomy, house set back from the avenue which winds along the north bank of the St. Lawrence at Lachine. In the summer Mrs. Packard and the children may go to Kennebunkport in Maine or some other spot on the seashore. Then will the husband and father spend all the hours of daylight at the Royal Montreal Golf Club, the oldest golf club on this continent, with a clubhouse whose very wide veranda is 300 feet long and whose two eighteen-hole courses are a test of good playing. In the evening he likes to get in three friends, including M. Henri B——, a notary of an old Quebec family, for bridge. Monsieur B—— and his friend, the writer, are likely to have exchanges in French, even though Packard insists that his French is somewhere short of perfection and less good, even, than in his youth when he was a student at Liége. If Robert H. Davis, editor of Munsey's Magazine, or some other old friend from New York is a house guest he will be golfed by day and admitted to the bridge game by night. There are, also, occasions for talk . . . and there are superlative meals, whether at the Royal Montreal, the University Club in Montreal, or at the Packard house. Not only these meals, but the hours between the meals, are made more grateful to many a visitor by the fact that the Province of Quebec is not dry. In fact, the Province is in the liquor business, to the exclusion of all private selling. By establishing government shops where liquor is sold in bottles only, the Province has abolished the saloon and made unnecessary a Provincial income tax.

A few years ago Robert H. Davis used to be able to lure Packard up North on camping and hunting expeditions in which a truly incredible degree of hardship was endured in the name of recreation and healthful exercise. But lately Packard has refused to go. He is content to take his healthful exercise at the Royal Montreal and have a little physical comfort with it.

He is not tall. He has a weathered face, blue eyes, and a grim-looking mouth that is never through smiling. He has been pretty much around the world. Back in 1912 (I think) he sailed from Montreal to Cape Town and then went on to Melbourne and Sydney in Australia. From there he stepped over to Auckland, New Zealand, and investigated Maoriland. He continued through the Pacific, visiting Tonga, Samoa, Fiji and Hawaii. At Samoa he went from Apia to one of the smaller islands, where he lived for a couple of weeks in a chief's hut in native fashion.

Again, in 1923, he went to South America.

Twelve years Mr. Packard waited while an idea that he came upon in the course of his round the world trip took shape. *The Locked Book* is in characteristics somewhat like *The Four Stragglers*. It begins with a yacht drifting, disabled, in Malay waters and proceeds without hesitation to the moment when Kenneth Wayne finds on a barbaric altar a book bound in leather, very old, clasped by the design of a dragon in thick brass, and locked in a strange fashion. The dragon's tail and mouth meet over the edges and the tail is solidly brazed into the mouth. One cannot move the covers by the fraction of an inch. It seems probable that the book holds the secret of a Rajah's treasure in gold and jewels. . . . The reader, after the first flush of enjoyment has passed, will be distinctly interested in analyzing Mr. Packard's methods in the plot and his use of the plot as a vehicle for effects more important.

He believes in having a story. If you ask him to write something about fiction he will emphasize two things: the story and the character of the story, the moral character, that is, and the "moral responsibility" of those who write.[4] And once, certainly, his sense of drama and his sense of the ideal fused in a story of such simplicity and force and elevation as to be intrinsically a work of art. No faults of execution can take away that core of beauty from Frank L. Packard's legend of *The Miracle Man*.

BOOKS BY FRANK L. PACKARD.

1911   *On the Iron at Big Cloud*
1913   *Greater Love Hath No Man*
1914   *The Miracle Man*
1916   *The Belovéd Traitor*
1917   *The Adventures of Jimmie Dale*
1917   *The Sin That Was His*

[4] "The Story—The Precious Corner Stone," by Frank L. Packard in The Photodramatist for November (1923?)

FRANK L. PACKARD UNLOCKS A BOOK

1918   *The Wire Devils*
1919   *The Further Adventures of Jimmie Dale*
1919   *The Night Operator*
1920   *From Now On*
1920   *The White Moll*
1921   *Pawned*
1922   *Doors of the Night*
1922   *Jimmie Dale and the Phantom Clue*
1923   *The Four Stragglers*
1924   *The Locked Book*

SOURCES ON FRANK L. PACKARD

In addition to those cited in the text of the chapter: Robert
H. Davis, 280 Broadway, New York, N. Y.

22. All Creeds and None

i

THIS ought to be the most interesting chapter in this book. For it deals with the subject of belief. Belief is of many kinds—religious, scientific, philosophical—but when one ceases to believe in anything at all, one dies.

In Chapter 10, I tried to indicate how the interest in religious belief has already begun to reflect itself in current fiction. In this chapter I am to deal with books which vary profoundly but are all straightforward efforts to express a belief held to be worth while. For the difficulty is not a lack of things to believe in, but a choice among them, a reconciliation (sometimes) of one with another; and very often a search for the thing that will mean more than life itself.

Can anything mean more than life itself? Yes. Men and women have sacrificed their lives for such.

Are the terms of belief capable of a common expression, acceptable to all men and women? No; at least, not yet.

Is it even necessary to know what one believes, in the sense of being able to give it a satisfactory expression? No; not if one lives it.

Can anything be achieved by reading books on belief? Yes. I suppose you may show surprise if I say that disagreement is often more useful than agreement. But agreement leading to a placid inactivity is against the very principle of life itself.

[348]

ALL CREEDS AND NONE

Disagreement causes thought.. Thinking always enlarges our living. For what we then do is done more consciously, more knowingly, than before. To that extent—and in no other way is it possible—we live more fully.

Which among the books to follow you ought to read or in what order they are for your reading, no one like myself can determine, for an answer depends on your belief, tastes, the extent of your reading and the extent of your thinking. Such a book as L. P. Jacks's *Religious Perplexities* is safely commendable to anyone, anywhere. But such studies as Lord Balfour's *Theism and Thought*, full of refinements and instinct with intellectual subtlety, are for the scholarly taste. Dr. E. Y. Mullins's *Christianity at the Crossroads* is fundamentalist in its position. Dr. Joseph A. Leighton's *Religion and the Mind of Today* is the work of a churchman who is also a philosopher and a teacher; it adopts the liberal attitude. And a number of these books concern themselves with health, the mind, the will and the spirit—those factors which so often determine not only belief, but the possibility of believing in anything.

If I start with Ernest Renan's *Life of Jesus*, a work now many years old, I do so because this Frenchman's extraordinary book remains undisplaced by the current great success of Papini's *Life of Christ*, but also because the popularity of Papini's book shows where the average interest lies. For when men begin contending about the forms of creeds and the facts behind phrases which have become sacred formulas, the instinct of the ordinary man is to go straight to the essentials and the beginnings. Let doctors argue the Virgin Birth; he rather asks himself what sort of Man was this Son born of Mary. It is the assertion of this instinct, joined to the timely appearance of the *Life of Christ* with its undeniable interest and eloquence, which made the success of Papini's volume. Such a success is fleeting. Like other converts and re-converts to Catholicism, Papini exhibited a marked tendency toward a belief that little had happened in the centuries preceding his accession. Not so, Renan. To go from the Italian to the Frenchman is to pass from painted scenery to the clear air and the sublime altitude of mountain peaks. There is something beyond eloquence, and Renan has it. With him both reflection and emotion are controlled; they lift him high and sustain him there. "Disastrous to Reason the day when she should stifle religion!" exclaimed this author of the *Life of Jesus*, adding: "Religions are false when they attempt to prove the infinite, to define it, to incarnate it; but they are true when they affirm it. The greatest errors they import into that affirmation are nothing compared to the value of the truth which they proclaim. The simplest of the simple, provided he practice heart-worship, is more enlightened as to the reality of things than the materialist who thinks he explains everything by chance or by finite causes."

Renan was repeatedly called an atheist; but none of the books discussed in this chapter are atheistic. I should present any which were, but I think it significant that none is. Lord Balfour's *Theism and Thought*, a strictly philosophical treatise in sequence to his *Theism and Humanism*, is a deliberate attempt to consider whether theism—that is, belief in God—is necessary or good. And every Balfourian conclusion is in favor of theism. Dr. L. P. Jacks, with his marvelous simplicity of expression, deals in *Religious Perplexities* with the two questions that every man asks: Why am I here? Why am I, and not some other, here and now? But the answer to both of these questions, stated as Dr. Jacks states it, for men of every sort, Christian and non-Christian, presupposes a God.

The three most recent books by Dr. Jacks vary considerably. *The Lost Radiance of the Christian Religion* is simply an address in which he makes a moving appeal for the recapture of Christian joyousness. *Realities and Shams* is a series of essays produced by reflection on events of the last nine years, continuous in the thread of their thought, which is the few and simple tests to tell the genuine from the false; and Dr. Jacks applies these tests to some public affairs. *A Living Universe* is directly related to *Religious Perplexities;* its point is that education without religious feeling is lifeless, just as a universe in which education does not proceed is a dead universe.

Such books as *Realities and Shams* and *A Living Universe* are directly related to Felix Adler's Hibbert lectures, now published under the title, *The Reconstruction of the Spiritual Ideal.* The distinguished founder of the Ethical Culture Society has never been one to deal with abstractions. In this book he brings his spiritual ideal to bear upon the problem of marriage, the labor problem, and the problem of a society of nations. The essence of his teaching, which employs both Jewish and Christian ideals of holiness, is his conception of a "weft of souls" in which each individual soul has intrinsic worth but all share in, and contribute to, a spiritual commonwealth. He strongly opposes attacks on the permanency of marriage, and for marriage itself he insists on a loftier standard. The problem of labor seems to him one of perfecting personal relations in industry, though it be necessary to reshape industry to achieve it. And though provisional solutions of the problem of a society of nations seem to Dr. Adler inadequate and futile, he is at pains to establish the principle on which such a society can, he thinks, be founded.

Religion and the Mind of Today, by Joseph A. Leighton, asks for careful definition. The author is a priest of the Protestant Episcopal Church. He is now professor of philosophy in the Ohio State University, the author of *Man and the Cosmos* and of an introductory book on philosophy used in many colleges. Dr. Leighton, in a sense, offers himself as living evidence that acceptance of modern science is not inconsistent with a deep and satisfying religion expressed in a formal creed. His book consists of three parts. The first studies the indispensable rôle of religion in a civilization, and aims to show the relation of religion to culture and its function in human society. The second part is a study of Christianity; it argues the superior ethics of Jesus to other systems of ethics; and endeavors to apply Christian ethics to problems of modern life. The third part of the book is on the validity of religion. Dr. Leighton finds religious belief entirely compatible with scientific discovery. He also, in special chapters, does his best to clear such religious problems as the nature of faith, the origin of the universe, the incarnation of Christ, the efficacy of prayer, and the immortality of the soul.

His work, which is general, leads me directly to the new book by Shailer Mathews and others, which is specific. If there is one thing which can be said about *Contributions of Science to Religion*, it is that the book gets down to bed rock. Dr. Mathews, dean of the Divinity School of the University of Chicago, one of the best known educators and editors in America, conceived the idea of getting representative scientists to tell compactly of those portions of the world, or life, which were their special provinces: He wanted to see what the resulting picture would be like. He asked bluntly: "After the scientists have explained the construction of the universe, the earth and man, is there any room left for God?" He felt, as he says in the opening sentence of this book, that "a man's religion must not give the lie to the world in which he lives." And he also felt, as he says in his introduction, that "if scientific knowledge could really destroy faith in God it would do so—and it *should* do so."

He got thirteen chapters by some very distinguished men, to which he prefixed a chapter of his own, then writing a final summarizing chapter; and this is the book. Among the scientist contributors are W. E. Ritter, director of the Scripps Marine Biological Laboratory of the University of California, who writes on the scientific method of reaching truth; Robert A. Millikan, the physicist who was the first to succeed in isolating an electron; and Edwin S. Frost, director of the Yerkes Observatory. The arrangement of chapters is ingenious and even dramatic. For example, one goes from the contemplation of invisible atoms made up of electrons to that of a universe, made up of electrons infinitesimally small but containing bodies many million times the size of our sun.

There is neither religion nor theology in these thirteen scientific chapters, which may be read, and can most profitably be read, by anyone who seeks simply a bird's-eye view of what science has found out. Dr. Mathews sums up ably; yet his case is practically stated in Professor Ritter's remark that "seeing God in the Universe is no more *difficult* than seeing electrons there."

But in praising this striking and admirable volume, I fully recognize that its very sharpness and definite-

[353]

ness make it extremely provocative—though therefore all the more interesting. To the mind purely mystical, *Contributions of Science to Religion* must remain all beside the point; and to Dr. Mathews's assertion that "a man's religion must not give the lie to the world in which he lives," the mystic will reply that that, precisely, is what *his* religion is for. And with many the question does not take the form in which Dr. Mathews puts it, but rather the form in which Dr. E. Y. Mullins, president of the Southern Baptist Theological Seminary, puts it in his *Christianity at the Crossroads:* "Will Christianity continue its redemptive work in the world, or will it cool into a reform movement, without redemptive power?" So asked, the answer may well be different. Dr. Mullins argues—and without appeal to authority of any kind—that the Christian religion is free and autonomous, and that efforts to transform it have failed. And if it is to be Christianity against a new religion, he has no doubt as to where the victory will lie.

ii

Sir Oliver Lodge's *Making of Man* has something in common with the books I have discussed and some relation to the books I am coming to; but first I wish to ward off a misconception. Sir Oliver's views of an after life, his experiments and speculations are well-known; but *Making of Man* is not in any sense a spiritualist volume. It is a study in evolution; a short, simple account of physical science which the author then relates, so far as our knowledge permits, to the history of the soul. His own special beliefs are kept out of the way; his point is that what we know from physics and other branches of science makes immortality of the soul an irresistible conclusion. As he says: "It is beginning to seem possible that the conservation of matter and energy may have to be supplemented by the conservation of life and mind. . . . I feel sure of this: that the Universe is a much completer whole than we had imagined. Every kind of real existence is permanent; and our activities do not cease when we change our instrument." The book is brief, very sincere, and of interest to readers of every class and shade of opinion.

In *Evolution: the Way of Life*, Vernon Kellogg, the zoölogist, has written a book designed for the general reader who wants exact but simply expressed knowledge concerning the theory. The author has been at pains to tie up his discussion to the evolution we all can see in ourselves and in the Nature about us. This is decidedly a book to clear up and make definite the reader's conception of what evolution is and is not, and of its significance to mankind.

The two remaining impersonal books I have to present are both purely scientific, though almost startlingly diverse; and then I shall go on to speak of books distinctly personal to the reader.

And first I offer a work of science keenly interesting to the general reader. George Grant MacCurdy of Yale is known wherever anthropology is known. For many years he has been gathering the materials for a history of man before recorded history begins. The interest of pre-history, as the subject is called, needs no emphasis. Its appeal has been shown by the success of such books as Henry Fairfield Osborne's *Men of the Old Stone Age* and by the fascination most readers confess to feeling for the earlier chapters of H. G. Wells's *An Outline of History*. But pre-history, sketched by Wells, dealt with partially by Osborne, had never been fully written in a single, up-to-date

work. Dr. MacCurdy has done it in the two volumes
of his *Human Origins: A Manual of Pre-History.*

Human Origins is a great book. It must be remembered that all we know about prehistoric man is the
discovery of the last hundred years, discovery that has
come thick and fast, but which has remained scattered. I shall say nothing about the work involved
in writing *Human Origins;* its immensity is apparent.
But it is sheer luck that we have in Dr. MacCurdy a
writer whose imagination and sense of the dramatic
turn the whole affair into a superlative story.

Man, emerging as a distinct species, entered upon
the Old Stone age, testified to by flint implements
which we can just begin to see bear evidences of
human shaping. The Old Stone Age lasted a long
while. During it, in intervals of thousands of years,
ice swept down over Europe and North America in
four successive glaciations. The three warm intervals
between these four ice epochs are the lower, middle,
and upper paleolithic periods. In each, prehistoric
man made some rude advance toward better tools and
weapons. He even progressed in art to the extent of
painting on cave walls. Then the ice came down
again, and for thousands of years man lost nearly all
the gain he had made.

He reappears in the New Stone Age using chipped
and polished flints, mining the flints in certain places,
working them in certain places. Pottery-making began, and some idea of weaving was gained. Religious
ideas were first entertained. Fire was conquered and
put to man's use, the wheel was invented, animals were
domesticated. Then came the Bronze Age, with its
discovery of how to smelt copper, tin, gold, silver.
The Iron Age arrived when man had acquired sufficient skill in smelting this more durable metal and

could use it to replace all others in things of hard use.

Approximately 400 illustrations, of a fascination at least equal to the text, appear in the two volumes of *Human Origins*.

If the new book on *Haunted Houses* did not bear the name of so distinguished a scientist as M. Camille Flammarion, it would find no place, I am afraid, in this chapter. M. Flammarion is fully aware of the skepticism he must encounter, and is at pains to refute it as fully as possible in his book. But great as the interest of this controversy is, I think most readers will find the mere subject irresistible, and I am certain that everyone, even he who pooh-poohs all the evidence, will be captivated by the strange stories to be read in *Haunted Houses*. Dwellings that are variously authenticated for their troublesome character are discussed in chapter after chapter—a chateau at Calvados, a habitation in Auvergne, the house of La Constantine, a parsonage, a teacher's house, the fantastic villa of Comedada at Coimbra in Portugal, the maleficient ceiling at Oxford, Pierre Loti's mosque at Rochefort. And after so much, a chapter providing "A General Excursion Among Haunted Houses"! Flammarion then classes the phenomena as of two kinds—those associated with the dead and those not so attributable. But he is no mere credulous believer in haunting. He devotes a chapter to houses spuriously haunted. His book concludes with a search for causes and an assertion, or reassertion, of belief in certain evidence; "the unknown of yesterday is the truth of tomorrow." It is interesting to note that there has been legal recognition of haunted houses.

iii

Two of the personal books before me are by Dr. James J. Walsh, medical director of Fordham University's School of Sociology, professor of physiological psychology at Cathedral College, and author of that remarkable history of fakes and faith-wrought miracles, *Cures*. In *Health Through Will Power*, Dr. Walsh is dealing with a subject which, more than any other one thing, has been made the foundation of new and powerful religious sects. But Dr. Walsh's interest is in the application and the uses of will power in the individual.

He therefore shows the preventive and curative power of the will in such universal ailments as coughs and colds, intestinal disorders, rheumatism, and the like. But most importantly he shows the rôle of the will in dealing with mental disturbances and in a therapeutic application to bad habits as diverse as self-pity, yielding to pain or succumbing to sentimentalism in sympathy, and irregular and insufficient exercise.

Health Through Will Power is untechnical. Anyone can read and understand it.

Success in a New Era, Dr. Walsh's other book, shows that the application of the will is the most important factor in achieving success of any kind. Is education important? Yes, but "it is not for lack of knowledge but for lack of will power that men fail to accomplish what they want to. Men have powers or energies far beyond what they usually think, and the men who use them up to something like their capacity make a success of life."

Next to will power comes work; and work must be offset by recreation, though proper recreation calls for the expenditure of mental or physical energy as great as work.

I am not sure that Dr. Walsh's warning about reading is needed in America. "Reading," he says, "requires the least mental labor of almost any pursuit, and hardly a person but sooner or later finds himself putting off something that ought to be done by pretending that he is accomplishing more by his reading. Reading in itself is excellent, but it is vastly overused to excuse the inaction of weak and lazy people." No doubt; but of 961 people I personally know well, 857 spend every evening listening to the radio, attending a moving picture, or playing cards and dancing. Of the remaining 104, only eighty-one read.

Yet Dr. Walsh is dead right when he says that "the best good habit in the world is the proper use of time" —though the acquisition of more hours in a day would be helpful—and his *Success in a New Era* is a singularly honest and helpful book, free from even one patent formula for attaining "success."

The Foundations of Personality, by Abraham Myerson, M.D., though on more general lines, is of no less value. Dr. Myerson analyzes the elements of character—which is not, of course, the same thing as mind. Character is intimately related to mind, as the brain and body are intimately related. Character may be affected by both the mind and the body; it is not dependent on either. Dr. Myerson describes the general types of character, the tradition of each and its social heredity; and he follows the energies of men as they expend themselves in instinct and emotion and intelligence. Although a physician and a psychologist, he writes from the standpoint of one who deeply shares the everyday aspirations and conflicts of his fellows. His comments on the influences exerted upon character, and on the expression of character in work, play, humor, sex and religion are of acute interest. His book's great practical value is dual: it helps toward self-understanding and it gives a good deal of help toward insight into the characters of others—a matter which usually has an important part in determining our own success or failure in life.

Simpler than *The Foundations of Personality* because of a much narrower scope is Arthur Holmes's *Controlled Power: A Study of Laziness and Achievement*. This popularly-written book by a professor of psychology is almost a handbook on the subject of laziness, its causes and cure. For not all laziness comes from the same cause, and not all apparent laziness is laziness in fact. There is such a thing as the indolence of genius, well-illustrated by Professor Holmes in the cases of Dr. Samuel Johnson, Oliver Goldsmith, and the naturalist, John Muir. There is the languor of youth, when the rapid growth of the body may produce a kind of inertia either physical or mental. The aversion of the normal boy to study is easily explained, Professor Holmes holds. What people have done much they like much to do; and what they have done little they like little to do. What the human race has not done very long is hard for individuals of the race to do. The human race has hunted and fished for thousands of years; it has studied for a very few centuries, and studied in the mass for only about one century. Of course the boy will prefer to hunt or fish!

Controlled Power is so entirely readable that one feels as if it should be put in the hands of every parent and school teacher. Its wisdom could do much for them, as well as for the child.

Teachers and many parents could read advantageously also *The Normal Mind*, by William H. Burnham, professor of pedagogy and school hygiene in Clark University. If our knowledge of what we call mental hygiene shows us anything, it shows us that most people do not utilize the brains they have. The whole purpose of mental hygiene is to teach how to make the most of one's inborn ability. The power to think with clearness means usually the throwing off of bad mental habits.

Professor Burnham, teaching at G. Stanley Hall's institution and with a background of many years' experience and observation, has produced a book which most satisfactorily compends what we know about mental hygiene to date. His presentation of the school task, of mental attitudes, of suggestion and mental hygiene, of success and failure and discipline offers in practical form the wisdom we have regarding mental health and how to attain it.

Twelve Tests of Character, by the Reverend Harry Emerson Fosdick, D.D., has amply proven its popularity; indeed, it has for months been among the ten best-selling books of non-fiction throughout America. Dr. Fosdick's tests are tests of character in action, not conventional qualities nor abstract traits. Written with reference to Christian teaching, the book is nevertheless one of extreme popular appeal. Nothing of the sort has more "rush" of style and pointedness, more irresistibility in brushing aside objections and obstacles. Undoubtedly the wealth of illustrative instances and anecdotes has greatly enhanced its popularity.

iv

But my chapter runs too long. I have saved for the end, and will not quit leaving unmentioned, Albert

Payson Terhune's *Now That I'm Fifty*. Is Mr. Terhune's outspokenness a bit brutal? I do not think so. He is fifty and knows whereof he writes; why should he not tell what he knows? Is it cruel to say that one should have money, such money as he can acquire, with which to meet fifty? No, it is common sense. Is it bitter to point out, with unmistakable instances, that fifty cannot do the things that twenty does? Most decidedly not; for Mr. Terhune points out those other things that twenty cannot do, and that fifty can. Fifty cannot run five miles; twenty can. Very well; when Mr. Terhune was in his twenties and tried to work a few hours at night after the work of the day, he went all to pieces. But now, at fifty, he can work better than ever before in his life; longer hours, harder work; and come out of it smiling. In fact, in *Now That I'm Fifty* he practically says: "Look at the things I used to be able to do and can do no longer; and thank the Lord I can't!" This little book of Terhune's, not much more than an extended essay, is so honest, so merry, so frank and so mellow that I think fifty can safely put it in the hands of those who aspire to be fifty.

23. J. C. Snaith and George Gibbs

i

CERTAIN novelists there are who, if they chance upon worthy material, need ask odds of no writer of fiction now living. I think at once of two Englishmen in this class, and one of them is John Collis Snaith. In such books as *The Coming* and *The Undefeated* he has had material of the first order and has wrought greatly with it. And at all times he is a novelist and entertainer of much more than ordinary competence.

The outstanding matters about J. C. Snaith are several. The first is his steady productivity through twenty years; for the number of novelists who sustain their work so long is not large. The second, and a more important matter, is Snaith's striking variety. As Henry Sydnor Harrison, the author of *Queed*, has said, Snaith "is absolutely his own man, always doing his own things in his own way and refusing to be deterred; and this quality gives to his published works a remarkable range." I wonder how many realize what courage, and even what sacrifice, such a course entails? Not many, probably. But the simple fact is that we all insist on putting a storyteller in a particular compartment in our minds. Let a man please us with a tale of a certain kind and we reject a tale from him of any other kind. This is very discouraging to the novelist, who, after all, is not producing Ford cars. As readers of fiction we should select a good chassis and give our novelist complete rope on the custom-built body.

J. C. Snaith was born of Yorkshire folk in Nottinghamshire, 1876. As a youth he played for his county in cricket, football and hockey. His health became impaired and he had to give up athletics. He lives down on the North Shore at Skegness but spends some time in London (where he may be found in a goodly company of novelists at the Garrick Club). But whether in the country or in town, as he says: "Outside of my work, I have no story to tell. I am always submerged in a novel. My life has been singularly uneventful. It seems to begin and end in the writing of novels. I study them continually and each one I write is in the nature of an experiment. In my humble opinion, the art of novel writing is in a state of continual development. To me a good novel is a mental tonic, exhilarating, educative, humanizing."

It will be to the point, then, with this modest man to give, chiefly, some sketch of his work. His first novel, *Broke of Covenden* (1904) is such a portrait of the English squire as no one else, I think, has given us. Those who were delighted by Sheila Kaye-Smith's *The End of the House of Alard*, and those who count as a great experience Galsworthy's *The Forsyte Saga* should lose no time in reading *Broke of Covenden*. Richard Mansfield longed for a play from Snaith's novel so that he might act as Broke. Well, it is not too late to fashion the play for some one like Lionel Barrymore.

William Jordan, Junior (1907) shares with *The Coming* (1907) first place in Snaith's own estimate of the comparative merit of his novels. The two have a certain remarkable likeness. Jordan is a poet of "uni-

versal power given to no other person in the modern or
the ancient world"; an utterly unworldly youth and
man; a symbol of the artist or prophet or poet who
comes with a message for all mankind and who finds
mankind unready to listen—who is, besides, caught in
the coil of a life he does not understand and to which
he has no real relation. *The Coming*, exquisite and
powerful, suggests in its principal figure the re-
appearance of Jesus Christ in England during the
World War. These novels are therefore really expressions of the human spirit done with extraordinary force
and unusual directness. They are, however, unsenti-
mental, reticent, quiet in tone and they do accomplish
in terms of the novel with many accents of realistic
detail what men have generally been driven to express in fable, allegory, legend or poem—in other
words, with a pretty complete divorce from everyday
actuality. Snaith never quite sacrifices that. It is his
distinction (unique, I think) to have been able in these
two books to take a lofty and sublime subject and
bring it to earth without shearing its wings.

The same effect is partly realized in *The Sailor*
(1916), supposed to have been suggested by the career
of John Masefield; but here the whole treatment is
more markedly realistic and perhaps more open to a
charge of sentimentality. Yet *The Sailor* by virtue of
its extreme realism (except the short period on shipboard, which bears only the most fantastic relation to
such an actual experience) is richer than either
William Jordan, Junior or *The Coming* in the elements of popular interest and appeal. If it at moments approaches hysteria, so did A. S. M. Hutchin-
son's *If Winter Comes;* if Henry Harper's rise taxes
ready belief, the drama of his upward struggle from
dirt and obscurity to freedom and success and power

is a drama on which the reader's interest hangs breathlessly throughout.

Many, and with justice, consider *The Undefeated* (1919) the best novel Snaith has written. Certainly this can be said for it: Appearing at a time when the public utterly refused to read "war books," this simple story of a little English greengrocer and his family in time of war became a best seller without any perceptible delay. Even today, perhaps, *The Undefeated* is most abidingly in demand of all the Snaith novels. "The kind of person Snaith writes about is the kind of person that fascinates me and that I try to write about. How I wish I could do it with his big simplicity!" exclaimed Edna Ferber, when she had finished the book. "A thing of finest spirit. It is one of the few works of fiction I have been able to read through since August, 1914," was Tarkington's comment, and other authors were not silent. Among an hundred novels and would-be novels and fact-books about the war, all loud as so many shrieks, this quiet voice could make itself heard. For among many merits in *The Undefeated* the greatest was the restraint with which Snaith wrote; and he contrived both by tone and by speech to say what H. G. Wells and others, alike in pulpits and on soapboxes, could never seem to utter.

There is another Snaith, the man of amusement who entertains himself and the reader with light fiction. Sometimes it is an engaging romance on the order of his *Araminta;* again it is a divertissement of youth, like *The Principal Girl;* most recently it is the friendly fun, by no means unalloyed with admiration, of *There Is a Tide.* The title is taken, of course, from the familiar, "There is a tide in the affairs of men which, taken at the flood leads on to fortune." Mame Durrance, of Cowbarn, Iowa, aided by an aunt's legacy, and weaponed with her own pluck, seeks her fortune first in New York and then in London. As Miss Amethyst Du Rance, European correspondent of the home-town newspaper, she seems destined to fail in her object. But when her affairs are most discouraging she finds friendship with Lady Violet Trehem, and the gayest pages in Snaith's novel record Mame's adventures in English society. Mr. Snaith obviously likes his heroine. He avoids burlesque and his comedy is a laugh with, and not a laugh at. The impossible type of ending is dexterously avoided; and if there is any fault to find it is with the author's prodigious and incredible assimilation of American slang. He really knows it, though perhaps he doesn't discriminate with nicety between last year's and this; but the result is a little like a cook unfamiliar with garlic and using it for the first time.

The main delight in Snaith's work is unchanging—it is the delight of adventurousness. One may not know in what precise field his new novel will take one, but one goes with him in the certain and satisfactory knowledge that the exploration will be a finished job. "To me a good novel is exhilarating, educative, humanizing." All three qualities mark his own work.

ii

Like J. C. Snaith, George Gibbs became a novelist for the love of writing novels, and like Robert W. Chambers he is both novelist and painter-illustrator. I say "for love of writing novels" when perhaps I ought to say for love of telling stories; and then the likeness with Mr. Chambers could be extended. The love of telling stories may seem to lie at the base of any novelist's career; but there are certainly differences. But what one has in mind in the case of Mr. Gibbs is a certain natural activity rather than a studied, deliberate and conscious choice.

He began to write very young, doing newspaper articles of a popular cast on scientific and naval topics. Then his work as an illustrator became more important. For a long while he illustrated his own stories and novels, as well as those of other men. As his skill in fiction developed and a really large audience grew up for the novels, Mr. Gibbs let illustration drop into the background. However, in recent years he has turned again after a ten-year interval to painting in oils. Now that his footing as a writer is secure, he says that to turn from a novel to painting rests him. But at first he wrote only in late afternoon and evenings when the light was too bad for work at the easel.

George Gibbs was born 8 March 1870 at New Orleans, the son of Benjamin Franklin Gibbs and Elizabeth Beatrice (Kellogg) Gibbs. The father was an officer in the United States Navy and died at Trieste while serving as fleet surgeon of the European squadron. Part of the son's schooling was got near Geneva, Switzerland, and afterward he was entered at the United States Naval Academy where he generally neglected trigonometry in favor of a sketch book and the writing of verses. On leaving Annapolis he entered the night classes of the Corcoran School of Art and the Art Students' League, Washington, D. C. "My days," he says, "were devoted to writing very poor short stories which steadily went the rounds of all the magazines of the country, only to be returned. I got in debt and began to write special articles for New York newspapers with sufficient luck to finish my art courses." He came to Philadelphia before he was 30. Cyrus H. K. Curtis had just bought the

Saturday Evening Post and Gibbs got work as an illustrator. In 1901 he married Maud Stovell Harrison of Philadelphia and he has been a Philadelphian ever since, living in Rosemont and having an office on Chestnut Street and appearing now and then in the agreeable company gathered at the Franklin Inn Club.

His first book was a collection of boys' stories on great naval heroes. Then he wrote a long, leisurely French historical novel, *In Search of Mademoiselle.* After another of the same sort he struck his *metier* with *The Medusa Emerald.* With his next novel but one, *The Bolted Door*, he became an author whose work goes to press early and often. The book went through a dozen editions and Mr. Gibbs, like Robert W. Chambers, decided that illustration was not the better part of valor.

He was frankly glad. "Inventing plots, people and situations is a thousand times more interesting than drawing scenes," he says. He had long since discovered that when one does both writing and painting different personalities are exercised. And he had in his own case an amusing experience which should greatly console those authors who have suffered from what seem to them the vagaries of the illustrators of their work. Mr. Gibbs soon found that he could not illustrate his own stories perfectly!

"When I approached my stories to illustrate them it always seemed as though they had been written by another person. I got the trained illustrator's idea from a situation. It never worked out exactly like the picture I had in mind when I wrote the passage. Before I begin a story, I can see every character's face and how he will move and what he will be doing at various climaxes. But when I come to paint him, I don't give it."

CARGOES FOR CRUSOES

A George Gibbs novel is characterized by a certain substance and power which make a comparison with the most successful work of Robert W. Chambers rather too natural and too easy to be trusted. Mr. Chambers, by his own admission, has always written the story which, at the moment, it amused him to write. Mr. Gibbs, with an equal equipment, has become steadily more intent on his work, both in the choice of subjects and in the treatment. He has never been without an interest in and a respect for character; and even in novels which are essentially novels of intrigue and suspense, like *The Yellow Dove*, the characterization is far from superficial. When he has a descriptive passage to write he takes his time to find the words, and his work shows the painstaking. Perhaps Mr. Chambers of some years ago and Mr. Gibbs of today are most alike in their distinct flair for the absorbing, even the fashionable, subject. Mr. Gibbs, perhaps owing to his painter's side, is unrestricted by place or social stratification. *The Yellow Dove* opens with excellent Cockney talk; *The Secret Witness* moves with assurance in central Europe; *The Golden Bough* details an American soldier's adventures in Germany; *The Black Stone* has scenes in Arabia; *The Splendid Outcast* is vivid with bits of the Paris underworld; *The House of Mohun* chronicles the rise and fall of an American family stranded between its town house and its Long Island estate; and the heroine of *Fires of Ambition* is a red-haired Irish girl, an obscure employee of an obscure cloak and suit concern.

A change in Mr. Gibbs's work, the result of a definite intention which he avowed at the time, can be seen beginning with *Youth Triumphant* (1921). It resulted from a wish to do novels more truly representative of American life than any he had done. He had come to feel, as Swinnerton expresses it, that romance should spring from a personal vision of life and not merely from that kind of romantic material which has been so much used and which has only the makeshift value of stage properties. The deepening treatment is noticeable in *The House of Mohun*. It is continued in *Fires of Ambition*, where Mary Ryan, having conquered life, asks herself: "What are these things I have fought for? What are they in comparison with the love I might have had?" Most observable is the maturer study of character and destinies in George Gibbs's latest and most competent novel, *Sackcloth and Scarlet*.

This is the history of two sisters of whom the older, Joan, is a responsible person and the younger, Polly, begins in weakness and progresses toward destruction. The development is smooth and unhurried and the characterization has a certain skill and a gradual intensity which is scarcely to be found in Mr. Gibbs's earlier books. The scene moves to Brittany, to Washington and to Atlantic City as the story proceeds; and in each case the novelist establishes his people firmly in the new setting. There is very little artifice and what there is works quite simply and directly to show the interrelation of just the three most important people. And yet, in an ordered fashion, the book does bring up very momentous questions—such a question as the difference between motherliness and motherhood, and the graver question of accident and destiny in the existence of a child.

In his fiction George Gibbs has now come to have more points of resemblance and contact, perhaps, with Arthur Train and Rupert Hughes than with other contemporary American novelists. He can, at any rate,

[371]

be depended upon for sincere and ambitious work, executed by a practiced hand.

BOOKS BY J. C. SNAITH

1904	*Broke of Covenden*
1906	*Henry Northcote*
1907	*William Jordan, Junior*
1909	*Araminta* [republished 1923
1910	*Fortune*
1910	*Mrs. Fitz*
	Lady Barbarity
	Anne Feversham
1912	*The Principal Girl*
1914	*An Affair of State*
1915	*The Great Age*
1916	*The Sailor*
1917	*The Coming*
1918	*Mary Plantagenet*
	The Time Spirit
1919	*The Undefeated*
	In England: *Love Lane*
1920	*The Adventurous Lady*
1922	*The Council of Seven*
1923	*The Van Roon*
1924	*There Is a Tide*

SOURCES ON J. C. SNAITH

Excellent descriptive notes on many of Mr. Snaith's novels will be found on page 155 *et seq.* of R. Brimley Johnson's *Some Contemporary Novelists* (Men), published by Leonard Parsons, London.

An appreciative review of *The Sailor* forms a short chapter in S. P. B. Mais's *Some Modern Authors* (Dodd, Mead & Company). See page 133 *et seq.*

"J. C. Snaith," by W. M. Parker, in The Bookman (London) for April, 1922.

J. C. SNAITH AND GEORGE GIBBS

BOOKS BY GEORGE GIBBS

1900 *Pike and Cutlass: Hero Tales of Our Navy*
1901 *In Search of Mademoiselle*
1903 *American Sea Fights.* Portfolio of colored drawings
1905 *The Love of Monsieur*
1907 *The Medusa Emerald*
1909 *Tony's Wife*
1911 *The Bolted Door*
1911 *The Forbidden Way*
1912 *The Maker of Opportunities*
1913 *The Silent Battle*
1913 *Madcap*
1914 *The Flaming Sword*
1915 *The Yellow Dove*
1916 *Paradise Garden*
1917 *The Secret Witness*
1918 *The Golden Bough*
1919 *The Black Stone*
1920 *The Splendid Outcast*
1921 *The Vagrant Duke*
1921 *Youth Triumphant*
1922 *The House of Mohun*
1923 *Fires of Ambition*
1924 *Sackcloth and Scarlet*

SOURCES ON GEORGE GIBBS

"Illustrates His Own Books" (article and interview), The Sun, New York, 18 February 1911.

"George Gibbs on His Work." Interview by Francis Hill in the Philadelphia Public Ledger. Date uncertain: 1912 or 1913.

"George Gibbs, a Novelist, and His Ideas." Interview by Theodocia F. Walton in the Philadelphia Press, 21 March 1920.

Who's Who in America.

CARGOES FOR CRUSOES

NOTE: George Gibbs's prowess as a painter in oils deserves a special note. He has painted some splendid nudes which have been widely exhibited, in particular one called "The Gold Screen" which has been at the Corcoran Gallery in Washington, the Chicago Institute of Fine Arts, the St. Louis Gallery, the Pennsylvania Academy of Fine Arts and other exhibitions. He has done some striking marines which have been shown at the Pennsylvania Academy and the Corcoran Gallery and are now (April, 1924) on view in Baltimore. He has become a portrait painter much in demand with more commissions offered him than he cares to accept.

In painting as in fiction his effort has been to achieve a steady progression into more serious and more ambitious work; and the difference between some early illustration of his and "The Gold Screen" is scarcely greater than between his first few novels and such work as *The House of Mohun* or *Sackcloth and Scarlet*.

24. Mary Johnston's Adventure

i

THERE lives in the city of New York a large, blond man who knows many authors and editors and publishers and who goes between them. That is his business, and yet, in spite of this dreadful occupation he is a merry man with a childlike countenance and a cheerful and carefree manner. Insouciant words bubble from his lips while his head rolls round on his shoulders; his invariable air is one of entire helplessness even in propitious circumstances; his tone is a tone of gay despair. His attitude toward all authors is fatherly and tender, and so is his attitude toward editors and publishers; he as much as admits that literature is a deplorable affair all around, and his expressive eye and accent say: "Courage! We shall yet make the best of this situation. You, who are about to buy, salute us." At times a strange gleam comes into his face and on more than one such occasion I have heard him murmur that some day he will turn publisher and bring out two books which were published, indeed, but not read. And one of those books is *Michael Forth*, by Mary Johnston.

Miss Johnston was read before the publication of *Michael Forth* and she has been read since. Her best work of one kind lies before it; her best work of another and more significant kind has followed it. *Michael Forth* is simply a chrysalis, escaping notice, from which was to come, in place of the writer of superb historical romances like *To Have and To Hold* and historical novels like *The Long Roll* and *Cease Firing*, an author as strange as William Blake, a woman whose proper company in American literature is Emily Dickinson, Emerson, Thoreau, Whitman, Margaret Fuller and Melville.

"She is a mystic bent upon the expressive embodiment of what eye hath not seen and ear hath not heard until she saw and heard it," concludes an anonymous writer.[1] The account of Mary Johnston's adventure given by this writer is as unsatisfactory as secondhand versions of a mystical experience must necessarily be. Miss Johnston may or may not write the story; Emerson said that "the highest cannot be spoken," and, most certainly, it cannot with adequacy be written. Miss Johnston has made some attempt to put her adventure on paper, but the result so far discourages her. In what follows I am merely trying to convey the quality of her strange experience. I have not her sanction for what I say; I had rather not make the trial. But there is really no escape. If we are to understand the growth of the writer we must have some notion of the thing that befell.

ii

The child was not strong, and her Scots grandmother first, an aunt afterward, taught her. She grew up in the village of Buchanan, Botetourt County, Virginia, still in the 1870s a place of canalboats and the stage-coach. Major John William Johnston was a Confederate veteran, a lawyer and ex-member of the Virginia

[1] "The Literary Spotlight: Mary Johnston," in The Bookman for July, 1922. Reprinted in *The Literary Spotlight* (book published 1924).

Legislature. Naturally the house was not without books. Mary Johnston found the histories particularly engrossing. Then the family moved to Birmingham, Alabama, and this daughter was sent to school at Atlanta. She was then sixteen. In a few months her health compelled her to return home where, a year later, her mother died. As she was the eldest of several children the direction of the household fell to her. She suffered intermittently from illness for many years. In her twenties and while living in a New York apartment she began a romance of colonial Virginia in the seventeenth century, writing much of it in a quiet corner of Central Park, so as to be outdoors. She had been writing short stories which editors sent back to her and which she burned on the first rejection. It is said that the late Walter H. Page, at the time with Houghton Mifflin Company, discovered her.[2] The historical romance, *Prisoners of Hope* (1898) became her first book and was successful; her second novel, *To Have and To Hold* (1900) was a record-making best seller and had literary merits most exceptional in the flood of historical fiction then running. Miss Johnston traveled considerably in Europe in quest of better health. After the death of her father she lived for some time at 110 East Franklin Street, Richmond. Then she built a home, "Three Hills," near Warm Springs, Virginia, where she has lived since. Knowing that her Civil War novels, *The Long Roll* and *Cease Firing*, owe much to Major Johnston's analyses and recollections, some Southerners have said that Mary Johnston's father was at least equally responsible with her for the splendid performance in her earlier novels. They quite misunderstand the nature

[2] "What You Should Know About American Authors: Mary Johnston," in the New York Herald for 21 June 1922 (book section).

of the inspiration he undoubtedly gave her. Of direct help—which is what these people really have in mind —he gave much, as she has acknowledged; it was, however, unimportant. Direct help can as well be got from books. If today you tell Miss Johnston how well you liked such a novel of hers as *Lewis Rand* (1908), she will probably respond: "Of course you realize that the picture of those times is idealized." In other words, although hers is one of those natures which must seek the ideal, possess and be possessed by it, the conception of the ideal has completely changed. Where once she found it in the bright glints of an earlier American day, now she finds it in our day and every day, past or present or to be—the pure silver of the human spirit that runs in a deep if irregular vein through the worn old rock of human destiny.

For she is like silver herself, like old silver choicely patterned. The small, oval face and pointed chin are serene in expression beneath a fine forehead and crisp hair with a great deal of its blackness still in it. Her manner is reposeful, friendly, unaffected and sympathetic. She talks readily about anything and everything but you have a feeling that she is also, at moments, somewhere else—this quite without any sacrifice or lessening of her hereness and attentiveness. I now come to the personal experience which, to be intelligible to most of us, must be put in a crude and simple kind of paraphrase.

If one has suffered much from illness and pain, one is very likely to have occasional moments in which one returns to life newly-washed, like the world in trembling freshness and sunlight on a morning after storm. If one stands on a Virginia hill, or a hill anywhere, one may sometimes have a distinct awareness that the length and breadth and depth round about and below are only a kind of length and breadth and descent to a creature measuring them with his legs; even the eye seems to declare that genuine dimensions are elsewhere. Stand on the hill one day, return to it one, five or ten years afterward, standing in the same place. It is quite possible that nothing has changed in the scene about you. A certain time has passed, but you, to yourself, haven't changed. You have grown a little older, but the essential *you* is not anybody else. Suddenly you realize that time is not a dimension, either, any more than the length and breadth round about or the drop to the valley below; and that as long as you are *you* and no one else, the day, the year or the century would make no genuine difference. The only distance or direction lies between the unchanging *you* and somebody else. You are really no farther from Balboa discovering the Pacific from a Panama summit than if you were standing beside him now sharing the discovery; the direction is from your spirit to his, from his to yours, and the distance is neither lessened nor increased by race, nationality, religion, leagues or centuries.

That is, instead of merely acquiring the notion of the fourth dimension of mathematics, you have come to see that all the so-called dimensions, length, breadth, height, time and imaginable others are merely conveniences of earthly existence, or necessities of earthly existence, like eating and breathing.

As you stand on the hill, you are alone and yet not alone. The physical *you* is alone, as always; but the unchanging *you* is one of a company whom you can identify only to the extent of what you may have read or heard about them. In the company will be Francis of Assisi, Joan of Arc, Spinoza, Ludwig van Beethoven, Cardinal Newman, William Blake, Walt Whitman—to mention a few of various times and countries —as well as countless others.

Then will follow the strangest part of the experience and the part most difficult to put in words. It is, however, something of which some intimation comes even to the humblest pair of lovers, just as it is the passionate fulfillment of the great, the immortal lovers of legend.

There is a feeling so intense that it can find coherent expression only in poetry which holds it securely in the rigid mold of metre and rhyme; there is another feeling, or degree of feeling either more intense or more delicate which can communicate itself only in a language of cunningly-related sounds which we call music. And there is even a pitch of feeling greater than these, higher and very tranquil and most piercing in its intensity and loveliness. This feeling has only one expression—love. The object of that love is immaterial to it. That object may be, outwardly, the body of the beloved. It may be a person or an idea. It may be anything. The effects of this feeling are almost infinitely various. You will find some of them described in William James's *Varieties of Religious Experience*. The feeling itself is a religious feeling but it may not expend itself on a religious object. The feeling made Francis of Assisi the Clown of God. It brought visions to Joan of Arc and put her at the head of a victorious army. Under its influence Beethoven wrote symphonies, Blake made pictures, and Whitman wrote *Leaves of Grass*. Sometimes, when the effects are tranquil, we say that the Lover has found peace—to which has sometimes been added a phrase of further description, "the peace that passeth understanding."

Nearly all these aspects of a continuous human experience came to Mary Johnston. There was the not unusual preliminary circumstance of invalidism. There was the loss of a father, much-loved. There were the Virginia hills she walked upon and there was frequent solitude. The sense of passing the boundaries of time and space was facilitated by two things: first, her devotion to history, and second, her strongly-developed novelist's imagination. Shortly after she was forty, therefore, she came to a day when, for an hour or part of an hour, she had access to a state of knowledge, of sympathy, of understanding which is so sane that it infuses its sanity into every act of living and so joyous that those to whom the experience is vouchsafed can throw aside every lesser joy. After that first experience Mary Johnston waited for it to renew itself, and gradually what had come as a miracle remained as a human faculty; so that since then she has acquired the apparent power or privilege of leaning out from the gold bar of Heaven, of letting earth slip without loosing herself from earth. You know how your mind will pass behind the stars while your feet yet continue to tread firm soil as you go on walking. That is a feeble likeness to the thing.

iii

It was bound to affect her writing, and perhaps the first traces of it are in *The Witch* (1914), but it was clearly apparent in *Foes* (1918), where, as I have said before this, "upthrusting through the surface of a stirring historical adventure, we had the evidence of the author's breathless personal adventure." It is one thing to be by temperament a mystic; quite another to become, as Miss Johnston had now become, a mystic by the witness of some inner illumination. In some

cases the change has brought with it a proselyting spirit
of great fervor; in Miss Johnston's there was a complete absence of any such missionary zeal. All the
same she could not go on writing novels in which the
picture of some bygone time was idealized simply for
the sake of a charming picture. *Foes* has been correctly described as "a dramatic story of eighteenth century Scotland with a lasting feud, a long chase, and a
crescendo of hatred and peril." But it is also a story
of sublime forgiveness, as much so as John Masefield's
The Everlasting Mercy. In *Michael Forth* (1919)
and *Sweet Rocket* (1920) there was, as in certain
novels of Herman Melville's, notably *Pierre*, more
transcendentalism than story. It was inevitable that
she should be inarticulate for a while, but it was only
for a while. For in 1922 appeared her story, *Silver
Cross*, a tale of England in the time of Henry VII.
and of two rival religious establishments. *Silver
Cross* was both beautiful and intelligible. For the
prose style I like best Stewart Edward White's word,
"stippling." It has also been said of what was to
be her mode of utterance for a book or two: "Written in a clipped sort of prose stripped of 'a' and 'an'
and 'the' and other particles as well as articles, the
text is a highly mannered English replete with ca-
denced sentences and animated by nervous rhythms.
The very diction bears poetic surcharges, and the
whole effect on the reader is to distill in his soul a
delicate enchantment or else to exasperate him to
death." [3] The core of the tale is irony, irony directed
at religious bigotry and religious intolerance; it lies
there at the base of the flower and from it the reader

[3] See "The Literary Spotlight: Mary Johnston" in The Bookman
for July, 1922. Reprinted in *The Literary Spotlight* (book published
1924).

may make his own bitter honey. Or, if he have no stomach for that, he may take his satisfaction and pleasure in the rich sound of ecclesiastical trumpets, the green England, the pageant of a simple world unrolled before him.

In the same year with *Silver Cross* Miss Johnston's *1492* was published. The book is, of course, the story of Columbus, told with the accurate historical coloring and the poetic feeling one would expect of the author; but it uses a technical device which, while not novel, is deserving of attention from the analyst of fiction. This is the employment as narrator of the story of Jayme de Marchena, a fictional person, represented as a Jew who has been banished from Spain under the decree of exile promulgated by Ferdinand and Isabella. Miss Johnston makes of him a man of philosophical mind, an "obscure Spinoza" whose thoughts are a constant commentary on the voyage from Palos and the succeeding voyages. Thus, without distorting history or creating an imaginary portrait of the Genoese sailor and discoverer, the book (in form a novel) gives us one of the great events in human affairs in a perspective that neither history nor biography affords. Again what we have is the vision of one standing on a hilltop, alone and yet not alone— of one who is at the same instant standing in the night watches on the deck of a caravel and listening to the cry from the man on lookout. . . .

iv

Slow turns the water by the green marshes,
In Virginia.
Overhead the sea fowl
Make silver flashes, cry harsh as peacocks.

Capes and islands stand,
Ocean thunders,
The light houses burn red and gold stars.
In Virginia
Run a hundred rivers.[4]

The fine opening of Miss Johnston's poem might serve as an evocation, except in the detail of the lighthouses, for her novel, *Croatan* (1923). The mere fact of her return to the Virginia of colonial days must have served to entice many readers to this book —who were held, I think, by the tale itself, once they had begun it. The legend of Raleigh's lost colony of Roanoke and of a first white child born in Virginia, "Virginia Dare," is skilfully utilized for a romance quite the most perfect Miss Johnston had imagined. The story of the three young people who grew up together in the forest—English girl, Spanish boy and Indian youth—is one of many overtones deftly sounded. Is Miss Johnston proclaiming a creed of racial tolerance and interracial understanding? Then the proclamation is made pianissimo and with muted strings, not with brass instruments. And the forest scenes—what delicious notes from oboes!

It is very natural to contrast Mary Johnston and Ellen Glasgow, both Virginians and both novelists of distinction as well as contemporaries. Their very agreeable personalities are, however, markedly different. Miss Glasgow is a product of her background and her time, as much so, for example, as Edith Wharton; Miss Johnston has a great deal more likeness to, let us say, Miss May Sinclair. Where Miss Glasgow tends to concern herself with Virginia of the last half

[4] Opening lines of "Virginiana," by Mary Johnston, in The Reviewer for February, 1922.

MARY JOHNSTON

century, Miss Johnston, from going back to the beginnings of her State, is quite as likely to plunge effortlessly forward into the farthest imaginable future. For a witness of what she can do in that direction one does well to read such a short story as "There Were No More People," [5] dealing with the extinction of man and the slow emergence of "a creature who must be classed among *aves*. He was small, two-footed, feathered and winged. . . . Slowly, taking aeons to do it, he put out, in addition to his wings, rudimentary arms that grew, taking a vast number of generations to accomplish it, into true arm and hand. At the same time he began, very, very slowly, to heighten and broaden his skull. Man would have thought him—as he would have thought man—a strange looking creature. . . . It took time, but at last there dawned self-consciousness. The old vehicle for sensation, emotion, memory and thought that had been called man was gone. But sensation, emotion, memory and thought are eternals, and a new vehicle has been wrought. It is not a perfect vehicle. In much it betters man, but it is not perfect. The new Thinker resembles the old in that he knows selfishness and greed and uses violence. . . . It remains to be seen if he can outwear and lay aside all that and remain—as man could not remain."

V

Carl Van Doren's words about Miss Johnston, in his *Contemporary American Novelists*, 1900-1920, that she brings to the legends and traditions of the Old Dominion no fresh interpretations, have been made

[5] In The Reviewer. Reprinted in The World Tomorrow for February, 1924.

obsolete by *Croatan*, and are, of course, so far as they are made applicable to legends in general, denied by her last half dozen novels. It is most true, though, that Miss Johnston is an historian and a scholar in her tastes. To the series of fifty volumes interlocking to form a complete American history, and published by the Yale University Press under the general title, *The Chronicles of America*, Miss Johnston contributed the volume on *Pioneers of the Old South*. The book deals with Maryland, the Carolinas and Georgia as well, but Virginia is, of course, the principal subject. The period is 1607-1735 and Miss Johnston's short account is an admirable piece of writing, concise, accurate, uncontroversial; alive with crisp human portraits and touched with poetry and imagination in its occasional descriptive passages.

Miss Johnston's new novel, to be published late in 1924, under the title, *The Slave Ship*, is a story of the American slave trade in the eighteenth century. David Scott, a prisoner after the battle of Culloden, is sold into slavery on the American plantations. The cruelty with which he is treated hardens his conscience, so that when he escapes he goes without much hesitation or scruple into a slave ship and then into slave trading. The novel follows with intensity and compassion the career which takes him from this most abominable traffic to an understanding of what it means. The novel is, therefore, a story (like *Foes*) of one who journeyed on the road to Damascus. But I recall no story which pictures with more vividness and power the Middle Passage of infamous memory. *The Slave Ship* is notable, too, for the greater suavity of Miss Johnston's prose style; the "a's," "an's," and "the's" are recovered and there are less tangible changes—all for the better.

[386]

"Nothing can be done but by being greater than the thing to be done" is a piece of wisdom uttered in Miss Johnston's fable, "The Return of Magic." [6] A writer is, or should be, capable of growth in two directions—as an artisan and as a source of emotion to be communicated in terms of beauty. The number who show growth in either fashion is not large; the number who grow both ways is very small. Five years ago I had occasion to survey the work of thirty-five American women novelists, three of whom have since died. One or two others have produced no new work in the period since. With the most liberal disposition toward the thirty or so others, it does not seem to me that more than a half dozen show growth either as writers or artists. Possibly three have produced work in these five years indicative of a mind enlarging as the hand serving it has grown more certain. Mary Johnston is one of the three.[7]

BOOKS BY MARY JOHNSTON

1898 *Prisoners of Hope.*
        In England: *The Old Dominion*
1900 *To Have and To Hold*
        In England: *By Order of the Company*
1902 *Audrey*
1904 *Sir Mortimer*
1907 *The Goddess of Reason.* Poetic drama.
1908 *Lewis Rand*

[6] In The Reviewer for April, 1922.
[7] It must be premised that "growth" in an artist is a term upon which agreement as to definition is probably impossible. Nevertheless it is loosely used by all of us to denote a certain progression in the work of such a writer as Henry James or Thomas Hardy. It may or may not, I suspect, mean greater or more enduring work, but it almost invariably must mean work of a more marked idiosyncrasy, more stamped with the personality of the author, and probably written with a noticeable idiom of style. Subject is hardly a safe test.

1911 *The Long Roll*
1912 *Cease Firing*
1913 *Hagar*
1914 *The Witch*
1915 *The Fortunes of Garin*
1917 *The Wanderers*
1918 *Foes*
       In England: *The Laird of Glenfernie*
1919 *Michael Forth*
1920 *Sweet Rocket*
1922 *Silver Cross*
1922 *1492*
       In England: *Admiral of the Ocean-Sea*
1923 *Croatan*
1924 *The Slave Ship*

SOURCES ON MARY JOHNSTON

Besides those referred to in the text of the chapter and in footnotes, the following are suggested:

The Women Who Make Our Novels, by Grant Overton. Moffat, Yard, 1918, 1919, 1922; Dodd, Mead, 1924. There is a chapter on Miss Johnston.

"Silver Cross, by Mary Johnston." Circular published by Little, Brown and Company, 1922.

Carl Brandt, Brandt & Kirkpatrick, 101 Park Avenue, New York, N. Y.

INDEX OF PRICES

NOTE: Prices given are net and are subject to change. Inquiry should be made of a bookseller for titles not listed.

ADDINGTON, SARAH,
   Round the Year in Pudding Lane, $2.00

ADLER, FELIX,
   The Reconstruction of the Spiritual Ideal, $1.50

ALCOTT, LOUISA M.,
   Little Men: Life at Plumfield with Jo's Boys, $1.50
   Little Women: or Meg, Jo, Beth and Amy, $1.50

ALEXANDER, ELIZABETH,
   Rôles, $2.00

ALLEN, LUCY G.,
   Choice Recipes for Clever Cooks, $2.00
   Table Service, $1.75

ALTSHELER, JOSEPH A.,
   Apache Gold, $1.75
   Border Watch, The, $1.75
   Candidate, The, $1.75
   Eyes of the Woods, The, $1.75
   Forest Runners, The, $1.75
   Forest of Swords, The, $1.75
   Free Rangers, The, $1.75
   Great Sioux Trail, The, $1.75
   Guns of Bull Run, The, $1.75
   Guns of Europe, The, $1.75
   Guns of Shiloh, The, $1.75
   Herald of the West, A, $1.75
   Hosts of the Air, The, $1.75
   Hunters of the Hills, Thë, $1.75
   In Circling Camps, $1.75

ALTSHELER, JOSEPH A.—*Cont'd*
   Keepers of the Trail, The, $1.75
   Last of the Chiefs, The, $1.75
   Last Rebel, The, $1.75
   Lords of the Wild, The, $1.75
   Lost Hunters, The, $1.75
   Masters of the Peaks, The, $1.75
   My Captive, $1.75
   Quest of the Four, The, $1.75
   Riflemen of the Ohio, The, $1.75
   Rock of Chickamauga, The, $1.75
   Rulers of the Lakes, The, $1.75
   Scouts of Stonewall, The, $1.75
   Scouts of the Valley, The, $1.75
   Shades of the Wilderness, The, $1.75
   Shadow of the North, The, $1.75
   Soldier of Manhattan, A, $1.75
   Star of Gettysburg, The, $1.75
   Sun of Saratoga, The, $1.75
   Sun of Quebec, The, $1.75
   Sword of Antietam, The, $1.75
   Texan Scouts, The, $1.75
   Texan Star, The, $1.75
   Texan Triumph, The, $1.75
   Tree of Appommatox, The, $1.75
   Young Trailers, The, $1.75

ARLEN, MICHAEL,
   The Green Hat, $2.50
   These Charming People, $2.50
   "Piracy," $2.50

[389]

ASQUITH, HERBERT HENRY,
The Genesis of the War, $6.00

BAKER, S. JOSEPHINE, M.D.,
Healthy Babies, $1.25
Healthy Children, $1.25
Healthy Mothers, $1.25

BALDERSTON, JOHN L.,
A Morality Play for the Leisure Class, 50c

BALFOUR, ARTHUR JAMES,
Theism and Thought, $4.00
Theism and Humanism, $1.75

BANNING, MARGARET CULKIN,
A Handmaid of the Lord, $2.00

BARBOUR, RALPH HENRY,
The Fighting Scrub, $1.75
Follow the Ball, $1.75

BARKER, GRANVILLE,
Anatol, $1.50
Exemplary Theatre, The, $2.00
Madras House, The, $1.50
Marrying of Ann Leete, The, $1.50
Secret Life, The, $1.50
Three Short Plays: Rosco, Vote by Ballot, Farewell to the Theatre, $1.50
Vosey Inheritance, The, $1.50
Waste, $1.50

BARKER, LEWELLYS F., M.D., AND COLE, N. B., M.D.,
Blood Pressure, $1.25

BARNHAM, HENRY D.,
The Khoja: Tales of Nasr-Ed-Din, $2.50

BARRETTO, LARRY,
A Conqueror Passes, $2.00

BARTLETT, JOHN,
Familiar Quotations, $4.50

BARRY, DAVID S.,
Forty Years in Washington, $3.50

BARRY, FLORENCE V.,
A Century of Children's Books, $2.00

BEACH, LEWIS,
Ann Vroome, $1.50
A Square Peg, $1.50
Goose Hangs High, The, $1.50

BECK, JAMES M.,
The Constitution of the United States: Yesterday, Today—Tomorrow? $3.00

BENNETT, ARNOLD,
Elsie and the Child, $2.50
Riceyman Steps, leather, $2.50; cloth, $2.00

BENSON, E. F.,
David Blaize of King's, $2.00

BINYON, LAURENCE,
Ayuli, $1.50

BIRKENHEAD, EARL OF
The Inner History of British Politics, Vol. I, $6.00

BLOCK, ETTA,
One-Act Plays from the Yiddish, $2.00

BOWER, B. M.,
The Bellehelen Mine, $2.00

BOYD, ERNEST,
The Contemporary Drama of Ireland, $2.50

BRADLEY, ALICE,
The Candy Cook Book, $1.75

BRIDGES, ROY,
Rat's Castle, $1.75

BRIMMER, F. E.,
Autocamping, $2.00

INDEX OF PRICES

CURTIS, CAPT. PAUL A., JR.,
The Outdoorsman's Handbook, $1.50

DARK, SIDNEY,
The Book of England for Young People, $2.50
The Book of France for Young People, $2.50
The Book of Scotland for Young People, $2.50

DAVENPORT, EVE, and MAUDE RADFORD WARREN,
Mother Hubbard's Wonderful Cupboard, $2.50
Adventures in the Old Woman's Shoe, $2.50
Tales Told by the Gander, $2.50

DAVIS, OWEN,
Icebound, $1.50
The Detour, $1.50

DE LA MARE, WALTER, AND OTHERS,
Number Two Joy Sheet, $2.50

DICKINSON, EMILY,
The Complete Poems of Emily Dickinson, $3.50

DICKINSON, THOMAS H.,
The Contemporary Drama of England, $2.50

DIXON, THOMAS,
Black Hood, The, $2.00
Fall of a Nation, The, $2.00
Foolish Virgin, The, $2.00
Man in Gray, The, $2.00
Man of the People, A, $1.75
Sins of the Father, The, $2.00
Southerner, The, $2.00
Way of a Man, The, $2.00

DODGE, DANIEL KILHAM,
Abraham Lincoln, Master of Words, $1.50

DONHAM, S. AGNES,
Marketing and Housework Manual, $2.00
Spending the Family Income, $1.75

DOYLE, A. CONAN,
Memories and Adventures, $4.50

DULAC, EDMUND (Illustrator),
Tales from Hans Andersen, $3.50
Edmund Dulac's Fairy Book, $3.75
Shakespeare's Comedy of "The Tempest," $3.50
The Sleeping Beauty and Other Fairy Tales from the Old French, $3.50

EGAN, MAURICE FRANCIS,
Recollections of a Happy Life, $5.00

ELLIOTT, MAUD HOWE,
Three Generations, $4.00

EMERSON, WILLIAM, R.P., M.D.,
Nutrition and Growth in Children, $2.50

ERSKINE, LAURIE YORKE,
The Laughing Rider, $1.75

ERTZ, SUSAN,
Madame Clair, $2.00
Nina, $2.00

ESPINA, CONCHA,
The Red Beacon, $2.00

FAIRBANKS, DOUGLAS,
Youth Points the Way, $1.25

FARMER, FANNIE MERRITT,
Boston Cooking School Cook Book, The, $2.50
Food and Cookery for the Sick and Convalescent, $2.50

INDEX OF PRICES

GIBBS, PHILIP,
Heirs Apparent, $2.00
Little Novels of Nowadays, $2.00
Middle of the Road, The, $2.00

GOING, CHARLES BUXTON,
David Wilmot, Free Soiler, $6.00

GREGOR, ELMER RUSSELL,
Stories, each $1.75
Captain Jim Mason,
Jim Mason, Backwoodsman,
Jim Mason, Scout,
Running Fox,
Spotted Deer,
Three Sioux Scouts,
War Trail, The,
White Otter,
White Wolf, The,

HALL, G. STANLEY,
Adolescence, $10.00
Aspects of Child Life and Education, $2.00
Educational Problems, $10.00
Founders of Modern Psychology, $3.00
Jesus, the Christ, in the Light of Psychology, $7.50
Life and Confessions of a Psychologist, $5.00
Morale, $3.00
Recreations of a Psychologist, $2.50
Senescence: The Last Half of Life, $5.00
Youth, $2.00

HAMILTON, COSMO,
Another Scandal, $2.00
Blindness of Virtue, The, $2.00
Blue Room, The, $2.00
Door That Has No Key, The, $2.00
Four Plays: The New Poor, Scandal, The Silver Fox, The Mother Woman, $2.50
His Friend and His Wife, $2.00
Miracle of Love, The, $2.00
Rustle of Silk, The, $2.00

HAMILTON, COSMO—*Cont'd*
Scandal, $2.00
Sins of the Children, The, $2.00
Unwritten History, $4.00
Who Cares, $2.00

HAWTREY, CHARLES,
The Truth at Last, $5.00

HELLMAN, SAM,
Low Bridge and Punk Pungs, $1.25

HENDERSON, HELEN W.,
A Loiterer in London, $5.00
A Loiterer in Paris, $5.00
A Loiterer in New England, $5.00
A Loiterer in New York, $5.00

HENSHALL, JAMES A., M.D.,
The Book of the Black Bass, $4.50
Bass, Pike, Perch and Other Game Fishes, $3.00

HERBERT, A. P., AND OTHERS,
Double Demon and Other One-Act Plays, $2.00

HICHENS, ROBERT,
After the Verdict, $2.00
Last Time, The, $2.00

HILL, FREDERICK TREVOR,
On the Trail of Grant and Lee, $2.00
On the Trail of Washington, $2.50
Washington, the Man of Action, $6.00

HILL, JANET MCKENZIE,
Canning, Preserving and Jelly Making, $1.75
Cooking for Two: A Handbook for Young Housekeepers, $2.25

HOLDEN, DR. GEORGE PARKER,
Streamcraft: An Angling Manual, $2.50

INDEX OF PRICES

HOLLIDAY, ROBERT CORTES,
Literary Lanes and Other Byways, $2.00
Walking-Stick Papers, $2.00

HOLMES, A.
Controlled Power: A Study of Laziness and Achievement, $1.75

HOLT, L. EMMETT, M. D.,
The Care and Feeding of Children, $1.25

HOUGH, EMERSON,
Broken Gate, The, $2.00
Covered Wagon, The, $2.00
Girl at the Half-Way House, The, $2.00
Man Next Door, The, $2.00
Magnificent Adventure, The, $2.00
Mother of Gold, $2.00
North of 36, $2.00
Story of the Cowboy, The, $2.00
Way Out, The, $2.00

HOUSMAN, LAURENCE,
Echo de Paris, $1.00

HUDDLESTON, SISLEY,
Poincaré: The Man of the Ruhr, $2.50

HUDSON, HOLLAND,
Action, 50 cents

HUDSON, WILLIAM JAY,
Abbe Pierre, illustrated gift edition, $3.00
Abbe Pierre, regular edition, $2.00

HULIT, LEONARD,
Fishing with a Boy, $2.00
Salt Water Angler, The, $3.50

HUXLEY, ALDOUS,
Antic Hay, $2.00
On the Margin, $2.00

HUXLEY, ALDOUS—*Cont'd*
Young Archimedes and Other Sketches, $2.00
Crome Yellow, leather, $2.50; cloth, $2.00
Mortal Coils, $2.00
Leda and Other Poems, $2.00
Limbo, $2.00

IWASAKI, Y. T., AND HUGHES, GLEN,
Three Modern Japanese Plays, $1.50

JACKS, L. P.,
A Living Universe, $1.00
Religious Perplexities, $1.00
Realities and Shams, $1.50
The Lost Radiance of the Christian Religion, 50 cents

JACKSON, HELEN HUNT,
Nelly's Silver Mine, $2.00
Ramona, $2.00

JACQUES, MARIE,
Colette's Best Recipes: A Book of French Cookery, $2.00

JERITZA, MARIA,
Sunlight and Song, $3.00

JEWETT, ELEANORE MYERS,
Egyptian Tales of Magic, $2.00

JOB, HERBERT K., AND OTHERS,
Birds of America, 3 vols., $17.50

JOHN, GWEN,
The Prince, $1.50

JOHNSON, OWEN,
Blue Blood, $1.75
Prodigious Hickey, The, $1.75
Skippy Bedelle, $1.75
Tennessee Shad, The, $1.75
Varmint, The, $1.75

JOHNSON, ROBERT UNDERWOOD,
Remembered Yesterdays, $5.00

CARGOES FOR CRUSOES

JOHNSTON, MARY,
Croatan, $2.00
1492, $2.00
Silver Cross, $2.00
Slave Ship, The, $2.00

JONES, HENRY ARTHUR,
Representative Plays, 4 Vols.,
$10.00

JORDAN, DAVID STARR,
Fishes, $7.50

KELLOGG, VERNON,
Evolution, $2.00

KELLY, GEORGE,
The Show-Off, A Play, $1.75

KENLON, JOHN,
Fourteen Years a Sailor, $2.00

KEYES, FRANCES PARKINSON,
Letters From a Senator's Wife,
$2.50

KING, BEULAH,
Ruffs and Pompoms, $2.50

KNEVELS, GERTRUDE,
Dragon's Glory, 50 cents

KUMMER, FREDERIC ARNOLD,
The First Days of Man, $2.00
The First Days of Knowledge,
$2.00

LAUT, AGNES C.,
The Quenchless Light,

LAWRENCE, DAVID,
*The True Story of Woodrow
Wilson*, $2.50

LEIGHTON, JOSEPH A.,
Man and the Cosmos, $4.50
*Religion and the Mind of To-
day*, $3.00

LINCOLN, JOSEPH,
Cap'n Eri, $2.00
Rugged Water, $2.00

[396]

LINCOLN, NATALIE SUMNER,
The Thirteenth Letter, $2.00

LITTLE THEATRE SHORT PLAYS
SERIES,
Ten titles, each 50 cents

LODGE, SIR OLIVER,
Making of Man, $2.00

LUCAS, E. V.,
Advisory Ben, $2.00
*Little Wanderings Among the
Great Masters: Michelan-
gelo, Leonardo da Vinci,
Frans Hals, Murillo, Char-
din, Rembrandt*, each, $1.50
Giving and Receiving, $2.00
*Roving East and Roving
West*, $2.00
Adventures and Enthusiasms,
$2.00
The Hausfrau Rampant, $1.75
Cloud and Silver, $1.75
Genevra's Money, $2.00
Luck of the Year, $2.00

LYND, ROBERT,
The Blue Lion, $2.50

LYTLE, HORACE,
Breaking a Bird Dog, $2.00

MacCLINTOCK, LANDER,
*The Contemporary Drama of
Italy*, $2.50

MACLAY, EDGAR STANTON,
*A History of American Pri-
vateers*, $3.00

MacCURDY, GEORGE GRANT,
Human Origins, $10.00

MACKENZIE, COMPTON,
The Altar Steps, $2.50
The Parson's Progress, $2.50
The Heavenly Ladder, $2.50

MacMILLEN, MARY,
Pan and Pierrot, 50 cents

INDEX OF PRICES

[397]

MOORE, ANNE CARROLL,
  Joseph A. Altsheler and American History, Free
  New Roads to Childhood, $2.00
  Roads to Childhood: Views and Reviews of Children's Books, $2.00

MORLEY, CHRISTOPHER, and DON MARQUIS,
  Pandora Lifts the Lid, $2.00

MOROSO, JOHN A.,
  Cap Fallon, Fire Fighter, $1.75
  The Listening Man, $1.75

MOSES, MONTROSE J.,
  A Treasury of Plays for Children, $3.00
  Representative British Dramas: Victorian and Modern, $4.50
  Representative Continental Dramas: Revolutionary and Transitional, $4.50
  Representative One-Act Plays by Continental Authors, $3.00

MOSES, MONTROSE J., AND GERSON, VIRGINIA,
  Clyde Fitch and His Letters, $4.00

MOTT, A. S., EDITOR,
  Fifty New Poems for Children, $1.00

MULLINS, E. Y.,
  Christianity at the Crossroads, $1.75

MYERSON, ABRAHAM,
  The Foundations of Personality, $2.25

NEWTON, W. DOUGLAS,
  The Brute, $2.00

NICHOLSON, KENYON,
  Garden Varieties, $2.00

NIELSEN, KAY (Illustrator),
  Fairy Tales by Hans Andersen, $6.00

NIELSEN, KAY (Illustrator)—
  Cont'd
  East of the Sun and West of the Moon, $3.50
  The Twelve Dancing Princesses, $3.50

NORWOOD, EDWIN P.,
  The Friends of Diggeldy Dan, $1.75

NORTON, THOMAS J.,
  The Constitution of the United States: Its Sources and Its Application, $2.00

OPPENHEIM, E. PHILLIPS,
  A Maker of History, $2.00
  Great Impersonation, The, $2.00
  Great Prince Shan, The, $2.00
  Great Secret, The, $2.00
  Michael's Evil Deeds, $2.00
  Mystery Road, The, $2.00
  Passionate Quest, The, $2.00
  Seven Conundrums, The, $2.00
  Way of These Women, The, $2.00
  Wrath to Come, The, $2.00

OVERTON, GRANT,
  Authors of the Day, $2.50
  Cargoes for Crusoes, 50 cents

PACKARD, FRANK L.,
  Doors of the Night, $1.75
  Four Stragglers, The, $2.00
  Jimmie Dale and the Phantom Clue, $1.75
  Locked Book, The, $2.00
  The Adventures of Jimmie Dale, $1.75
  The Night Operator, $1.75

PARK, E. A., AND BELKNAP, M. B.,
  Princeton Sketches, $2.00

PARKER, WILLARD,
  The Manuscript of St. Helena, $2.00

INDEX OF PRICES

The Complete Poems of Charlotte Brontë, leather, $7.50; cloth, $3.00
The Complete Poems of Anne Brontë, leather, $7.50; cloth, $3.00
The Complete Poems of Emily Jane Brontë, leather, $7.50; cloth, $3.00

SINCLAIR, BERTRAND W.,
The Inverted Pyramid, $2.00

SLEMONS, J. MORRIS, M.D.,
The Prospective Mother, $2.00

SMITH, O. W.,
Casting Tackle and Methods, $3.00

SNAITH, J. C., Novels, each $2.00
Adventurous Lady, The,
Araminta,
Coming, The,
Council of Seven, The,
Sailor, The,
There Is a Tide,
Time Spirit, The,
Undefeated, The,
Van Roon, The,

SQUIRE, J. C.,
A Book of American Verse, $2.50
Essays on Poetry, $2.50

STANFORD, ALFRED,
A City Out of the Sea, $2.00

STANISLAVSKY, CONSTANTIN,
My Life in Art, $6.00

STEELE, WILBUR DANIEL,
The Giant's Stair, 50 cents

STEUART, J. A.,
Robert Louis Stevenson: A Critical Biography, $8.00

STEWART, DONALD OGDEN,
Perfect Behavior Abroad, $2.00
Perfect Behavior, $2.00

STEWART, DONALD OGDEN — Cont'd
A Parody Outline of History, $2.00

STEVENSON, GERTRUDE SCOTT,
The Letters of Madame, 1661-1708, by Elizabeth-Charlotte of Bavaria, $5.00

STOCKBRIDGE, BERTHA E. L.,
The Practical Cook Book, $2.00
What to Drink, $1.50

STODDARD, CHARLES COLEMAN,
Shanks' Mare, $2.50

SURGUCHEV, ILYA,
Autumn, 50 cents

SWINNERTON, FRANK,
R. L. Stevenson, $2.00
George Gissing, $2.00

TERHUNE, ALBERT PAYSON,
Now That I'm Fifty, $2.00
The Heart of a Dog, $3.00

TILTON, GEORGE HENRY,
The Fern Lover's Companion, $3.00

TOLSTOI, COUNT LEON L.,
The Truth About My Father, $2.00

TOMLINSON, EVERETT T.,
Fighters Young Americans Want to Know, $2.00
Mysterious Rifleman, The, $1.75
Pioneer Scouts of Ohio, The, $1.75
Places Young Americans Want to Know, $1.75
Pursuit of the Apache Chief, The, $1.75
Scouting in the Wilderness, $1.75
Scouting on the Border, $1.75
Scouting on the Old Fontier, $1.75
Historical Story for Boys, The, Free

INDEX OF PRICES

CARGOES FOR CRUSOES

INDEX

INDEX

INDEX

INDEX

INDEX

Ferber, Maurice, *Lord Byron*, 261

Fern Lover's Companion, The, George Henry Tilton, 34

Field, Eugene, 328

Fifty Contemporary One-Act Plays, ed., Frank Shay and Pierre Loving, 254

Fifty-four Forty or Fight, Emerson Hough, 236, 245

Fifty New Poems for Children, 94

Fighters Young Americans Want to Know, Everett Tomlinson, 243, 250

Fighting Scrub, The, Ralph Henry Barbour, 88

Fires of Ambition, George Gibbs, 371, 372, 374

First Days of Knowledge, The, Frederic Arnold Kummer, 86

First Days of Man, The, Frederic Arnold Kummer, 86

Fishes, David Starr Jordan, 32

Fishing with a Boy, Leonard Hulit, 40

Fitch, Clyde, *Clyde Fitch and His Letters,* 203, 204; *Plays of Clyde Fitch,* 257

Flammarion, M. Camille, *Haunted Houses,* 358

Foes, Mary Johnston, 382, 383, 387, 389

Follow the Ball, Ralph Henry Barbour, 88, 89

Foote, John Taintor, 36, 91; *A Wedding Gift,* 36; *Dumb-Bell of Brookfield,* 36; *Pocono Shot,* 36

Food and Cookery for the Sick and Convalescent, Fannie Merritt Farmer, 123

Fordyce, Dr. Claude P., *Trail Craft,* 35

Forgotten Shrines, John Farrar, 286

Forty Good Night Tales, Rose Fyleman, 84

Forty Years in Washington, David S. Barry, 208

Fosdick, Rev. Harry Emerson, D.D., *Twelve Tests of Character,* 362

Foster, Maximilian, *Humdrum House?* 180

Foundations of Personality, The, Abraham Myerson, M. D., 360, 361

Founders of the Empire, Philip Gibbs, 18, 26

Four Plays, Cosmo Hamilton, 190, 195, 258

Four Stragglers, The, Frank L. Packard, 339, 342, 343, 344, 346, 348

Fourteen Years a Sailor, John Kenlon, 95

Fox, Fannie F., *Fannie Fox's Cook Book,* 116

French, Allen, *The Story of Rolf and the Viking's Bow,* 93

French, Joseph Lewis, 28, 29; *Pioneer West, The,* 28, 29

Friends of Diggeldy Dan, The, Edwin P. Norwood, 94

From Now On, Frank L. Packard, 339, 348

Further Adventures of Jimmie Dale, The, Frank L. Packard, 340, 348

Fyleman, Rose, *Fairies and Chimneys,* 84; *Forty Good Night Tales,* 84; *Rose Fyleman's Fairy Book,* 84; *The Fairy Flute,* 84; *The Fairy Green,* 84; *The Rainbow Cat,* 84

Gaige, Grace, *Recitations—Old and New for Boys and Girls,* 287, 288

Galwan, Ghulam Rassul, *Servant of Sahibs,* 211

Game Ranger's Note Book, A, A. Blayney Percival, 38, 39

Ganoe, William A., *A History of the United States Army,* 318, 319

Garden Varieties, Kenyon Nicholson, 255

Gaze, Harold, *The Goblin's Glen: A Story of Childhood's Wonderland,* 94

Geister, Edna, *It Is To Laugh,* 85; *Let's Play,* 85; *What Shall We Play,* 85

Genevra's Money, E. V. Lucas, 217, 230

George Villiers, First Duke of Buckingham, Philip Gibbs, 20, 26

Geste of Duke Jocelyn, The, Jeffery Farnol, 75, 78, 81

Giant's Stair, The, Wilbur Daniel Steele, 262

Gibbs, Arthur Hamilton, 315; *Gun Fodder,* 316

Gibbs, George, *see* Chapter xxiii, 364-375; *Fires of Ambition,* 371, 372, 374; *In Search of Madamoiselle,* 370, 374; *The Medusa Emerald,* 370, 374; *Sackcloth and Scarlet,* 372, 374; *The Black Stone,* 371, 374; *The Bolted Door,* 370, 374; *The Golden Bough,* 371, 374; *The House of Mohun,* 371, 372, 374; *The Secret Witness,* 371, 374; *The Splendid Outcast,* 371, 374; *The Yellow Dove,* 371, 374; *Youth Triumphant,* 371, 374

Gibbs, Philip, *see* Chapter i, 15-27, 315; *Adventures in Journalism,* 17, 18, 20, 22, 27; *Founders of the Empire,* 18, 26; *George Villiers, First Duke of Buckingham,* 20, 26; *Heirs Apparent,* 25, 26; *King's Favorite,* 20, 26; *Little Novels of Nowadays,* 25, 26; *Men and Women of the French Revolution,* 20, 26; *Now It Can Be Told,* 23, 27; *People of Destiny,* 23, 27; *The Middle of the Road,* 23, 24, 25, 26; *The Street of Adventure,* 19, 26; *Wounded Souls,* 23, 26

Gissing, Frank Swinnerton, 282

Giving and Receiving, E. V. Lucas, 219, 220, 221, 223, 230

[407]

INDEX

INDEX

INDEX

INDEX

INDEX

[412]

INDEX

[413]

INDEX

[414]

INDEX

[415]

INDEX